Personality Marketing

Targeting, Creativity and Performance Basics for Traditional, Owned, and Social Media plus Video Sites and Personal Contacts

Michael W. May

Published By

Supertext ®

Supertext Publishing
P. O. Box 26
Billings, MT 59103
Phone: (406) 259-7900
Fax: (406) 248-4320

EMAIL: info@supertextpublishing.com

Personality Marketing

Targeting, Creativity and Performance Basics for Traditional, Owned, and Social Media plus Video Sites and Personal Contacts

Michael W. May

ISBN-13: 978-0-9861909-0-2
ISBN-10: 098619090X

Library of Congress Catalog Control Number: 2015908749
Supertext Publishing, Billings, MT

DISCLAIMER: Nothing in this book is intended as legal advice. The material covered in this book is intended only as a broad summary of topics and terms that are in use at the time of this writing. Consult an attorney for legal advice on any topic covered in this book.

This book is dedicated to the musicians and other performers, writers, and producers who helped me find my way around lots of stages and studios; to the fellow broadcasters who have displayed their amazing creativity in action; to the teachers who stressed that learning is never finished; to the students who have always fueled the never-ending search for more effective ways to explain concepts; to the committed staff members and professional associates with whom I've worked throughout the years; to those who team up with me currently on promotional ideas and methods, as they've done for more than a dozen years now: Brian and Chad Randash, Bill Carey, Larry Davidson, Yami Mathieu, and Pat, John and Bill Bruski; to the guidance, innovation and courage of Ed Randash, who always stressed that the most important things in business are honesty, integrity, and caring about the customer; and to my family, who showed me that the most important things in life are caring for and loving each other.

Table of Contents

Introduction: About the Book 1

Part One: Customer Personalities 5

Chapter One: Personalities in the Marketing Cycle 7

    Customer-Centric Marketing 7

    The Marketing Journey 9

    What Is Personality Marketing? 11

    Communicating Our Message 13

    Listening Skills 14

    Personality in the 4-P's of Marketing 15

        Product 15

        Price and Place 16

        Promotion 16

    Internal Marketing 16

Chapter Two: Segmentation and Targeting Essentials 17

    Research 18

        Geographic Segmentation 18

        Demographic Segmentation 19

        Psychographic and Lifestyle Segmentation 19

Chapter Three: Buying Motivations and Consumer Behavior 23

    Human Behavior 23

        Positive Motivations 24

        Negative Motivations 24

    Consumer Behavior and the Buying Cycle 26

        Attention 27

        Interest 27

        Desire 29

        Action 30

Chapter Four: Teaching Concepts for Marketing 31

   Motivation...31

   How People Learn...32

   Learning Domains and Levels...32

      Cognitive Domain 33

      Affective Domain...33

      Psychomotor Domain...33

   Learning Personalities...33

   Get It Right and Drill It In..34

   Perceptions and Insight..34

   Attention and Interest Are Job One 35

   Retention of Our Ad Message 35

   Transfer of Learning..36

Part Two: Product Personality and the Elements of the Marketing Mix............37

Chapter Five: Product, Price and Place...39

   The Product...39

      Our New and Existing Products...40

      Product Line Extension or Expansion.................................42

   The Price 43

      Pricing Based on Cost...45

      Pricing Based on Demand...45

      Price and Quality Perceptions 46

      Promotional Pricing...47

      Payment Methods..48

   The Place...48

      Retail Selling 49

      Direct Response Marketing...50

      Personal Selling...51

Exporting and Importing...52

Packaging and Shipping 52

Chapter Six: Advertising, Publicity & Sales Promotions...................53

Promotional Budgets...56

Strategies 57

Advertising...58

Publicity and Public Relations 61

Sales Promotions 62

Chapter Seven: Principles of Personal Selling 65

Selling Means Listening 66

The Five P's of Personal Selling.................................66

Product Knowledge...66

Prospecting...67

Pressures and Motivations 67

Performance...69

Presentation 71

Part Three: Marketing Plans and Media Overview 79

Chapter Eight: SWOT, Strategic Thinking, and Marketing Plans 81

Marketing Plan Overview...81

SWOT Analysis...82

Objectives, Strategies, and Tactics 82

Mission Statement 83

The Annual Marketing Meeting.................................84

What...84

How...85

Where...86

Who...86

Why 87

When 87

A Written Marketing Plan 88

Executive Summary 88

Mission Statement 88

The Team 88

Present Situation 89

Competitive Analysis 89

Objectives 89

Strategic Elements 89

Tactical Details 90

Controls and Tracking 90

Chapter Nine: Promotional Planning and Media Selection 91

Media Options 91

Market Research 93

Population Segments 94

Understanding Media Audience Estimates 95

Audience Measurement Types and Terms 95

Reach and Frequency 95

Media Rates 96

Comparing Media Costs 98

Traditional Media 99

Broadcasting 100

Print 103

Outdoor and Out-of-Home 105

Specialty and Premium Advertising 105

Trade Shows, Exhibitions, and Events 105

Point-of-Purchase 106

New Media: The Internet, Mobile Devices, and Digital Advertising
.... 106

Our Website... 108

Content Marketing for the Web and Mobile Devices 111

Social Media and Sharing Sites.. 112

Search Engine Marketing... 112

Online Auctions 115

Email Marketing.. 115

Multimedia, Streaming, and Webcasting.................................. 115

Part Four: Creativity Tools.. 117

Chapter Ten: Visualization 119

The Craft of Mental Imagery 119

A Method for Visualization.. 121

Chapter Eleven: Elements of Wit and Humor............................. 123

The Psychology of Wit 123

Wit, Humor and Comedy Compared....................................... 124

Why People Laugh... 126

Analyzing Jokes as Building Blocks for Creativity....................... 127

The Value of Humor... 129

Premise of the Joke: Situational Humor................................... 130

Switching 131

Polishing 133

K-Words... 134

Monologue 134

Straight Character vs. Comic.. 135

Topical Setups 135

Our Basic Writing Formula 136

Joke Structures 136

Laughter Reason #1: Surprise.. 136

Laughter Reason #2: Defense or Escape Mechanism.................. 142

Laughter Reason #3: Victory..144

Laughter Reason #4: Superiority 146

Chapter Twelve: Copywriting - Selling Ideas, Feelings, Images, and Action..149

Targeting and Consumer Behavior for Copywriting......................151

Some Commercial Types and Formulas..152

Commercial Types..152

Commercial Formulas...155

Branding, Imaging, Positioning, Differentiation, the Offer, and Action 158

Marketing Vehicle Selection 159

Demand States..162

Strategy and Intent...163

Hook, Body, Hook 164

Opening Hook..164

Body Copy...165

Closing Hook..166

Example 166

Use of Narrative..167

Idea Sources..168

Commercial Creativity, Wit and Humor.......................................169

Engagement, Entertainment, Education, Persuasion, and Action .170

Topical Observations 171

Word Association..173

Chapter Thirteen: Principles of Video and Audio........................179

Video for Marketing 179

Video Hosting 179

Creative Video Production on a Budget..180

Producing for Content Marketing and Local Media....................180

Production Phases 181

    Preproduction 181

    Production 183

    Postproduction 189

Basics of Audio and Acoustics 193

Sound Effects 195

Production Music 196

Recording and Editing Audio 197

    Frequency 198

    Amplitude 199

    Time 200

    Quality 200

    Intensity 201

    Noise 203

    Stereo 203

Microphones 204

    Impedance and Frequency Response 205

    Microphone Pickup Patterns 205

    Microphone Construction 207

    Working the Mic 207

Part Five: Personality Performance Basics 209

Chapter Fourteen: Vocal Performance 211

Tools of the Craft 211

Dialects 212

Articulation 212

    Vowel and Diphthong Formation 212

    Vowel Sounds 213

    Diphthong Sounds 213

Consonant Sounds 213

Articulation Errors...215

Grammar and Vocabulary Errors...................................215

The PIPPs 216

    Pitch...216

    Intensity 220

    Pauses 222

    Pacing 224

Outline of the PIPPs 225

Copy Notations 226

Long-Term and Short-Term Impressions....................227

Character Voices 228

Vocal Skills Exercises 229

Chapter Fifteen: The Subtext - More than Words 231

Objectives, Strategies, and Tactics.............................231

Tactical Subtext 232

Strategic Subtext 232

Spine of a Character...232

Circumstances of a Character.....................................233

Unit Objectives, Intentions, Actions and Activities 234

Bringing Scripts to Life 236

Superobjectives and Through-Actions 236

Meter: The Flow of Our Performance 236

Being In Character..237

Sample Ad Copy Marked for Subtext...........................238

Chapter Sixteen: Becoming the Part with Characterization...............241

Building a Mental Image 242

Defining, Scripting, and Portraying Characters 244

Character Construction...244

    Physical 244

    Mental 245

    Emotional...245

    Speech 245

    Social 245

Character Modeling..246

Portraying Characters...247

    Affective Memory and Imagination 248

    Sense Memory 249

    Performance Triads 249

    Performance Triad Exercises 251

    Emotional Recall 252

    Body Language 253

    Facial Expressions...253

Psychophysical Communication Planning....................................255

About the Author..257

Resources and Recommended Reading...259

Index 265

Introduction: About the Book

New technology has democratized publishing and broadcasting. In addition to using traditional media, we can all now employ our owned media, including our company website, plus social media and video sharing sites to put our messages out to the masses. *Personality Marketing* is a foundational text and reference for anyone who wants ideas and systems that can help them be both more creative and strategic in any contacts designed to entertain, inform or persuade in personal contacts or in any media. This includes management, sales and customer service personnel, as well as any other staff members from virtually any business that are now involved with or want to learn to do broadcast or webcast performances, on-air or online advertising, content marketing, presentations, customer service contacts, training, or personal selling. The book is also a good overview for broadcasters, webcasters, agencies and other content creators in some basics of performing, copywriting, and promoting.

We begin with a review of the elements of the marketing mix from conception to consumption, looking at personality's role in each step. We cover topics including product awareness, branding, imaging, positioning, differentiation, and calls-to-action. We also outline creative techniques for copywriting and scripting, including the use of visualization, wit and humor to transfer the right ideas, feelings, and images. We address the use of traditional media, the web, and mobile devices as promotional vehicles. We cover the principles of good video and audio for content marketing, training, and advertising in traditional and new media. And we outline vocal techniques, the subtext, and characterization methods for performing as personalities and marketers, and for training our personnel to project the right personalities in all of their contacts.

Whether we're promoting our own business interests or someone else's, we should remember that entertainment, education, and marketing are all pretty much the same thing. Whenever we're doing one, we're doing a bit of the others as well. Many of us, particularly in small business, simply don't have big budgets for flashy production and big-dollar ad buys, so targeted creative communication can help us compete against fatter wallets. Buying decisions often involve just one person who believes in us and our product, so it's critical that we transfer the right ideas and feelings to targeted individuals. Personality in the marketing cycle includes defining our products, knowing our target audience and customers, understanding why they might want what we have, training our personnel, and outlining our intentions.

Bob Dylan once said that "he who is not busy being born is busy dying." Marketing can help keep our business being born. However, particularly in small businesses, we know that it's very easy to spend promotional dollars ineffectively. Advertising pioneer John Wanamaker once said, "I know that half my advertising is wasted. I just don't know which half." Marketing decisions are part art and part science, and they aren't getting any easier. But thankfully, better marketing is becoming more accessible to those of us without big bank accounts. This book features focused, quickly readable sections on real-world topics for promoting with limited dollars. It contains tools for the nuts and bolts that we need to ratchet into place for frugal marketing using traditional media, new media including the web and mobile devices, and personal selling.

After our review of these basics, we address creative strategies plus performance techniques for personalized communications. It can be difficult, frustrating, or even intimidating to try to "be ourselves" once we're in front of a live audience, the microphone is on, or the camera is rolling. This book is designed to help make these and other tasks easier for those of us who want to perform better in our roles as managers, salespeople, customer service personnel, broadcasters, webcasters, or trainers.

In small businesses, our job description is "*pretty much everything*" and our promotional budget is "*not much of anything.*" And there are plenty of small businesses out there. In the United States, small business makes up a big chunk of the economy. Counting those that have 1 or more employees, the U. S. Bureau of Labor Statistics says that about 63% of all U. S. companies have fewer than 5 employees, while almost 90% have fewer than 20 employees. These figures do not include corporations that list zero employees, and there are also lots of those.

The percentages for small businesses are even higher in some other developed nations. A 2009 report from the Center for Economic and Policy Research quotes data from the 22 richest democracies compiled by the Organization for Economic Cooperation and Development (OECD). According to the OECD data, almost all of the other rich nations have both a higher percentage of self-employed workers and of small businesses overall in their economies.
(http://www.cepr.net/documents/publications/small-business-2009-08.pdf).

So small businesses make the developed world go 'round. They're a huge part of the U.S. economy and even bigger elsewhere. And good performances help sell small business products and services.

Wherever we are, communication requires engagement. This can mean both entertainment and education which, like marketing, depend on transferring ideas and feelings to targeted individuals. If we're in entertainment, we need to relate to our audience. If we're educating or training, we must understand our students. And in business we have to know and communicate well with our stakeholders. That's anyone who has an interest in our products. These can include the business owners or shareholders, employees, suppliers, prospects, and customers.

Certainly we should all study the in-depth works of experts in marketing. To name just a few, we have books by the likes of Peter Drucker, Philip Kotler, Gary Armstrong, Al and Laura Ries, Jack Trout, and Alexander Hiam. Direct response thought leaders include Bob Stone, Ron Jacobs and Dan Kennedy. In sales there are Zig Ziglar, Keith Rosen, and Tom Hopkins. Online marketing experts include Lorrie Thomas, Liana Evans, and David Meerman Scott. Let's not forget great motivators like Napoleon Hill and Earl Nightingale. And there are scores of others in all these fields. But sometimes we just want to review the fundamentals that are most relevant to communicating our message and doing bigger things with a small budget. Those basics are what this text is all about.

This book is presented in five parts. They're designed to work either sequentially or as stand-alone units. For the easiest understanding of their interrelationship, the book is designed for reading the parts in order from beginning to end. For reference use on specific subjects, particularly by those who already have extensive marketing, production or performance knowledge or background, each subject area can be read in no particular order.

In Part One of the book, we look at how personality fits into the marketing effort. This includes the first fundamental of marketing, which is identifying our target customers and defining the reasons why they might buy. To get prospects to know us, trust us and like what we have to offer, we first have to get to know them and their needs. Part Two reviews the elements of the marketing mix from conception to consumption, including an overview of our products' personalities. We look at strategies for use in advertising, promotion, PR, and personal selling. Part Three covers the subject of designing and implementing a marketing plan, and looks at media options. Once we understand who we are, what we have, who we're trying to reach and why, we can build both effective performances and marketing plans on a tight budget. Part Four introduces creative tools for crafting our marketing messages. We explore copywriting for both traditional and new media. Part Five ends the book with techniques for performing in person or in media. These are used to effectively project our defined message, feelings and images to an audience, whether we're trying to entertain, inform, persuade or do some combination of the three. These personality performance basics can come in handy in all of our contacts with prospects, customers, and others who are involved in some way with us.

Now let's have some performance and promotional fun. Let's engage all our audiences and stakeholders with communication that's entertaining enough to get their attention and hold their interest. Let's create some desire by teaching them our ideas, images and feelings. And let's work on ways to get them to take our intended action.

Part One:
Customer
Personalities

Chapter One: Personalities in the Marketing Cycle

As mentioned in the Introduction, the web and mobile media have stopped traditional media from being the exclusive gatekeepers for messaging. We can now all be publishers and broadcasters using owned media, including our company website, plus social media and video sharing sites.

Personality is important in every area of the marketing cycle, whether we're using traditional or new media or making personal contacts. This includes identifying and understanding our customers, creating our product, and training our personnel. We all know that people buy products they like from folks they know and trust. So, if we want others to know and trust us and to like what we're offering, the first thing we need to do is to make a good effort to get to know them and their needs. We should understand who they are, where they live, how they think, and what they feel. Then, we need to define the personalities that we want our product and company to project. Once we understand who we are, what we have, and who we're trying to reach, we can be more effective in our marketing efforts…no matter what venue we're in, what media we're using, or what we're promoting.

Customer-Centric Marketing

We should avoid *marketing myopia*, which is the tendency to focus on our company instead of our customers. This means that we should be *customer-centric* in our marketing, as opposed to being *company-centric*. Perhaps, instead of having a sales meeting where we haul out a whiteboard showing the sales numbers we want to hit and discussing shareholder value, we might instead talk about ways that our product can benefit our customers. A 2014 article in *Forbes Magazine* lists 6 key steps to customer-centric marketing. These are: (1) Connect with buyers by understanding their "personas"; (2) Engage across multiple channels; (3) Optimize campaign effectiveness through performance analytics; (4) Use intelligent content to deepen customer relationships; (5) Leverage social media, and (6) Manage your database to enhance its value.

http://www.forbes.com/sites/oracle/2014/05/05/6-key-steps-to-customer-centric-modern-marketing/

Here's a little history. As a business discipline, marketing is now said to be entering its fourth major era. The first was the *production era*, with a focus on making products efficiently. It lasted from the late 1800's until about 1930. The second was the *sales era*, focused on personal selling techniques. This lasted through about 1950. Then the *customer era* began, with a focus on customer satisfaction and relationship marketing, and it continues today. Meanwhile, though, technology is bringing us to a new stage that's being called the *interactive era*. It's filled with an ever-growing number of media choices for marketers, and with more information and buying options available to consumers. So with customer power increasing and with a bewildering plethora of marketing choices to make, it's important that we as small business marketers stay grounded in the basics while we explore this brave new world.

Personal communication and promotional messaging are not just about our words. They're also about how we look and how we sound. Whether or not we intend it, every message we transmit to another carries meaning far beyond what we actually say. Sure, the words themselves are vital. But they're only a part of the ideas and feelings that we transfer. Subtextual meaning is conveyed in the structure and tone of written communications including a letter, a print ad, an invoice, or on the company's website. And in spoken contacts, communications guru Dr. Albert Mehrabian maintains that the words themselves are actually only about 7% of the message. He says the other 93% is conveyed in our vocal sounds plus our facial expressions and bodily movements.

Engagement, entertainment, education, and persuasion are all tied together in marketing. Whenever we're doing one, we're doing a bit of the others as well. An engaging marketing campaign is entertaining enough to grab and hold attention, it teaches the viewer or listener what we want them to know and it persuades them to take some sort of action.

Those of us who are small business owners or managers have to wear a lot of hats, including the marketing one. Here in our real world, a buying decision usually comes down to just one person who believes in us and our product. For us, marketing is more about effective person-to-person communication than flashy production and big-dollar ad buys. Hey, it's great to watch ads on a top-rated primetime TV program, or on a huge sporting event like the Super Bowl or the World Cup. Wonderful communication can be accomplished by spending millions of dollars on the production of a 30-second TV spot and then forking over a few million more to run that new gem. But for most of us, big promotional budgets are just not available.

The good news is that we probably don't need to plop down big bucks. As businesspeople, we know that it's a waste to spend money reaching people who are not potential customers. So instead of trying to reach the largest possible audience, we employ *targeting* to zero in on actual prospects. Even though we don't have a big marketing department we have some huge competitive pressures, not the least of which is that our bigger challengers have much larger budgets. So we have to be a bit spunky when we fight back, and one of our best weapons is personality.

Local traditional media are great for achieving some of our little-guy marketing objectives with TV, radio, print, outdoor, and specialty advertising. So are the Internet and mobile technology using our owned media and the social web plus video and photo sharing sites. With a little technique and creativity, we can maximize the use of our limited promotional dollars in both traditional media and the new media outlets. And if we want, we can instantly have access to markets all over the world…just like the big guys.

The Marketing Journey

An advertising schedule is sometimes called a *flight*, so let's compare a marketing plan to an airplane trip. As a pilot for over 30 years, I've learned that a successful cross-country journey requires five things. First, we have to be aware of exactly where we are right now. We also need to know our intended destination. Next, we must define a precise route that's made up of a series of shorter-term waypoints to be reached sequentially. Fourth, we have to have a vehicle that's capable of getting us there. Finally, we need the skills to fly the danged airplane and navigate our course.

Obviously, this simple five-step formula can be applied to virtually any journey in life. This includes our personal goals such as learning to play a sport or a musical instrument, as well as our company goals. For our business purposes, one of the first things we need is a good understanding of the elements of marketing. This helps us build a clear definition of each of our marketing objectives. We'll probably simultaneously use a variety of avenues to reach our prospects. Those we choose at any given time will likely be a mix of traditional media, personal contacts, the web, and mobile devices. Communication is the skill set that we use to fly our marketing vehicles and navigate the course. After successfully reaching each of our course waypoints along the route, we just have to look out the window. We're now at our destination.

The main focuses of this book are to understand the personalities of our target audience, to try to ensure that our product itself projects a compatible personality, and to build interpersonal communication skills so that each of our personnel exhibits our company's intended personality. We'll also look at the steps of setting marketing goals and selecting promotional vehicles. Our basic idea is always simple. We have a message that we use to transfer specific ideas and feelings from one person to another. Our personality is an important part of those feelings. It's the perception by the receiver of our traits and intentions.

Comedian Johnny Carson once commented that he believed that about 95% of people who go into the entertainment business do so because they need applause. And marketing certainly involves the psychological fact that a lot of us need recognition and rewards. Some fundamentals of teaching and learning are also included in this book, since they're an important part of the persuasion process. Performance techniques are a big part of what this book is about, because the skills of working in front of an audience can be a big help in all of our business communications. As businesspeople, we might consider regularly getting in front of a crowd in some way. This can be done by giving speeches in Toastmasters, or through a service club. We might teach an adult education class, join a community theatre group, play in a band, or sing karaoke. Working on a platform or stage in front of others forces us to think about the exact ideas and feelings that we want to convey, and about how we want to be perceived. These skills transfer to all sorts of pressurized situations, including business meetings and presentations of all kinds. Particularly in theatre and in singing, we must think about conveying emotions. As we practice thinking about the ideas and emotions we're communicating, we learn to avoid accidentally communicating unintended feelings or perceptions. And performing is not only beneficial. It's just plain fun.

What Is Personality Marketing?

It's often said that all of politics is local. We could also think of marketing that way, because in the end it's one-on-one. It all comes down to a buying decision from an individual. So let's define personality marketing as *an integrated program across multiple communication channels that is designed to display specific aspects of our persona, product or company to a targeted individual that we have defined in terms of characteristics and needs.* A spokesperson is often used. Examples could include the business owner, a hired celebrity, a satisfied customer, a baby, a personified animal, an animation, or a fictional human character.

Personality is a big deal in marketing. Big companies and large agencies do it very, very well. They pay huge amounts of money to use famous folks such as actors and athletes to advertise and endorse their products. In other cases the products themselves become the personalities, or fictional characters are created by actors or animators to represent them. Examples include Flo for Progressive Insurance, Captain Obvious for hotels.com, the Budweiser frogs, the California Raisins, the Geico gecko, and Leo Burnette's classic product personalities including Tony the Tiger, Charlie Tuna, the Jolly Green Giant, and the Pillsbury Doughboy. The list goes on and on and changes daily.

Big budgets help the top copywriters, producers, marketers, performers and agencies emphasize personality in their work. The good news is that at the local level we can accomplish similar personality campaigns using home-grown talent and not spending much. And with just a little directing, company personnel can be among the most effective personalities. It's great when the firm's owner or manager becomes a local celebrity. Personality should be a fundamental consideration when we're planning all of our marketing communications. First, we'll define our appropriate market segments by sex/age groups, income, and other lifestyle factors. Second, we need to identify reasons why these people might want what we're offering. Third, we must decide which of our product's features create what desirable benefits for each targeted group. Then we can define product traits, positioning, and differentiation that appeal to the target. Finally, we should understand that every customer contact by anyone associated with our company should communicate, reinforce, or at least not conflict with, the intended characteristics of our firm and its products.

For a simple example of how personality and emotions can be used in marketing, let's begin with a peek at the new songs that continually transform the music business. Hey, at its core music is pretty simple. It only has 12 notes, and they haven't changed in the 2,500 years or so since Greek mathematician Pythagoras stretched some strings and came up with the chromatic increments of an octave that are still in use today. But these 12 notes can be put together in infinite ways, and fresh-sounding music comes out every day. That's because artists, writers and producers combine them differently at any given time depending on which personalities they're trying to reach and what feelings they want the music to transfer through a song.

The same concept is just as true in writing and performing advertising and other marketing communications. We might think of personality marketing as a kind of guerilla strategy. Once our message has been defined, we must plan beyond just what we say. In our subtext, a product's personality profile can be transferred throughout various media in an integrated campaign, in all contacts with customers and prospects across all parts of the marketing mix.

Communicating Our Message

As mentioned in the Introduction, marketing depends on effective communication with all stakeholders in the business, including owners or shareholders, managers, employees, suppliers, prospects, and customers. Communication occurs when one person sends ideas or feelings to another. We all studied our grammar, vocabulary and composition skills in school, and these were certainly important. Yet the fact is, particularly in spoken communication, the words themselves carry only a relatively small part of our total message.

Communication models have been around for a long time. The Shannon-Weaver model proposed six elements: *source, encoder, message, channel, decoder, and receiver*. In 1954, Wilbur Schramm expanded it to also include *feedback* from the receiver to the source, plus *field of experience* for both the source and the receiver. This includes an individual's values, beliefs, customs, and experiences both as an individual and as a part of a group to which the source or receiver belongs. I like the FAA's simple explanation of the communication model. It includes the source who decides on the message and encodes it using symbols such as words and images, and the receiver who decodes the message. The receiver then sends feedback to the source, which is used to adjust subsequent encoding as necessary. We human beings are just 5-channel receivers who see, hear, feel, smell, and taste. So we select one or more of these channels for sending our encoded message.

As the rock group "The Animals" once sang, *"I'm just a soul whose intentions are good. Oh Lord, please don't let me be misunderstood."* On the receiving end, our target fights through all the noise that exists in our chosen communication channel, and receives our encoded message. The receiver decides whether to ignore the message or to pay attention to it. If attention is gained, the message is decoded by the receiver and interpreted according to his or her understanding of it. This can vary widely according to the receiver's perception of the meaning in our words plus subtextual meaning in our movements, gestures, facial expressions and the way that we sound. These can unknowingly transfer unintended meaning.

The receiver's perceived meaning of our message can also vary according to his or her sex, age, culture, customs, belief system, attitudes, income, lifestyle, and present circumstances. The source hopes for useful feedback from the receiver. Once encoded by the receiver and sent back to the source, this feedback enables the source to strategically adjust the message according to the source's decoding and understanding of the feedback. And the process starts all over. The communication's *effectiveness* is judged by the similarity between the idea transmitted and the idea received. Communication is *successful* when the desired results have been achieved.

The fact is that consumers are exposed to hundreds of marketing messages every day. Most have little or no apparent effect on the potential receiver's circumstances and are simply ignored. Only those relevant messages that cut through the noise and grab the prospect's attention receive any interest or consideration. If we're to have a good chance of sending out effective marketing messages, we have to employ both strategic thinking and creativity in our marketing communications. We have to somehow grab the attention of a qualified prospect in a well-defined market segment. Once we've settled on the human sensory channels for our communication effort, we need to decide on media. There are more of them than ever before, and making decisions about which to use seems harder than ever. But the marketing goal remains consistent throughout all media considerations. We have to cost-effectively reach the right individuals and convey the desired message.

Listening Skills

A critical part of interpersonal communication is to listen carefully to others involved. This becomes especially difficult when we're working impromptu with no outline or script because we sometimes tend to focus on what we're getting ready to say next, rather than on what the other person is presently saying. We must always do our best to listen, because we can't communicate effectively if we don't know what the other person just said or meant.

Personality in the 4-P's of Marketing

Characterization is the process of deciding what personality traits we want to communicate in our messages. We have to make sure that our non-language communications are as effective as the words themselves.

At this point, let's be careful to not confuse promotion with marketing. There's a tuna/fish relationship here. Just as all tuna are fish but not all fish are tuna, all promotion is marketing but not all marketing is promotion. The classic marketing mix is a concept that was developed by E. Jerome McCarthy. It's called the 4-P's, which are product, price, place, and promotion. Marketing is involved in every product at every phase from conception to consumption. In Part Two of this book, we take a more in-depth look, but for now let's just peek briefly at each of them.

Product

The *product* should appeal to the personality or idealized self-image of our target customer, depending on his or her needs, emotions, lifestyle and other circumstances. Products can be goods, services, ideas, or persons. Examples include widgets, accounting, social issues, and political candidates.

A product can be personalized by assigning human qualities to it and giving the product a distinct personality, such as the personification of a tough, durable and hard-working pickup truck with a mind of its own. We might want to build a product image that's compatible with the prospect's idea of personal perfection like a sleek, fast and prestigious sports car. We could focus on satisfying pleasure needs with a beer that's cold and refreshing and has uncompromising brewing quality. Positioning and differentiation are also important in defining the image and personality of our product, and are covered in more detail later.

Price and Place

For *price*, a simple example of our personality strategy is deciding where we want to fall in the customer's price/quality perception. In the *place* step, the product's personality traits might be perceived differently if the product is being marketing at a high-end retailer than if it is sold via direct marketing on, say, an auction website.

Promotion

In the *promotion* phase, personality can be conveyed in any number of ways depending on the channels we employ and the media we choose plus the advertisements and other publicity that we write and produce. After our target has been defined in geographic, demographic, and psychographic terms, we need to understand and address the buying motivations of our prospects. Our approach could be quite different depending on whether we're introducing an exciting new product, attempting to build momentum in the product or category's growth cycle, trying to gain market share from competitors in the maturity phase, or simply reminding customers of our product during a category's decline. It's often said that opportunities walk around dressed as problems and that success lies in creating solutions for them.

Internal Marketing

Finally, our internal marketing is very important. The desired customer, company and product personality traits should be communicated to all persons involved in any way with prospect and customer contacts. The right personality message should be incorporated in every contact point throughout an integrated marketing campaign. This becomes increasingly important as segmentation replaces mass marketing and technology moves us into more interactive marketing. Using basic communication tools like those covered later in this book, people everywhere in the marketing mix can increase their effectiveness as members of the marketing team.

Chapter Two: Segmentation and Targeting Essentials

A good first step in any promotional campaign is to decide who might want our product. Our *target market* is simply a group of people who have needs and wants that make them likely prospects for whatever it is that we're selling. We break down populations through the process of *segmentation*, dividing a large group into smaller sections that contain common attributes. We can segment a population in terms of geography, demographics, psychographics, and lifestyles as well as by categories such as initial or repeat purchasers and light or heavy users. The terms *lifestyle* and *psychographic* analysis are often used as a single concept. Some separate the two, using the term psychographic data in reference to attitudinal and other psychological traits, and the term lifestyle to refer to income category and leisure activities. In this book we'll keep it simple by using the terms interchangeably and combining them as *qualitative data*, which is covered more in the next section.

Our target market can be business-to-business (B2B), industrial buyers, governmental agencies, or end consumers (B2C). Although this book primarily addresses consumer markets, many of the principles such as personal selling also apply to other types of marketing.

The consumer market can be either a *mass market* or a *segmented market*. *Mass marketing* is appropriate for products that have appeal to a wide chunk of the population. It tries to reach the widest possible audience and is sometimes called a shotgun approach or undifferentiated marketing. *Targeted marketing* aims at specific market segments and is often referred to as a rifle approach, concentrated marketing, or niche marketing. Segmentation and customer-oriented thinking help make it possible for the little guy to compete against larger companies that market to the masses over a wide area.

17

Research

Targeting and segmentation require research. Chapter Nine includes more expanded information on market research, but for now let's take a quick overview. *Quantitative research* deals with numbers, such as an overall population of persons in a demographic group. *Qualitative research* deals with the specifics of a group including such components as lifestyles, social classes, attitudes, opinions, and buying habits. Research may be primary or secondary. *Primary research* is that which is done specifically for our purposes, and it's the expensive kind. *Secondary research* was originally done for other purposes and has been adapted to our use. This is the most economical research method, and it's what we should do first before we go out and start commissioning our own primary research.

Geographic Segmentation

The first and most fundamental way that we segment is by geography. Our market may be global, international, or national, but most small businesses focus on a regional, statewide, area, local, or neighborhood market.

The most obvious source for geographic data is the official national census. In the U. S, the Office of Management and Budget and other federal agencies use the term *Metropolitan Statistical Area* (Metro) to describe a place that has a core urban population of at least 50,000. It uses the term *Micropolitan Statistical Area* (Micro) for one that has an urban core of at least 10,000. Both are abbreviated MSA. The term *Core Based Statistical Area* (CBSA) applies to both. The CBSA consists of one or more counties. It includes those containing the core urban area, as well as any adjacent counties that have a high degree of social and economic integration with the urban core, measured by commuting to work.

A major marketing consideration is population density, which is calculated by dividing the total population of a geographic area by its area in square miles or kilometers.

Demographic Segmentation

Demographics is the term referring to the study of human populations with reference to age, sex, family size, and other statistics including population density and distribution. Demographic segmentation is the method used most frequently in defining the groups making up a population's universe. Demographic groups or *cells* are often used for marketing purposes, such as 18-49 or 25-54.

Generational clustering is a simple example of demographic segmentation. Going back to 1900, the U. S. generations are generally recognized as being the G. I. Generation (1900 – 1924), the Silent Generation (1925 – 1945), Baby Boomers (1946-1964), Generation X (1965 – 1979), Generation Y or Millennials (1980-2000), and Generation Z (2001 – present).

Psychographic and Lifestyle Segmentation

Once we have our geographic area defined and the population broken down by demographics, the next step is to look at lifestyles and attitudes. *Psychographic* or *lifestyle marketing* is consumer behavior segmentation relative to income, attitudes, leisure activities, and other factors. We'll look at income and occupation plus things like dwelling status including neighborhoods, renters and homeowners. We'll analyze *disposable income*, which refers to income after taxes, and *discretionary income*, which refers to the after-tax income left over after buying necessities including food, shelter, and transportation.

Our marketing strategy will depend on many factors, including the available population and whether we want to promote *downmarket, midmarket,* or *upmarket* in terms of quality and price. If we go upscale, we're focusing on persons with high incomes or education levels. We may want to target the upwardly mobile. Or we might target lower income individuals. Whatever our target, we'll want to do some benefit segmentation to isolate those groups that might want or need our product. Then our next step is to find cost-effective ways of reaching them.

One useful lifestyle segmentation tool is the generally accepted *Family Life Cycle Stage Segmentation System*. It utilizes nine groupings by age, marital status, household size, working status, and income. These are:

1. *Single Stage* – Unmarried young people not living at home
2. *Newly Married* – Young couples with no children
3. *Full Nesters – Stage I* – Younger Couples with children, youngest is under age 6.
4. *Full Nesters – Stage II* – Middle-age couples with children, all age 6 or older.
5. *Full Nesters – Stage III* – Older couples with children, perhaps in college.
6. *Empty Nesters Stage I* – Older married couples, working, with no children at home.
7. *Empty Nesters Stage II* – Older married couple, retired.
8. *Solitary Survivor Stage I* – Single middle-aged or older, still working.
9. *Solitary Survivor Stage II* – Single, retired.

If we really want to get fancy, we can use a geo-demographic segmentation system from PRIZM (U. S.) or MOSAIC (U. K.) that divides specific geographies down to the neighborhood or postal code level, breaking their populations into lifestyle categories. PRIZM is the acronym for Potential Rating Index by Zip Market. It's a market segmentation service developed by Claritas, Inc., which is now available from The Nielsen Company. The PRIZM system uses U. S. Census data to segment consumer markets at the zip code level into 14 groups comprised of 66 demographic and lifestyle types. The 14 groups are organized into geographies of Urban, Suburban, Second City, and Town & Rural. They're then broken down by lower, middle and upper income groups according to the geography. Some basic PRIZM data is available for free on the Internet, and more detailed reports can be purchased for as little as $149 at the time of this writing. Visit www.mybestsegments.com.

And let's not forget our own data. If we keep good customer and leads databases we can employ *micromarketing* right down to the individual level. We can contact existing and former customers with, for instance, the perfect gift for an upcoming event such as a spouse's birthday. We can also make a new offer to someone who has previously been a prospect but who hasn't bought yet. Customer relationship management (CRM) software can be a good investment of time and money for such purposes. Many small businesses use *Microsoft Office Outlook* as their communications, scheduling, and contact management hub. It can be enhanced with *Microsoft Dynamics CRM for Outlook*. Other companies offer CRM plug-ins for Outlook, and there are a number of standalone CRM software options.

Chapter Three: Buying Motivations and Consumer Behavior

If we're going to try to sell products, we should try to figure out why people might want to buy them. Makes sense, eh? So now that segmentation and targeting have helped us determine who our prospects are, where they live, and how many of them are out there, we need to figure out what their motivations might be in wanting or needing our product, and what drives their buying decisions. Before we look specifically at consumer buying behavior, let's discuss basic human behavior.

Human Behavior

Maslow's Hierarchy of Needs is a good place to start in analyzing the human needs that create both positive and negative motivations. In his 1954 book *Motivation and Personality*, Dr. Abraham Maslow detailed a model of human behavior that classifies human needs into five tiers, each of which must be satisfied before the person can focus on moving up to the next level. At the base of his pyramid, Maslow lists *Physical Needs*. These include food, water, air, shelter, rest, bodily functions, and warmth. Next are *Safety Needs*, which include security related to the person's body, family, employment, and property. The third tier is *Social Needs*, which include love, belonging, friendship, family, and intimacy. *Ego* follows, including respect of and by others, self-esteem, self-confidence, independence and achievement. *Self-Fulfillment* tops the pyramid. It includes higher-level thinking such as the use of creativity, strategic problem-solving, and morality. While some people have circumstances that stall them at a certain level for an extended period of time, pyramid tier positions are not always static. People move around, and on a given day a person may have needs at one or more levels, with varying desires.

Positive Motivations

In marketing, we usually deal with positive motivations. These satisfy a person's physical needs or build the self-image, and can meet lower-tier, mid-level or higher-tier needs. A positive motivation occurs when someone is rewarded, and can be based on emotion or logic. Logical or intellectual motivating factors are sometimes called "stated" motivations, because a purchase may be justified based on logical factors even when the decision is actually driven by emotions. Some logical motivating factors include the desire to save or to make money, making a deal urgently to avoid losing out, and doing something to be more efficient by saving time or effort. Some emotional motivating factors include pleasure, love, acceptance, sentiment, self-improvement, excitement, inspiration, and pride of ownership.

A want is a desire to satisfy a recognized need in a certain way, such as by using a specific product. We should try to understand our product's general position on the hierarchy of needs. And we also need to know how it typically equates to our prospect's position there. For example, food can satisfy a base-level hunger need while dinner in a fine restaurant can also help satisfy social and self-esteem needs. Some foods may be just plain fun to eat while satisfying hunger. We're starving, and we just can't wait to get a pizza and some cold beer. Maybe later we'll think about writing that paper on the history of archaeology.

Negative Motivations

A negative motivation occurs when our safety, survival, or self-image is threatened. It happens when someone expects or receives some sort of punishment or undesirable consequence as a result of a particular action or behavior, or the lack thereof. Like positive motivations, negative motivations can also be logical or emotional. Negative motivations of a logical nature could include losing our savings. We might miss a deadline, lose some item that then makes a task become much harder or take longer, receive a failing grade, or get a bad review. Emotional factors of a negative nature include anger, disgust, dissatisfaction, sadness, sympathy, escape from pain or discomfort, the need to prove something, guilt, concern, fear, and survival. Negative motivations are often addressed in advertising copy. (Can you say "political"?) We might be selling casualty, life or health insurance. Or we might be positioning our widget against a competitor's.

In marketing, we may occasionally encounter a situation in which we need to overcome or get around a prospect's use of a psychological defense mechanism. Everyone has a need to protect the ego and the sense of personal worth, so sometimes one of these may be consciously or unconsciously used. *Compensation* is an attempt to hide a perceived weakness by emphasizing a perceived strength. *Projection* is blaming others for one's shortcomings, mistakes, desires and impulses. With *rationalization*, a person creates excuses that they believe seem plausible and acceptable, and they may even actually believe that their own excuses are reasons. *Denial of reality* means that a person just simply refuses to acknowledge some situation. *Reaction formation* is the process of developing outward or conscious attitudes and behaviors that are the exact opposite of those that the person is trying to hide. *Flight* means getting away from something physically or mentally. With *physical flight*, a person develops symptoms of ailments that give them excuses to remove themselves from an unpleasant situation. With *mental flight*, a person escapes with mind-numbing activities such as daydreaming. *Aggression* occurs when a person gets angry at someone or something in response to a situation. *Resignation* occurs when someone becomes so frustrated that they give up.

Here are some examples of when we might be dealing with a defense mechanism in marketing. We could sense and then try to smoke out a hidden objection during personal selling. We might be doing an ad for the new sedative Damitol. Or perhaps Captain Obvious is pointing out that if the significant other continues to have those intimacy-blocking headaches at bedtime every night, there's a great deal right now on booking a room at the Lonely Lodge.

Consumer Behavior and the Buying Cycle

Consumer behavior is a person's tendency to acquire products and services in certain ways and for reasons according to their needs, desires, and ability to purchase. Human motivations drive consumer behavior. Some purchases are considered over time and competitors are researched, while other purchases are made on impulse with little or no prior consideration. *Buying motivations* are the underlying, often unexpressed decisions that consumers make regarding purchases. One person's motivation may be different than another's for buying the same product, and the same person's motivation for buying the product may be different from time to time.

The *buying cycle* is a series of consumer behavior steps that a person goes through in making the decision to purchase. These include the recognition of a want or need, a search for information on available options, developing a preference for an option, analyzing data or other evidence to develop conviction, making the purchase, and then undergoing a post-purchase evaluation to confirm that he or she made the right choice. A number of buying cycle models exist out there.

Here, let's keep it simple with one that's both practical and easy to remember. That would be the AIDA formula, built on the acronym meaning Attention, Interest, Desire, and Action. This one has stood the test of time by having been around since the turn of the century. Not this past turn of the century, the one before that...St. Elmo Lewis came up with AIDA in 1898. Here's how it flows. First, a product or service comes to the attention of the consumer. Next, the consumer becomes interested in it by realizing a need in that product category. Then, something convinces the consumer to develop a desire to have that particular product fill the need. Finally, the consumer takes action. Let's look at some things to consider in each step of the AIDA buying cycle.

Attention

Before we can have any hope of selling anything to anyone, we have to get their attention. In advertising, this often means cutting through the clutter of surrounding ads. People pay selective attention, so we must be aware of *cognitive consistency* and *cognitive dissonance*. These terms mean that a listener, viewer, or reader of an advertising message tends to pay attention only to messages that are consistent with his or her current wants, needs, beliefs, attitudes, or opinions. And we must be mindful of *intrusiveness*, which is the level of irritation caused by an advertisement.

Advertising can be done for a lot of reasons. We might be trying to generate *product awareness* or a direct response purchase. We might want to attract people to a weekend sales event. We might be doing reputation management. We might be *positioning* or *repositioning* by attempting to establish or modify the image of our product or its benefits and value relative to competitors. We might be doing *differentiation*, explaining how our product is better or unique. We might have an infomercial in which we're talking about a *paradigm shift* that involves adjustments in beliefs, thoughts, values or ideas required by some major change, which of course means trying our revolutionary new product. Or we might be doing *reminder advertising* on a billboard or transit ad in conjunction with more detailed ads in other media.

We discussed marketing myopia in Chapter One, which involves a company's natural tendency over time to focus on its product rather than on the wants and needs of the customer. The attention-grabber in our opening is generally more effective when it's customer-centric, addressing some logical or emotional motivation of our buyer, as opposed to being feature-oriented. Wants and needs drive behavior, and that includes paying attention.

Interest

The next thing in the buying cycle is that the consumer must become interested by realizing that he or she has a want or need related to the benefits of a product in our category. Lots of things come into play here. For example, economics can be a big factor in consumer spending. Consumer confidence and spending patterns are very different in the business cycles of downturns, recessions, recoveries, and booms. *Macroeconomic factors* like the unemployment rate, national or regional economic growth, and the rate of inflation are beyond the control of a company, but may have an impact on the prospect's attitudes or ability to purchase. *Microeconomic conditions* are those concerned with particular companies or individuals and the economic relationships between them. These may also have a direct impact on a prospect's buying decisions.

Our product has to fit with the prospect's view of the *price/quality equation*. For example, an upscale buyer such as a wealthy businessperson, doctor, or lawyer might consider only higher-priced items, potentially gaining *psychic income*. That's getting an emotional benefit such as prestige from buying a product. In the middle, an upwardly mobile prospect who is trying to move up the socioeconomic ladder might spend more time in a cost-benefit analysis, comparing the cash spent to the expected benefits to be gained. He or she may consider *opportunity cost* before making a purchase. That's income not kept or some other benefit not received as a result of using the money to buy our product. At the lower end of the income scale, affordability becomes more important with a product of acceptable quality. Also, we might have something that a prospect really wants, but decides against buying after taking a look at his or her discretionary income.

Of course, *individual demand* is generally a primary consideration. This is the prospect's own historical, present, and future need for products in our category. Our product category may be very important to the customer's lifestyle, or it might be considered a luxury that gets cut as soon as money tightens. Demand might be seasonal. The prospect may have heard of our product or something similar through social channels such as conversations with friends or other word-of-mouth influences, but the prospect has never tried it. We may be offering something completely new that he or she has never considered before, but that now sounds interesting. Or we might have a product in a category that the prospect uses regularly, and for some reason our widget could be better than what's presently being used. Once our prospect has decided that we have a product in a category for which he or she has a present need and the ability to buy, we've accomplished the Interest Step.

Desire

Now that our prospect sees a need in our category, it's time to convince him or her that our product is the best way to fill it. Branding with our logo, slogan, or jingle is a good first step. The Small Business Encyclopedia at entrepreneur.com defines branding as "the marketing practice of creating a name, symbol or design that identifies and differentiates a product from other products." For our purposes in this book, we use the term *branding* to refer to our name, logo, slogan, or jingle. We consider differentiation, positioning, and imaging separately.

We'll use the term *differentiation* to express how we're better, and hopefully unique. The *Unique Selling Proposition* (USP) is a concept that originated with Rosser Reeves of the Ted Bates Advertising Agency in New York. He detailed it in his 1961 book, *Reality in Advertising*. The concept is that every ad needs to offer a special benefit which should be unique to the product and strong enough to pull customers.

Positioning is a concept advanced by Al Ries and Jack Trout in their book *Positioning: The Battle for Your Mind*, with editions in 1981 and 2002. It refers to the way that customers perceive the value of our product's benefits relative to those of its competitors. A major point is that consumers are more likely to buy a product based on its perceived differences from similar products than they are to buy the product based purely on its own features and benefits.

Imaging means promoting our product in a way that appeals to either the personality or idealized self-image of our target customer. We might emphasize the actual mental picture we want the prospect to retain. We could personalize the product by giving it a personality of its own. Or we may stress how the prospect will feel when using it. Over time, we can build top-of-mind-awareness (TOMA) that causes the prospect to think of our product immediately when the need arises for something in our category. And of course we have to make a good offer or give a compelling reason why the prospect should do what we want. We should do everything possible to ensure that our prospect has a perceived value of our product that outweighs any perceived risk in choosing it. This includes reputation management with existing and former customers, because positive word-of-mouth can be a big influence in a prospect's decision to choose our product over that of a competitor. We should ask our happy customers for good reviews.

Action

The first factor in getting action is to make sure that we're addressing either the decision maker or a key decision influencer. Our focus can vary depending on the type of product we're marketing. For some B2B and industrial products, there's a formal decision making unit (DMU). This is the group responsible for making purchases for a business. While the big guys have formal teams, for us little folk this may just be the owner or the manager.

If we offer a revolutionary product, we have to deal with a concept called *diffusion*, which refers to the adoption of a product over time by a widening group of consumers. Diffusion of Innovation is a concept developed by Everett M. Rogers in 1962. It breaks the adopters of an innovation into five groups: (1) Innovators (less than 5%); (2) Early Adopters (12 - 15%); (3) Early Majority (30 – 35%); Late Majority (35 – 40%); and (5) Laggards (15 – 20%).

For most consumer products, the individual prospect is the actual purchaser. An influencer could be the child who sees the McDonald's arches and causes the family car to make a stop. Pricing strategy is a major factor in influencing action. We'll talk more about that in Chapter Five. And we want to remember the *Least Effort Principle*. This means that we make it as easy as possible for customers to purchase.. And whether we're doing an advertisement or making a personal sales presentation, we generally want to actually ask the customer to take some sort of action. This could be buying now, going to a sales event, sampling a product, calling a phone number, returning a business reply mail (BRM) card, visiting a website, remembering the product's image, or by assigning it a mental position relative to others in our category.

Chapter Four: Teaching Concepts for Marketing

Our essential tools include talent, knowledge, reasoning, skill development, and the investment of time if we want to build success in anything from playing the guitar to dribbling a basketball to producing commercials to closing sales. We'll call it the *BAT formula*, for brains, abilities, and time. In marketing, we're in the education business. Our "students" are our prospects, customers, and others with whom we do business. Learning has been defined as a change in behavior due to experience, while teaching is the process of transferring knowledge and skill. Knowing something is one thing, and teaching it is quite another. In marketing, sometimes we try to influence knowledge, thinking, memory, attitudes or behavior. Other times we want to train someone how to do something with, for example, a content video on the web. We're always trying to educate to some degree, whether we're doing a 30-second commercial or a 30-minute presentation.

Education requires both teaching and learning. The teacher can teach, but only the student can learn. It's the teacher's job to make learning more effective by understanding the motivations people have that might make them want to learn what we have to teach, and to convey the message effectively. Let's take a marketing view of some principles of teaching and learning.

Motivation

Motivation is the main force in learning. It can be *intrinsic*, coming from within, or due to *extrinsic* factors caused by circumstances out of an individual's control. A negative motivation might be used to help stimulate a purchase by, for example, pointing out the possibility of financial loss without a product. Or it could show ways to use a product to avoid pain or injury. Positive motivations in marketing can stress things including financial gain, personal comfort, security, peer approval, or improving the self-image.

Marketing is influencing, so let's look at some fundamentals of how teaching and learning work. We'll begin by defining ability. *Ability* is made up of talent plus knowledge plus skill. In educating, we can't supply the talent. It's our job to affect the other two.

How People Learn

Learning depends in part on factors including psychosocial and moral development. Roles are also played by things including language skills, achievements, and attitudes on gender and sex. Learning depends on the processing of information coming into the brain, and on social interaction. A person has to recognize, sort and store the incoming information. And everyone's perception of incoming information is influenced by psychological factors including their beliefs and their attitudes, as well as those of their peers. As mentioned earlier, this is often referred to as the cognitive consonance or dissonance of a message. If it's in harmony with these attitudes and beliefs, they'll listen. If not, they probably won't.

Prospects process information differently. So we need to utilize a variety of communication channels to access the learning process that's most effective for different people. Some prospects are visual learners. Others are aural learners. Some respond better to logical information. Others are more influenced by emotions. Some are kinesthetic learners who respond best to hands-on training.

Learning Domains and Levels

There are four *levels* of learning. *Rote* learning is simple memorization. *Understanding* means to grasp the nature of something. *Application* refers to the ability to put something that has been learned into use. *Correlation* means that something has been understood, can be applied, and has been related to other things that have been learned.

Three *domains* of learning are generally accepted. These are (1) the *cognitive domain* (knowledge and understanding), (2) the *affective domain* (attitudes, beliefs and values), and (3) the *psychomotor domain* (physical skills). Here's an FAA summary designed for developing a program of instruction. This can be useful for planning live training, producing a web content video, or any other marketing purpose. It covers things to consider in each level of each learning domain.

Cognitive Domain

Knowledge: Describe, identify, name, point to, recognize, or recall.
Comprehension: Convert, explain, locate, report, restate, or select.
Application: Compute, demonstrate, employ, operate, or solve.
Analysis: Compare, discriminate, distinguish, or separate.
Synthesis: Compile, compose, design, reconstruct, or formulate.
Evaluation: Assess, evaluate, interpret, judge, rate, score, or write.

Affective Domain

Receiving: Ask, choose, give, locate, select, rely, or use.
Responding: Conform, greet, help, perform, recite, or write.
Valuing: Appreciate, follow, join, justify, show concern, or share.
Organization: Accept responsibility, adhere, defend, and formulate.
Characterization: Assess, delegate, practice, influence, revise, and maintain.

Psychomotor Domain

Perception: Choose, detect, identify, isolate, or compare.
Set (Knows & Relates Cues): Begin, move, react, respond, start, or select.
Guided Response: Assemble, build, calibrate, fix, or mend.
Mechanism (Performs Simple Acts): Same as above, but with greater proficiency.
Complex Overt Response: Same as above, except more highly coordinated.
Adaptation: Adapt, alter, change, rearrange, reorganize, or revise.
Origination: Combine, compose, construct, design, or originate.

Learning Personalities

Personality has a huge impact on how people learn our marketing message. *Dependent learners* require more individual attention and step-by-step sequential instructions. *Independent learners* may just want to get the big picture, and then off they go on their own. A prospect may be *silent, impulsive,* or may be more *tentative* about making changes. He or she could be *anxious, despondent, depressed,* or *vulnerable.* The prospect may be an *attention-seeker* out to impress the Joneses. Personality characteristics like these can be important considerations in defining targets for our marketing campaigns.

Get It Right and Drill It In

We need to keep our marketing messages relevant, engaging, and exciting. The *Law of Readiness* says that our prospects must be ready to learn. If we're to have any hope of them remembering our message we should keep in mind that, first and foremost, they must have or be given some meaningful reason to see or hear it. The *Law of Primacy* tells us that the first experience creates a lasting impression, so we want to make that one a good one. We need to provide pleasant or satisfying feelings. These are usually emotional, but can be physical. In training applications we may be able to incorporate some mental or physical drills to aid retention. And we should remember the *Law of Recency.* This states that the last things learned are remembered best. We can help with this by repetition of our key points, and by including the key thing to be learned or done in our closing summary.

Perceptions and Insight

Real meaning comes from within our prospect according to how he or she perceives our marketing stimuli, which must be experienced through the five human senses. According to the FAA, what we see leads the way by a long shot, at 75%, followed by hearing at 13%. Learning occurs most rapidly when multiple senses are employed in teaching.

Our perception is our reality. Psychologists say that our most basic need is to maintain and enhance the *organized self,* which is our perception of our past, present and future combined. Our body affects how we perceive things, and all perceptions are affected by our goals, beliefs, values, and our self-image. An element of threat tends to limit our attention to resolving that danger. *Insight* occurs when perceptions are grouped into meaningful associations with other things we know. True learning involves an understanding of how each thing affects each other thing. As marketers, we shouldn't assume that prospects will make these correlations on their own. We want to point out the relationships.

Attention and Interest Are Job One

As mentioned earlier, in our marketing material we want to either address an existing reason or give our prospect a new, clear one to want to learn what we wish to teach them. This is accomplished in our headline or opening summary, also called a grabber or hook. Once we have their attention, we have to keep their interest. We want our presentation to be entertaining and engaging, and to take sufficient but not excessive time. For instance, if we're teaching a skill in a content video, we want to make sure that we're providing a clear, step-by-step example. But taking too much time or providing too much detail can be counterproductive.

Retention of Our Ad Message

Obviously, we don't just want them to pay attention to what we have to say. We want them to *retain* it. The retention of the information we try to put across depends to a great degree on how entertaining and engaging it is. To be effective, our education attempts should include the creation of mental or physical experiences that promote learning. That means we have to relate our messages to our prospects' situations by telling them how changing their actions, thoughts, or reasoning helps them reach their goals. We back up our claims by providing logical or emotional supporting evidence.

Memory involves some sort of input to the sensory register. The brain quickly evaluates the information for relevancy. If the prospect sees the stimulus as important, it's sent to the working or short-term memory. In the short-term memory, the information is coded according to its subject matter. Then it's sent to the long-term memory for processing and for storage, where it becomes available for later recall.

The opposite of remembering is, of course, *forgetting*. There are a number of reasons why we forget things. Three of the biggest are disuse, interference, and repression. *Disuse* means that we tend to forget things that aren't used. *Interference* occurs when something new or similar has been learned that replaces what was previously learned. *Repression* means that people forget things that are unpleasant to recall or that produce anxiety.

The FAA lists five main factors that influence *retention* of what we've learned. These are praise, association, favorable attitudes, learning with all the senses, and meaningful repetition. Let's discuss each. The recall of *praise* brings positive memories, whereas the recall of negative criticism can cause repression of the memory. *Association* of new knowledge with something previously learned aids retention while unique, disassociated things are easily forgotten. A favorable *attitude* must be created toward the material, because people tend to learn and remember only things that they want to know. And although people tend to learn mostly what they see and hear, we should try to involve as many human senses as possible in our marketing efforts. Finally, meaningful *repetition* increases retention. Frequency of exposure works in marketing.

Transfer of Learning

In order to use new knowledge, the prospect or customer should know how it applies to things that he or she already knows. In order to apply a new skill, it should have been learned well enough that it becomes easy, and he or she must be able to recognize situations in which the skill should be applied. This is called *transfer of learning*. People interpret new things based upon their previous experiences, their beliefs, their attitudes, and their skills. This may aid or inhibit learning something new. For example, it may sometimes be harder to correct something that already exists than to teach something entirely new from scratch.

Part Two:

Product Personality and the Elements of the Marketing Mix

Chapter Five: Product, Price and Place

The term *marketing mix* refers to the way all the elements are combined throughout the entire process from product conception to consumption. We did a brief overview of the 4-Ps in Chapter One. Now let's look at each of them in more detail.

The Product

In this book, we use the term *product* to include goods, services, ideas, or people such as performers or political candidates. A *product category* is a group of similar products designed to satisfy related consumer wants and needs.

Every product category has a *life cycle*, and we need to pinpoint our product's position in it. The product category's life cycle position is plotted on a line through the stages of introduction, growth, maturity, decline, and withdrawal. A number of factors can play a role in the length of the category's life cycle, and a major one is technology. In days past, the intercontinental railroad spelled the end of the wagon train business and the automobile killed buggies. Today, smart phones are replacing land lines and tablet computers are taking sales away from desktops and laptops. *Market share* is calculated by dividing our product's sales by our category's total sales.

Once we know our category's life cycle position and our market share, we can describe our product using the classic terms from the Boston Consulting Group's *Growth/Share Matrix*. We'll consider both the category's life cycle growth position and our product's market share from low to high. A *Star* product has high market share in a high-growth category. A *Problem Child* or *Question Mark* has low market share in a high-growth category. A *Cash Cow* has a high market share in a low-growth category, and a *Dog* has a low market share in a low-growth product category.

Here are the investment and profit basics from the matrix. Stars require investment in the face of competition, and so their profits can be relatively low. Question Marks need high investments to try to build market share in growing categories, with resulting low profits. Cash cows face relatively little competition to maintain their position, and they generate high profits. Dogs generate low profits or losses.

Once we have an idea of where our present product sits in terms of category growth, market share, investment requirements and profitability, we can decide whether we want to invest more in marketing the product as it is, improve it, or develop a new product.

A *product line* is a group of related products offered by a company. The firm's *product mix* is the total of all its various product lines. The *depth* of a line refers to the number of related products in the line. The *width* of a company's products refers to the number of product lines in its product mix. A specialty shop goes deep, while a big box store like Wal-Mart goes wide. We should periodically analyze our product mix in terms of company goals, how each product in each line is meeting customer needs and expectations, and how our mix might be improved.

Our New and Existing Products

In our last thrilling section, we analyzed our current product's position in terms of category growth and market share. A good next step is to do a little brainstorming on the product, perhaps using a team approach to generating ideas. Our creative team should regularly brainstorm regarding both our current and new product options, reviewing the wants and needs of our potential and existing customers and how we can fill them with existing or new products.

New products should be, to the degree possible, designed and tested to meet or exceed both customer needs and expectations prior to their release, whether our product is marketed locally, regionally, nationally, or internationally.

Our *logo* is our brand or company's identifying symbol, usually made up of some combination of graphics and text. Our *slogan* is the phrase used to identify a product or service. Each may need some revision from time to time to make sure it's still representing our products well.

Our *intangible assets* include licenses, patents, trademarks and copyrights to which we have rights. The Lanham Trademark Act of 1946 is a federal law in the U. S. that protects registered trademarks and trade names. Copyrights are protected in the U. S. by the Copyright Act of 1976, as amended. The Digital Millennium Copyright Act (DMCA) implements two 1996 treaties of the World Intellectual Property Organization, and concerns digital rights management. From time to time we should look at our intellectual property to determine if our protections are current, if they need renewal, or if we need additional ones.

We might also look at our production capacity, as well as that of our competition, with an eye toward efficiency and profitability in the balance between demand and our ability to create supply. Perhaps a competitor has begun offshoring some of their operations, taking advantage of lower labor costs, lower taxes, or more favorable regulations in another country. Or maybe they're now hiring illegal workers, essentially getting offshoring with free delivery. How can we compete with those things? Could we outsource some of our own production, utilizing another company's products for components used in making ours? Could we benefit from outsourcing some of our company's non-production operations, such as payroll, accounts payable and receivable, or telephone answering? Is there technology we could add that would increase productivity? Are there ways we can achieve better economies of scale? Can we increase our vertical integration by strengthening our contracts with suppliers? Are our warranties adequate to provide customer security without being excessively costly to the company?

How about inventory? Do we have too much or too little on hand? Do we need excess supply for demand bursts, or do we want to conserve cash by keeping minimum inventory on hand and replacing it only when needed? Can we profitably use drop-shipping?

What are our costs per product sold? We can allocate production expenses to each product sold by using the *overall expenses method*. We just divide the total production expenses during a time period by the number of units sold in the same period. Our non-production overhead such as rent, telephone, and office utilities could also be allocated to each product using the same formula.

Product Line Extension or Expansion

An old cliché says that the secret to success is to find a gap and fill it. When we do *gap analysis*, we're looking at a market in search of unserved or underserved wants and needs. Sometimes that leads us to decide that we want to start selling something that we haven't previously offered.

If it's something we're going to make ourselves, this involves a number of different steps. First we need to develop the concept, do research and development, test the product, set up production, and then make pricing and distribution decisions. We have to give the product a name, calculate a break-even point, and then set our initial market penetration goals. We may do some test marketing to a representative demographic, psychographic, or geographic segment to gauge reaction to the product. Finally, we must decide on our promotional strategy including product awareness, branding, positioning, differentiation and imaging, and develop an advertising plan.

The new product that we've now decided to make or to acquire elsewhere might simply replace what we have now. It could extend our existing product line by deepening it. Or it might widen our mix by using horizontal or conglomerate diversification.

Product line *extension*, or *concentric diversification*, means adding products or *flanker brands* that are similar to what we presently offer but that are aimed at new customer segments. This is also called *deepening* the line. We're adding additional non-competitive but similar products to an established product line. This may be different varieties of a product for different segments of a market, such as a light beer or diet soda for weight-conscious drinkers. For a car dealer, it could be offering some

42

cars on a buy-here-pay-here basis in addition to those available through cash purchases or financed via traditional lenders. Other examples could include adding a big-and-tall size selection to a clothing product line, or a gluten-free version of a food product.

Whenever we extend a line, a product that is too similar to our main product can cause some *cannibalization*, which is a resulting reduction in our core product's sales. Cannibalization can also occur from adding an additional outlet that's too close to our present location. In some cases, adding our own flanker brands or products can help guard against flanking attacks from competitors.

Product line *pruning* is line extension in reverse. Pruning means reducing depth by eliminating less profitable products from a line.

Product line *expansion* can be either horizontal or conglomerate. *Horizontal diversification* means adding products that are unrelated to our core products but that appeal to our present market segment. One rationale for horizontal line expansion can be *derived demand*, which is a customer's new need for some product due to buying another product, such as the need for a swimsuit after purchasing a new ski boat, or for batteries after buying a child's toy. If we diversify with *conglomerate expansion*, also called *line stretching*, we're adding products that are both unrelated to our present offerings and that appeal to entirely new market segments.

Product line *retrenchment* is the opposite of product line expansion. Retrenchment means reducing line width by eliminating categories.

The Price

Our pricing and our credit policies bring us the income we need to sustain the business and hopefully cart off a little cash to the bank. Pricing and credit can be great competitive tools.

They can also unintentionally get us into hot water. This brief section is not intended to be all-inclusive, or to give legal advice. Rather, its purpose is to give some examples pointing out why it's a good idea for everyone in business to have a trusted attorney to consult in such matters. One area in which we may need to be especially careful is credit policies. Another involves any activities that could lead to allegations of predatory pricing or price-fixing.

The *Truth-in-Lending Act*, also known as the *Consumer Credit Protection Act*, is a federal law passed in 1968 that requires lenders to provide specific and accurate information that gives the full cost of borrowing. It can apply to many types of businesses extending credit terms, not just to banks.

Predatory pricing is an attempt by a seller to eliminate competitors by driving them out of a market through lowering prices to a level below those at which the competitors can offer the same products. This can be a never-ending battle for the little guy. For example, *Resale Price Maintenance (RPM)* agreements once offered some protection for small retailers against aggressive pricing by large sellers such as big-box outlets. These agreements between a manufacturer and a distributor set a price floor below which the distributor could not sell the product, or the manufacturer could stop doing business with the distributor. But the *Consumer Goods Pricing Act of 1975* fundamentally outlawed RPM agreements in the United States.

Then, in a 2007 decision, the U. S. Supreme Court ruled that *vertical price restraints* such as *minimum advertised pricing* are not per se unlawful but, rather, must be judged under the "rule of reason." Of course, since one of the basic ideas of free market competition is to keep prices down for consumers, it's generally great to advertise lower prices due to such things as lower overhead and volume purchasing.

The problem comes when the *intent* of lower prices is not to benefit consumers, but to drive out competition. Also, since doing things like getting together with your competitors to fix prices can create harm to consumers, that's a no-no too.

Again, we may need to get good legal advice regarding the extension of credit and aggressive pricing policies. It's been said that the best legal defense is to stay out of trouble in the first place. So now that we're back from our visit to the lawyer and we're confident that what we're planning to do is legal, let's look at some ways to set our prices.

Pricing Based on Cost

One of the first steps in calculating a price is to determine the *break-even point*, when gross revenues and total expenses meet. Some costs are fixed, such as real estate, utilities and salaries. Others are variable, such as packaging and shipping, increasing or decreasing in accordance with some factor such as total units sold. Some products have *zone pricing* to help account for this variability, with the price differing somewhat depending on the cost of shipping it to a particular geographic area. Costs as a percentage of sales can also vary according to how much product is sold at what quantity discounts based on volume purchasing.

Cost-plus pricing is a method wherein the selling price of something is based upon a multiple of the cost or a set percentage added to the seller's cost. *Target pricing* begins with a projected sales volume and then adds the desired rate of return on investment at that volume. *Milking*, also called *skim pricing*, is a cost-recovery pricing method that takes the largest amount of profit from a product in the shortest amount of time, particularly when a product is first introduced and there's little competition.

Of course, in addition to the price itself our prospective customer will likely consider the *cost of ownership*. That's the customer's total cost over time, including the product's purchase price plus operating and maintenance costs.

Pricing Based on Demand

Demand is estimated based on the past, present, and projected future wants or needs for our company's products. *Demand-based pricing* is a strategy in which we set the price of our product in accordance with demand projections, or on sales of similar products based on their demand. Prices can vary based on *excess capacity or demand*, which happens when supply and demand get out of balance.

Some products are more price sensitive than others, with demand varying according to price. This is called *price elasticity* or *elasticity of demand.* There's a fancy formula that big companies sometimes use to calculate the degree of this, which depends on keeping very accurate records of fluctuations over time. *Perfect unitary elasticity* is considered to be a value of 1.0, meaning that there is an exact relationship between price and demand. For example, with perfect unitary elasticity a 5% increase in price would result in a 5% decrease in demand, but gross sales receipts would remain the same. Since this formula has little relevance to small businesses, we won't cover it in detail here.

Price and Quality Perceptions

Let's look at the customer's perception of our product's *price/quality equation.* Sure, we'd like them to think that we have the highest quality AND the lowest price, but they're probably not likely to buy that idea. So whether we want to be seen as downmarket, midmarket, or upmarket can be a big factor in how we set our prices. Price points are often based on the customer's perceived value as opposed to a specific markup percentage.

In general, downmarket and midmarket consumers attempt to get maximum utility from purchases by seeking the best value for the least money. At the *downmarket* end, people don't generally expect the highest quality. They're looking for bargains on acceptable quality products. It's an adventure to go to the dollar store and see what's available for a buck. In the *midmarket* area, some sellers find that the best promotional strategy is to have relatively high list prices with frequent sales events that offer discount prices and specials. Others prefer to offer *everyday low pricing* (EDLP), a strategy used by stores such as Wal-Mart, Home Depot, Best Buy, and some other retailers to promote the concept that low prices are always there, without waiting for special offers or collecting coupons. The idea is that consumers generally like to expend as little energy as possible in making purchase decisions, so an EDLP policy helps them assume that they'll get low prices while they shop for good quality products.

At the *upmarket* end of the quality spectrum, *prestige pricing* equates a high price with exceptional quality. As mentioned earlier, psychic income becomes part of the deal, with emotional or psychological value placed on a product beyond its actual usage. For example, a Mercedes Benz automobile does essentially the same transportation task as a Kia Ria. But Benz customers are buying pride of ownership in a premium-priced product, so they expect to see a much higher sticker.

Promotional Pricing

Price lining is the practice of posting the same price levels for categories of products. For example, a clothing store might have several racks with each item on a particular one priced at $10, $15, and $20.

Odd/Even Pricing is a decision made by a seller as to whether to end the product's price in an odd number, such as $99.95, or in an even number such as $100.00. With many purchases, numbers ending in 5 or 9 have the effect of making the price seem much lower to consumers. Sellers of prestige products often don't want the price to seem lower and thus use even pricing ending in round numbers.

The *manufacturer's suggested retail price* (MSRP) is a list price at the retail level. This may be used as the actual selling price or as a reference for comparison of discount and sale pricing. A *temporary markdown* may be made for a number of reasons, including sales events and attempts to quickly gain market share. *Penetration pricing* is an attempt to gain market share by reducing the price of a product to a low level. It's often easier to increase a price after a temporary reduction than after reducing the list price. A *rebate*, which is the return of a portion of the purchase price to the buyer after the sale has been made, is an alternative to a markdown.

Some sellers use *leader pricing*. This is lowering the price of some items to cost or even at a loss to get customers through the door in the hope that they'll buy other regular-price items while they're in the store.

Specialty goods are products not available everywhere, such as those found at Sporty's Pilot Shop or Victoria's Secret. Consumers know they'll find unique things at these places, and generally expect to pay relatively high prices.

And sometimes we can just have the customer set the selling price for us. In an online auction such as those on eBay, we list our product and then just kick back to see what happens. We can have a buy-it-now price, set a reserve price that's the minimum bid which will be accepted, or have a no-reserve auction where the highest bid wins, period.

Payment Methods

We might just accept cash, check, or credit cards for payment. Or we may offer credit. B2B sellers often offer trade terms, such as net 10 or net 30. We might offer bank financing. Or we may offer our own installment terms, allowing customers to make scheduled payments over time. If we do the latter, we should have our attorney check our installment agreements for compliance with Truth-in-Lending requirements.

The Place

Place refers to all channels of distribution through which a product is delivered to end users. *Direct channels* include the Internet, telemarketing, infomercials, direct mail, and personal selling. These often utilize sophisticated customer databases. *Indirect channels* include the use of distributors such as brokers, agents, and wholesalers who sell to retailers. They're often also referred to as *middlemen*. If our product is a service, an idea, or a person it probably is marketed directly to the end consumer. Products that are physical goods can move through more complicated channels involving middlemen. *Channel management* is the process of overseeing the middlemen. An *exclusive distribution* agreement gives territorial rights to a distributor for a product. An *open distribution* arrangement gives any distributor the right to sell the product.

The term *push-pull marketing* refers to two different approaches designed to stimulate demand through an indirect channel. *Push* marketing refers to efforts to create demand by encouraging sellers to promote the product to their end users. Examples include *co-op advertising* programs in which the manufacturer or distributer pays some or all of the cost of advertising the product to end consumers, as well as *trade marketing* efforts directed at distributors including volume discounts, graduated commissions, and sales contests. *Pull* marketing refers to creating end-user demand that generates orders through the channels. If we're a manufacturer we may need to do some *selling-in*, which means teaching our distributors about our product and motivating them to sell it.

Production of the product is sometimes also called push and pull. Sales forecasts create *push production*. Actual demand, if greater than expected, creates *pull production*.

An important law regarding channels of distribution is the Clayton Act, which was enacted in 1914. This consumer protection legislation covers things like exclusive dealings and price discrimination in distribution channels. For example, it prohibits *tying agreements* from suppliers that force distributors to buy a second product in order to be able to get the first. The Robinson-Patman Act, passed in 1936, amends the Clayton Act. It adds further protection for consumers by prohibiting the big guys from setting up sweetheart deals that push smaller competitors out of distribution channels.

Retail Selling

Retailing means selling to the end user. Traditional brick and mortar stores generally purchase from middlemen such as wholesalers. Some large retailers buy directly from manufacturers through a central purchaser and maintain their own intermediaries in the form of distribution centers.

Retail outlets can range from a cart on a corner or a kiosk in a mall to a Mom & Pop single store operation to a franchise shop to a big box store. A *category killer* is a big box store that specializes in one product category, such as Office Depot or Lowe's. It has both exceptional line depth and width within the category, plus volume pricing. This combination makes it hard for other retailers to compete.

Location and the physical appearance of the store are important considerations in retailing. Merchandising displays are essential elements in point-of-purchase selling. Some selling at retail outlets is done via vending machines. It may also be done through self-service, with customers doing their own checkout and paying for products using a scanner and card reader. Inventory control is extremely important at retail outlets to make sure that sufficient stock is on hand without tying up excessive cash in inventory, particularly in slow-moving items. In addition to product sold off the shelves, retail inventory considerations often include some *shrinkage* due to theft or damage.

Retail selling can also be done through *direct response marketing*, also called direct marketing, or through *personal selling*. These techniques do not require the customer to go to a traditional brick and mortar store. They involve selling the product directly to the end user without middlemen as intermediaries. Let's quickly look at both.

Direct Response Marketing

This type of marketing seeks an immediate action from the prospect, such as an instant order or a visit to a website, with results that are directly measurable and attributable to the specific advertising campaign. It can be done through a variety of communications including direct mail, television infomercials, point of sale materials, or on the web. The Direct Marketing Association (DMA) is an organization that defines itself as serving "data-driven marketers" since direct marketing generally utilizes external or in-house databases to do very precise segmentation of prospects plus tracking of campaign results.

The Internet can be a good vehicle for direct response marketing through email campaigns, banners, search engine advertising, social media, or through an online auction channel such as eBay. The term *ecommerce* refers to business transacted on the Internet. It's often done by attracting a prospect to visit a company's website address, or URL, which is the company's location on the Internet. The prospect begins at a landing page and is directed from there through a hyperlink to the appropriate page to select a product, and the purchase is made through a shopping cart page. Some ecommerce sellers have their own huge warehouses and distribution centers, such as Amazon.com. Others utilize *drop shipping*, which is an arrangement through which the website (or other retailer) makes the sale for an item that it doesn't keep in stock. The manufacturer or intermediary ships the item directly to the customer once the retailer has submitted the order to the supplier.

Personal Selling

Chapter Seven is devoted to *personal selling*, sometimes also called direct selling, which means standing toe-to-toe with a prospect while giving our presentation. It can be done in our workplace, such as at a car dealership. It can also be done in the prospect's workplace, as is the case in much B2B selling. A *trade show* is a special event designed to attract individuals or firms interested in a certain type of product. Vendors rent booths where they set up displays in which they may do onsite sales. They might set appointments to provide a service. Or personal contact activities could be made that are designed to generate leads which can be pursued following the show. In the latter case names and addresses are collected using lead cards, business cards, contest entries, or BRM cards. Then, outbound telephone calls are typically made in which appointments are set to provide the service or to make a sales presentation.

Personal selling can also be done with prospects at their residences. Examples include bulk foods such as frozen seafood or steaks, and some home improvement items such as painting contractors or siding and window companies. Magazine resellers, political candidates, storm-chasing construction companies, and religious or charitable fundraising groups may send people to canvas a neighborhood by knocking on doors and giving their messages to prospects in their homes.

Another example of in-home personal selling is *multi-level marketing* (MLM). The MLM marketing method is based on pyramiding, and is also known as *network marketing*. In an MLM, salespeople are compensated for their own sales to end users plus those by persons below them on the pyramid, called their *downline*. Orders at the various levels are typically generated through the personal relationships of the salespeople involved, who often place more emphasis on building a downline than on personally selling products to end users. Some people have considered MLMs to be unusual, perhaps unethical, or have even questioned their legality. But the fact is, a number of highly successful companies have been built through MLM strategies. These include Tupperware, Amway, Avon, Herbalife, Shaklee and others.

Exporting and Importing

It's hard not to be involved in some way with importing. At least some part of something we sell is probably made in China, Mexico, India, or South America. So hey, we may want to try our hand at exporting, too. Global marketing means we've put on our big boy pants and now see the entire world as our market. But if we thought we had this segmenting thing all figured out, now it's a whole new game. In addition to demographics and psychographics, exporters also have to look at things like ethnicity, language differences, cultures, customs, and the political climate of each country. Ouch.

Packaging and Shipping

A product's packaging includes advertising on the container itself, which must tell the product's marketing story in a quick glance perhaps lasting less than one second. The packaging must also be easy to open while protecting the product from damage. If the product has been sold to an end user through channels such as online, direct mail or a catalog, it must also be packed for shipping. This is typically done in a box that's in addition to the product's original packaging. It contains packing material to protect the packaged product, plus a packing slip to identify the items contained in the box. Products shipped to intermediaries such as wholesalers are often sold by the pallet, which is a 40" x 48" wooden skid that can hold about one ton of product.

Chapter Six: Advertising, Publicity & Sales Promotions

Promotion is the fourth of the 4-P's, and is itself the mix of four elements. These are *advertising, publicity, sales promotions, and personal selling*. This chapter covers the first three, and the next chapter is devoted to personal selling.

It would be nice if promotion were a vaccination. Unfortunately, it's maintenance medication that must be applied regularly and consistently in order to work. As small business owners, we know all too well that what we do is a constant battle. If we don't aggressively defend and try to grow our market share, someone will take it away from us.

When we promote our product, we may need to start with making a prospect aware of our product or brand's existence. If it's something they haven't tried before, our goal might be to get them to try it. Our prospect will compare the cost of our product to its expected benefits. If it's in the category of something they already use, we want to build a preference for our product through branding, positioning, differentiation and imaging to show why what we have is better or more desirable.

We communicate through geographically, demographically and psychographically appropriate channels that we've selected through quantitative and qualitative research. Knowing that people are bombarded with marketing messages, we write or speak in terms that connect with the prospect's attitudes and beliefs. Everyone tends to pay selective attention, noting only those messages that are consistent with his or her current wants or needs, and with what he or she currently thinks and believes.

Consumers often buy based on information stored in their minds. For this reason, one promotional goal is to build top-of-mind awareness so that our product comes to mind when the prospect thinks of our category. And we want to have good customer service that helps build the positive word-of-mouth in which one person influences another about our product.

There are some laws and regulations that affect what we can promote and how, and for which we might get legal advice. One example of a regulated promotion is a *lottery*, which (except for a state lottery) is illegal in many instances. The components of a lottery are generally a *prize*, the element of *chance*, and *consideration* in the form of some purchase or expenditure being required in order to be eligible to win. Another regulated promotion is political advertising, which is often subject to special government rules. For example, in U. S. broadcast media the rates must be based on the lowest available during the defined political window.

On its website at FTC.gov, the Federal Trade Commission describes the key federal laws that regulate commerce, as follows:

"Congress passed the first antitrust law, the Sherman Act, in 1890 as a 'comprehensive charter of economic liberty aimed at preserving free and unfettered competition as the rule of trade.' In 1914, Congress passed two additional antitrust laws: the Federal Trade Commission Act, which created the FTC, and the Clayton Act. With some revisions, these are the three core federal antitrust laws still in effect today.

The antitrust laws proscribe unlawful mergers and business practices in general terms, leaving courts to decide which ones are illegal based on the facts of each case. Courts have applied the antitrust laws to changing markets, from a time of horse and buggies to the present digital age. Yet for over 100 years, the antitrust laws have had the same basic objective: to protect the process of competition for the benefit of consumers, making sure there are strong incentives for businesses to operate efficiently, keep prices down, and keep quality up.

Here is an overview of the three core federal antitrust laws.

The Sherman Act outlaws 'every contract, combination, or conspiracy in restraint of trade,' and any 'monopolization, attempted monopolization, or conspiracy or combination to monopolize.' Long ago, the Supreme Court decided that the Sherman Act does not prohibit every restraint of trade, only those that are unreasonable. For instance, in some sense, an agreement between two individuals to form a partnership restrains trade, but may not do so unreasonably, and thus may be lawful under the antitrust laws. On the other hand, certain acts are considered so harmful to competition that they are almost always illegal. These include plain arrangements among competing individuals or businesses to fix prices, divide markets, or rig bids. These acts are "per se" violations of the Sherman Act; in other words, no defense or justification is allowed.

The penalties for violating the Sherman Act can be severe. Although most enforcement actions are civil, the Sherman Act is also a criminal law, and individuals and businesses that violate it may be prosecuted by the Department of Justice. Criminal prosecutions are typically limited to intentional and clear violations such as when competitors fix prices or rig bids. The Sherman Act imposes criminal penalties of up to $100 million for a corporation and $1 million for an individual, along with up to 10 years in prison. Under federal law, the maximum fine may be increased to twice the amount the conspirators gained from the illegal acts or twice the money lost by the victims of the crime, if either of those amounts is over $100 million.

The Federal Trade Commission Act bans 'unfair methods of competition' and 'unfair or deceptive acts or practices.' The Supreme Court has said that all violations of the Sherman Act also violate the FTC Act. Thus, although the FTC does not technically enforce the Sherman Act, it can bring cases under the FTC Act against the same kinds of activities that violate the Sherman Act. The FTC Act also reaches other practices that harm competition, but that may not fit neatly into categories of conduct formally prohibited by the Sherman Act. Only the FTC brings cases under the FTC Act.

The Clayton Act addresses specific practices that the Sherman Act does not clearly prohibit, such as mergers and interlocking directorates (that is, the same person making business decisions for competing companies). Section 7 of the Clayton Act prohibits mergers and acquisitions where the effect 'may be substantially to lessen competition, or to tend to create a monopoly.' As amended by the Robinson-Patman Act of 1936, the Clayton Act also bans certain discriminatory prices, services, and allowances in dealings between merchants. The Clayton Act was amended again in 1976 by the Hart-Scott-Rodino Antitrust Improvements Act to require companies planning large mergers or acquisitions to notify the government of their plans in advance. The Clayton Act also authorizes private parties to sue for triple damages when they have been harmed by conduct that violates either the Sherman or Clayton Act and to obtain a court order prohibiting the anticompetitive practice in the future.

In addition to these federal statutes, most states have antitrust laws that are enforced by state attorneys general or private plaintiffs. Many of these statutes are based on the federal antitrust laws."

Promotional Budgets

Promotional budgets include everything related to advertising, publicity and public relations efforts, sales promotions, and personal selling. The promotional budget contains not only the direct costs, but expenses such as travel and entertainment required for sales calls, trade shows and conferences, and even collateral materials such as business cards and letterhead. Budgets may be set in a number of ways. A specific dollar amount or percentage may be allocated for use during a period based on projections or historical data. With the plowback method, a sizeable percentage of all revenues above break-even are used for promotion during a given period.

Individual demand is, of course, a primary consideration in budgeting. We need to understand and tap into the motivations that drive buying decisions. It can be helpful to consider Maslow's Hierarchy of Needs. This is the five-level model detailed in Chapter Three that breaks human needs into five groups, each of which must be satisfied from the bottom up before moving to the next higher level. At the lowest level are physiological needs, followed by safety, then social needs, upward to self-esteem, with self-actualization at the top. Our product is designed to address needs on one or more levels.

When budgeting, it's also important to consider the demand state for our product. Eight demand states are generally recognized in marketing. These are non-existent, negative, latent, declining, irregular, full, overfull, and unwholesome demand. They're discussed in Chapter Twelve.

Strategies

A strategy is a plan to achieve an objective through the use of available resources. A marketing strategy includes the promotion of product awareness, branding, positioning, differentiation, imaging, and action. It also involves selecting communication channels and media vehicles, building relationships, growing a customer base, and providing a superior product with exceptional service. Let's review some of the basics of setting our marketing strategy.

We make sure people know that our product exists, and we make it as easy as possible to buy. We have a recognizable and memorable logo and slogan. We also have a pricing policy that's attractive to potential buyers and that reinforces our price/quality position. If we're a retailer with many items, we may sometimes employ leader pricing.

We make our product as attractive and desirable as we possibly can. We try to create the desired mental picture of our product, and to build or reinforce our product's reputation. We work to create top-of-mind-awareness. We employ positioning or repositioning to affect how customers perceive our product's benefits relative to those of our competitors. We use differentiation to explain how our product is better or more desirable. And we employ relationship marketing to please our existing customers, increase repeat sales, generate referrals and build positive word-of-mouth.

We market to the segments that we've defined, within our product's geography. We make sure that our marketing message is consistent across all promotional vehicles and advertising media by using an integrated marketing campaign (IMC), reinforcing our message through repetition. And if we're a local merchant marketing a national product, sometimes we may be able to run a tie-in promotion that piggybacks on a national campaign.

In developing our strategy, it's also helpful to keep in mind our category's position in the Growth/Share Matrix. In a product category that's growing, multiple competitors can increase the size of their pieces as the entire pie is getting larger. However, in a category that's not growing, the pie isn't getting any bigger. For one company's slice to grow, its gains must come by taking business and customers away from others. That can mean war, so military terms are sometimes used to help define our strategies. A number of books have been written on this topic, including *Marketing Warfare* by Al Ries and Jack Trout (McGraw-Hill, 1986), and *Business War Games* by Benjamin Gilad (Career Press, 2009).

Defensive strategies include *position defense*. This means taking action to fortify our present position, such as promotional activities and aggressive pricing. A *flanking defense* could include introducing our own related product to discourage a competitor from attacking our flank. A *preemptive defense* means that we attack the competitor before they can attack us. A *counter-offensive defense* means we attack after having been attacked. A *mobile defense* means constantly changing positions so that we're a moving target that's harder to hit. A *contraction defense* means eliminating unprofitable products to conserve cash for other battles.

Offensive strategies include a *frontal attack*, in which a competitor tries to match another product feature-for-feature. In a *flanking* or bypass attack, a competitor attacks an opponent's weaknesses by skipping the opponent's main targets and trying to more effectively serve fringes. With a *guerilla strategy* the competitor attacks, withdraws, waits, and then comes back again using tactics such as price cuts. In a *leapfrog attack*, a competitor might wait for a new product to be released and then introduce its own version that adds new features. In an *encirclement attack*, the competitor comes from all directions at the same time.

Advertising

Advertising is paid promotion utilizing one or more media. An advertisement has a life cycle during which it will be noticed and remembered. To keep the forgetting rate low, advertising should be consistently applied and regularly refreshed. Frequency of exposure to an advertising message is important in aiding recall and in building top-of-mind-awareness. There are a number of considerations in buying advertising, and these are discussed in Chapter Nine.

Tracking advertising results is relatively easy to do with direct action ads that seek an immediate response. With indirect action ads that seek goals such as to remember something, including branding and imaging campaigns, a number of tracking methods can be used. A target sales increase, or payout, could be set with results tracked periodically or in a post-buy analysis. Tracking can be calculated based on total sales or on the sales increase over a time period. Measurement terms include cost per inquiry, cost per lead, cost per unit sold, and cost per average order. With some types of products an order code can be used, and tracking can be based on the individual medium and the specific campaign.

Advertising can be business-to-consumer (B2C) or business-to-business (B2B). Consumer advertising is directed at a product's end users. This can use a variety of media and strategies. B2B advertising refers to that done to reach businesses in order to provide components, products for resale, or services to those businesses. Trade advertising is done by product makers to reach distributors and retailers. This is often done in publications designed to provide content to a particular trade, or via direct mail.

Advertising to end users can be done by retailers or by the makers of a product or service. As mentioned earlier, direct marketing is that which is done straight to the consumer and which asks for an immediate sale. This can be done through a variety of media, including direct mail, the Internet, TV infomercials, radio spots, and newspaper ads or inserts. The customer might be asked to call a number, go to a website or return a card in order to get the product.

Let's take a quick glance at some advertising media options, with a more in-depth look in Chapter Nine. Advertising is done to reach prospects in two basic places: in their homes and out of their homes. *In-home advertising* options include newspaper, radio, television, and the Internet. *Out-of-home advertising* can be done with media including radio, billboards, transit, and mobile devices such as smartphones and tablet computers.

Reach is an estimate of the number of individuals exposed to a message. Unduplicated persons reached have different terms with various media. With a broadcast advertising schedule they're called the cumulative audience, or *cume*. In print media the term is *circulation* or *readership*. The web term for unduplicated individuals who visit a site is *unique users*. *Frequency* is the term for the estimated number of times the average listener, reader, or viewer is exposed to an advertisement in a given period of time.

Some businesses advertise on a continual basis. Others use *flighting*, which is the term for advertising for a period of time, removing the advertising for a period of time, then putting it back on for another period, removing it again, and so on. Some advertise only during certain periods, such as seasonally. In a situation where a business is waiting, for example, for the first snowfall in order to sell skis, it may prepare an advertisement and place a *wait order* so that the ad starts running as soon as the flakes fly.

All advertising media have their pros and cons. Traditional print and broadcast media are sometimes called *interruption advertising*. *Intrusiveness* is a term that refers to the irritation it may create. *Merchandising* refers to displays at retail outlets, and is also called *point-of-purchase* advertising. It can be very effective in influencing impulse buying, but is often ignored by shoppers except when products are being compared. Web advertising can be highly targeted to precisely defined segments. However, some web ads such as banners have a high level of irritation and are often ignored, while unwanted email (spam) is often discarded and may generate outright anger. Direct mail can be highly targeted both geographically and demographically, but is often discarded without being opened. Telemarketing refers to the use of the telephone in a marketing campaign. *Outbound telemarking* means calling prospects, which has a very high level of intrusiveness. This can be used as one-to-one advertising in direct marketing by calling prospects to try to make an immediate sale. It's also often used as an intermediate step to qualify prospects prior to making an extended presentation through personal selling. Both have high levels of hang-ups and rudeness by prospects, so outbound telemarketers need to have thick skins. *Inbound telemarking* answers calls from prospects who

60

are often responding to an ad in some other medium. *Billboards* and *transit* advertising can generate high frequency in a short period of time at relatively low cost and can be segmented geographically. However, the reach is difficult to segment demographically, so unless the product appeals to a mass market much of the reach and frequency may be to non-prospects.

Publicity and Public Relations

Publicity is the general term referring to the use of the press and other unpaid media such as interviews and talk show appearances, plus community involvement. Good publicity can positively influence public opinion. Its goal is to keep a favorable light on the company. Publicity received is sometimes measured in *equivalent advertising value.*

A formal program in *public relations* (PR) is the part of the publicity effort that involves news releases, press conferences, and other contacts with the media such as interviews. *Press releases* are announcements of some story or event related to a product or company. These can be distributed via postal mail, email, social media, a website, or a blog. A *press conference* is a meeting with journalists. A *press pack* containing relevant printed or multimedia information is often sent to members of the press, or distributed at a press conference location before the meeting starts.

Press conferences and news interviews sometimes involve *crisis communication*, which is a response to some negative event or unfavorable publicity. The projection of our personality and demeanor is important in all publicity and promotional efforts, but especially so in crisis communication. The way we look, act and speak can influence people to perceive us in a particular way.

Every business boat has to navigate rough waters sometimes. It may be a need to motivate a particular salesperson, a tense staff meeting, or a full-blown PR crisis with reporters circling like sharks. A good first step is to define the traits of the persona we want to project. Does the situation call for us to be wise, understanding, and motivational? Should we show ourselves to be in control, strong, and unwavering?

Do we need to display a demeanor that we're calm, concerned, and committed to finding a solution? Whatever we decide as the image we want to project, we should write down these key words or phrases and keep them at the top of our mind during the event. If we're giving a prepared speech, they could be written in the margins as subtext. If it's something quick and impromptu, we might just write the traits on a sticky note or even on our hand. But we should always remember that our effectiveness depends not only on our proposed solution, but at least as importantly on our performance.

Sales Promotions

A *sales promotion* builds product awareness and sales through special offers. For example, one might be designed to motivate intermediaries in distribution channels. A *sales contest* could be held to motivate a personal selling force, such as winning a trip with a certain volume of sales. Sales promotions can also be aimed at end users, including sweepstakes, premiums, discounts, rebates, trial offers, referral programs, and coupons.

A *sweepstakes* is a contest with a prize. A *premium* is an extra item added as an inducement to purchase something. The seller might absorb the full cost of the premium. Or the premium might be a *self-liquidator*, meaning that its wholesale cost is added to the selling price. A *semi-liquidator* is in the middle, with both the seller and the customer paying part of the premium's cost. A *discount* is a price reduction. With a *rebate*, the buyer is refunded a portion of the purchase price. A *trial offer* might guarantee a refund if the customer is not satisfied. It could also offer a free sample or an introductory price. In a *referral* sales promotion, someone is given a discount or a premium for referring another prospect. When *coupons* are offered, *redemption rates* must be projected. When applicable, expected slippage rates should also be calculated. *Slippage* is the term for those who've been given a coupon but who fail to use it.

A *cross-promotion* is using one product as an advertising vehicle for another, such as attaching a coupon for salsa to a bag of tortilla chips. *Cross-selling*, or *suggestive selling*, is promoting a related item at the time of another sale. This could be asking the purchaser of a major appliance if they'd like a maintenance agreement or a computer buyer if they want an extended warranty. Or it might be the fast-food server who realizes he has just sold a burger to a supermodel, and says "would you like a fry with that?"

Customer relationship management (CRM) software maintains records of sales calls, purchase histories, inquiries, service, and other information. It can be used for database marketing in offering sales promotions to present and former prospects and customers such as sending out cards or making special sales promotion offers for birthdays, anniversaries, graduations, and other events. The information can also be employed for *data mining* in looking for trends and patterns.

Sales promotions can also be part of our strategy at trade shows, events and exhibitions. These can be excellent places to meet face-to-face with prospects and customers who may have already been segmented into one huge group with an interest in our category. Foot traffic is highly segmented at both B2B and B2C trade shows, but less so at events like fairs and festivals. All these types of venues can be good places to sell products directly or to gather leads for follow-up.

Chapter Seven: Principles of Personal Selling

Particularly in B2B selling, the personality conveyed by company personnel is critical. It can account for a huge percentage, if not most, of the sale. Whenever we're taking a call on the telephone, conducting a staff meeting, handling a customer complaint, or writing a commercial for radio, television or the Internet, we're trying to convince someone to attach value to what we have to say. We're selling. Whether our message is designed to sell a product or an idea that we have, and whether it's going to be 30 seconds long or 30 minutes long, it needs to be grounded in the same fundamentals.

In a 2015 cover story, *Sales and Marketing Management Magazine* quoted authors Chris Wirthwein and Joe Bannon from their book *The People Powered Brand: A Blueprint for B2B Brand and Culture Transformation*. The article defined *owned media* as things that a company controls, including its website, office and plant facilities, literature, and the brand messages conveyed by company personnel. It called advertising channels *paid media*, while outside publicity and word-of-mouth were referred to as *earned media*. They contended that *"whereas the consumer goods method of media mix weighs heavily toward paid media...B2B considered purchases flip that model on its head and focus 75 percent or more of your efforts on owned media."* (www.salesandmarketing.com, January/February 2015).

Personal selling happens when we get one-on-one with a potential buyer or a customer. A sale results from making an effective presentation to a qualified prospect for a needed or wanted product. Remember that in this book, we use the term *product* to refer to physical goods, persons, services, and ideas. Selling is a test of our product knowledge and our ability to handle pressure, and it's a forum in which we display our verbal and non-verbal performance skills. No matter what our widget, service or idea might be, the basics of selling are pretty much the same.

65

Selling Means Listening

One fundamental rule of communication during a sales presentation is that we listen to understand and reach agreement, not to win an argument. If we remain focused and are really hearing what our prospect is telling us, we may in fact be able to answer a question, provide evidence that may be lacking, or correct some misunderstanding. Good listening requires that we both hear and understand feedback.

The Five P's of Personal Selling

For the purposes of this book, we'll use our own *5-P's of Personal Selling* model as an aid in organizing and remembering important elements in preparing for personal selling situations. These are product knowledge, prospecting, pressures and motivations, performance, and presentation. Let's look at each.

Product Knowledge

The more *product knowledge* we have, the better. We should continually study all aspects of our products, knowing how they work and how they benefit our customers. We also need to anticipate and prepare for possible objections, just like a politician prepares for questions or topics that might come up in an interview or a debate. Salespeople need the reflexes of prizefighters. If a boxer has to stop and think about the next punch, guess who's going to get his rear-end kicked.

For example, if we're in B2B sales of advertising services for a broadcast station, we may have anticipated that a prospect might offer the objection that "*I tried (radio or TV) and it didn't work.*" Our prepared, reflexive response could begin by agreeing that it's not very surprising that the prospect might say that. Being careful not to be overtly negative about a competitor, we could then note that there aren't many products that work well when they're poorly constructed. We might add that there are plenty of advertising reps who lack the depth of knowledge to put together an effective ad campaign, or who might simply be more concerned about moving the station's inventory than moving the client's. Here, our challenge is to convince the prospect to give it another shot. Without slamming the competition, we can gently point out that for a campaign to achieve good results the ad must be well written, creatively produced, and strategically placed. And then we try to convince the prospect that, if given the chance, we'll get it done right.

Prospecting

Prospecting is the term for the process of acquiring leads or "suspects" and then turning them into prospects through qualification and appointment-setting. The first step in prospecting is to organize our list of leads. Depending on how we plan to work them, we can organize leads by name, by address, or by category such as hot, warm or cold. We might organize them by frequency of contact such as weekly, monthly, or quarterly, or by type such as regular, developmental, or seasonal contacts. Once we have our leads organized we can begin working them.

As mentioned earlier, a lead becomes a prospect through qualification. This can be done by questioning our suspect through a mail or Internet survey form, in a telephone conversation, or through a personal visit. We qualify our prospects to avoid wasting valuable time and effort in making pointless presentations. A qualified prospect is one who has a need or desire for our product or service, can afford it, and is either the decision maker or a key influencer. The information we get in the qualifying process can help us customize a game plan for our sales presentation.

Pressures and Motivations

Pressures and motivations make up the fuel for the engines of both the salesperson and the prospect. They drive the prospect's buying decisions, and can be either positive or negative. Our application of them can be seen as either high-pressure or low-pressure. For the prospect, examples of positive motivations include saving time, saving or making money, gaining or protecting assets, and pride of ownership.

Negative motivations could include losing any of the above or missing out on an opportunity.

Pressure is a good thing. An engine won't run without it, and we can compare our brains to these machines. Our teakettle won't whistle until we light a fire under its bottom. However, it's human nature to want to relieve pressure when we feel it. And we can do that in one of two ways. We can use an escape mechanism that essentially opens a valve to release it, or we can use the pressure as a force to drive our engine. Energy becomes power when it's channeled. For example, energy is released whenever gasoline is burned, but it's probably of little or no value if we just pour the gas on the driveway and set it ablaze. However, we can transform it into useful fuel by filling our car's tank with it. Power itself is a double-edged sword. It's the *application* of it that's good or bad. It'll be good if we use the car for transportation or bad if we get behind the wheel drunk and cause an accident.

Our skill in pointing out benefits, costs, risks, scarcity or urgency can create pressure. Human nature causes the prospect to want to get rid of it, perhaps by putting off a decision on our offer. It's the job of the salesperson to skillfully guide the prospect to instead use that energy to address his or her problem by making a buying decision.

Of course, we also face our own pressures. Sales forecasting sets quotas for us to meet. There are bills to pay and mouths to feed. For the salesperson, examples of positive motivations include making good money, providing a better living for our family, and being able to afford the things that we'd like to have. Examples of negative motivations for us include the possible loss of commission on a sale, the loss of our job, and the inability to buy what we want.

We must accept the frustration and rejection that we feel when prospecting or when we lose a sale. In fact, we can use these pressures to our advantage by keeping track of our percentages. Successful athletes know the importance of stats. A salesperson should also tabulate his or her statistics, because ours is a numbers game just like sports. We should keep records so that we know how many leads it takes to qualify how many prospects, how many prospects we need in order to set how many appointments, how many appointments we need to set so that we can make how many presentations, and how many presentations we need to make to close how many sales, which will result in what dollar volume. We can then do a little math and help motivate ourselves by assigning an average dollar value to each contact that we make, whether its result is positive or negative. So instead of feeling frustration at an unset appointment or a missed sale, we can mentally count ourselves as being one measureable step closer to our goal. We should remember too that selling is not just an individual numbers game. It's also teamwork, and our sales manager's rather tough job is to visualize, systematize, strategize, recruit, train, motivate, track and report. To improve, we should get as much feedback as we can from management, other team members, and customers.

While the fundaments of selling don't change much according to the length of our presentation they certainly may bend, compress, or stretch. We need to cover the essential elements of attention, interest, desire, and action whether we have a 30-minute personal selling situation, a 30-second broadcast spot, a 6-second billboard exposure, or a 6-day training seminar.

Performance

Performance means that a good salesperson is both teaching and putting on a show. The client will perceive us according to how we look, how we behave, what we say and how we sound. Reality exists from a point of perception. Five people are singing right this minute in the room where you're reading this book. What? You can't hear them? Well, just turn on a radio and you can. They're here in the same time and space that you and I occupy. But our receiver, the human body, is not designed to perceive radio waves. So we need a device that translates them into signals that our body can process. Like every other human being, our prospect has just a five-channel receiver, perceiving us only through the five senses: seeing, hearing, feeling, smelling, and tasting. Prospects see how we dress, our gestures, movements, and the looks on our faces. They hear not only what we say, but also how we sound when we say it. And prospects can feel both the touch of our handshake as well as the emotional feelings conveyed in our messages.

Our voice and body language, consisting of movements, gestures, poses, and facial expressions communicate too. As mentioned in Chapter One, some experts say they communicate over 90% of the message received. The other two senses, smell and taste, play less common but still important roles in personal selling. Prospects can smell us, so that needs to be pleasant. We can't afford to have bad breath or body odor. And in some cases prospects may taste something during our presentation, such as when we're giving out food samples. In this event, taste is extremely important.

To paraphrase Shakespeare, the world is a stage and we're players on it. That's not a parable. It's the literal truth. As salespeople, we need to determine the traits we want to reveal and then play the role accordingly. We may choose to put emphasis on characteristics that differ a bit from one situation to another. In the movie *Patton*, as he prepared to give a speech meant to inspire his troops who were about to engage in a fierce battle, an aide asked the General: "Do they know if you're acting?" Patton remarked: "It's not important for them to know. It's only important for me to know." Performance techniques are covered in detail in Chapters Fifteen and Sixteen, but for now let's look at some basics.

Stanislavski's Triad

Constantin Stanislavski ran the Moscow Art Theatre in the early 1900's. He devised a method of acting that was designed to provide a means for stability in the performances of his players. Today, Stanislavski's work remains the most widely accepted system ever devised to comprise a total system for acting performance. Others including Michael Chekhov, Stella Adler, and Lee Strasberg have refined and added to it. But the essential elements spelled out by Stanislavski remain largely unchanged. It's now popularly known as "The Method", and has been studied by many, if not most, of the major acting performers that we see on stage, TV, and the movie screen. These elements are sometimes boiled down to just three words, known as "Stanislavski's Triad." They are relaxation, concentration, and truth. We'll briefly discuss each as it relates to our marketing performance objectives.

Relaxation

These traits are the "physical control" elements of our character as perceived by the prospect. They include the absence of unnecessary tension or movement, plus effective facial expressions and good vocal technique.

Concentration

On a stage, this refers to total belief in the reality of imaginary objects, props, and characters. In a sales presentation or other business communication, it's the ability to stay on track and not get rattled by interruptions or questions. It also means listening to feedback from the prospect and making adjustments as necessary.

Truth

Both onstage and in personal business contacts, this refers to the concept of naiveté which means remembering the natural performing skills we possessed as a child. John Lennon once said that "every child is an artist until some idiot tells him he can't draw." No one has to teach 5-year-olds how to play. They adlib and improvise with total conviction. Truth also means that we must have faith in the benefits of the product or service we're selling. We shouldn't try to sell something we don't believe in.

Presentation

Now that we have good product knowledge, have qualified our leads, understand the pressures they're facing, and have developed our performance skills, it's time to make a game-plan for our *presentation*. Call planning may involve both appointments and cold calling, and the purpose of a call may involve hunting or farming. *Hunting* means seeking new business, and *farming* is cultivating business from existing customers.

Three presentation plan strategies are canned pitches, consultancy, and a step plan. A *canned pitch* is a memorized presentation. With *consultancy selling*, also called relationship selling, the idea is to retain customers over the long haul by focusing on their wants and needs rather than on our sales. This builds customer loyalty, referrals, and positive word-of-mouth. With consultancy regular meetings are scheduled, conversations are held, information is gathered, and suggestions are made. A *step plan* combines elements of the canned presentation and consultancy. The steps are memorized, but information in each step can be easily customized for the individual prospect and situation. Questions are asked in each step, and the presentation can be modified on the fly according to the feedback received.

Strategic planning increases our effectiveness. We should remember that professional sports teams sometimes pay millions *per employee* to hire the best players. But even with the most skilled players, would any team ever show up at the stadium without a game plan? Of course they wouldn't. Coaches spend many hours preparing before meeting a quality competitor. Sure, adjustments are necessary during the game. Sometimes we get surprised when the other team doesn't do what we expected.

Especially when we're doing relationship selling through consultancy, but in any sale for that matter, we have to know what the problem is and why our solution is a good one. Selling success lies in offering effective solutions to problems, and these can occur over time. So whether we're doing one-shot B2C selling or recurrent relationship B2B selling, preparation equals effectiveness.

A step plan is a roadmap that makes our journey easier. It means we always know our position in a sales presentation, and we've laid out our straight-line path. So when we get taken off course for some reason, we know exactly where to re-enter to keep the presentation on course.

A mental map also builds confidence, helping reduce the chance that unwanted messages might be subtextually communicated. For example, we might really need this sale to meet a quota. But if our anxiety shows, it could communicate to the prospect that our needs are more important than hers. Uncertainty could also result from wondering if we've forgotten something important. Since we always know where we are in our step plan, we reduce the chances for this to subconsciously show. When a prospect detects anxiety or uncertainty, it could cause him or her to lose confidence in what we're saying, becoming less likely to want to buy even though the prospect might realize that he or she needs or desires what we have to offer.

Throughout all areas of our presentation we ask the prospect questions. These can be used to maintain involvement, to confirm understanding, and to verify agreement on key points. Two question types are open and closed. Open questions seek information, and can be thought of as the journalist's "who, what, when, where, why, and how." Closed questions are answerable with "yes" or "no." Questioning strategies include probing, leading, confirming, and rhetorical questions. A probing question is designed to gain knowledge in areas such as discovering attitudes, discussing strengths and weaknesses, uncovering problems, and revealing motivations. A leading question takes the prospect into a predetermined area. In this case, the questioner knows the answer he or she wants and phrases the question so that the prospect answers in a certain way. A confirming question is generally a closed question used to verify understanding or to seek agreement on key points. Rhetorical questions can be used to make a point or express an idea.

Below is a step plan based on the AIDA formula.

Attention

The attention step could also be called the warm-up. Our goal is to get the prospect's attention focused on us, rather than on what they were doing before we showed up. A business lunch is often used to accomplish this step in B2B selling.

If we're in the prospect's home or office, we remember that the root word of *business* is "busy" and we keep this part short. We might try to warm the prospect to our presentation by first discussing some of his or her areas of interest, such as sports, children, traveling, photography, painting, or gardening. We try to get the prospect talking. A well-placed and deserved compliment regarding something like the prospect's clothing or hairstyle could be good. We might ask questions without prying into the prospect's personal life. Here are some examples of warm-up questions: *Are these pictures of your children? Where are they now? You have a beautiful office (or home). Your team is doing great! When's their next game?*

Interest

The interest step is that part of the buying cycle in which a prospect develops a positive opinion or recognizes a need for a product in our category.

In the interest step, we try to get the prospect talking about things related to his or her individual situation or that might relate in some way to our product. Hopefully the prospect will bring up a situation where we can help or some problem that needs a solution. Sometimes we may discover needs or wants that we did not previously know existed. This can lead us to make a different offer than what we had originally planned. Remember, though, that our solution is not going to be proposed until the desire step, so this information is for future use. Here in the interest step, we're probing into potential need and want areas, saying things like "Tell me more about..." and asking questions designed to generate information. We may want to confirm a perceived need or want by saying something like "So as I understand it...is that right?"

Desire

In the attention step, we warmed the prospect to us so that we could begin without distractions. In the interest step, we did fact-finding and summarized our understanding of the prospect's potential need.

Here in the desire step, we offer our product as the solution to that need, providing support such as facts and figures that address the specifics. We might need to use some positioning or differentiation to explain how it compares to competitors, or to show some testimonials.

If this were a court of law, we'd be hauling out the evidence that would get us the conviction.

We also consider our prospect's individual buying motivations, which could be logical or emotional. We've tried to determine these so that we can more effectively phrase our proposal when we make it. What exactly does the prospect want to accomplish in addressing the need we've uncovered? Primary (logical) buying motivations include profit or savings to increase the bottom-line, improvement of some kind, competition with a rival, and efficiency in terms of time spent. Secondary (emotional) motivations include pride of ownership and the prospect's personal attitude toward the price/quality relationship.

In personal selling, we often use visual aids such as charts, graphs, brochures, articles, and testimonials. We may have a presentation book, and if so we can point out relevant facts in it. Let's discuss how we might approach needs and wants.

Let's first look at addressing needs. People tend to receive messages better in one channel or another at various times. Each person has a natural tendency to lean toward being, for example, a better visual learner, aural learner, or emotional learner. However, at a given time any individual may be tuned in more to one channel than another, so that he or she can be more effectively reached through emotions, for instance, than through logic. So in order for us to have the best chance of reaching a prospect with our message, we should effectively use sound, sight and feelings to reinforce each other. For the hearing channel, we can talk about features and benefits, give questions and provide answers. For the seeing channel, we can use charts and graphs, facts and figures, and newspaper or magazine articles. And for the feeling channel, we can use testimonials, emotional examples, stories, and meaning contained in our subtext. The subtext is covered in detail in Chapter Fifteen.

Now let's look at wants. It's entirely possible that we may convince the prospect that he or she needs what we're selling, but then they turn around and buy it from someone else. We need to convince the prospect that he or she should want to do business with *us*. For example, product knowledge transfers confidence. We may need to show that we'll provide service after the sale. Our vocal techniques, facial expressions and bodily movements all work together to transfer subtextual meaning that helps a prospect make the decision to do business with us. And we communicate subtextually whether or not we intend it.

Wants are at least as important as needs, if not more so. A want is a desired way to satisfy a need. We may be hungry and need food, and what we want is a Big Mac. We may realize that we need a lawn mower, so we want to shop for one at a store that's conveniently located, clean and well organized, and which has friendly, helpful personnel to show us the options. The same concept applies to any product or service. We establish a need in the interest step. In the desire step, we try to get the prospect to want to do business with us rather than someone else.

We make our specific proposal. We give the details of the offer, phrasing it in terms relative to the prospect's buying motivations. We explain how it meets the prospect's needs and wants, listing relevant features and benefits. We tell the prospect the cost of our proposal. The prospect must see an equivalent or greater benefit than the cost, or it's probably a no-sale.

Action

The action step is where we close the sale by getting a commitment from the prospect to do something. If we're not sure that the prospect is ready to buy, we may use a *trial close*. This is the equivalent of sticking our toe in the pool to test the water before we dive in. A trial close doesn't seek a commitment to buy. Rather, it's designed to solicit a positive or negative opinion, a question, or an objection. A positive opinion is a *buying signal* that tells us it's time to close. A negative response shows a lack of interest, one or more unanswered questions, or an outright objection. The trial close gives us a chance to uncover and deal with any potential problems before we ask the prospect to say yes or no to our offer. Here are some examples of a trial close question: "Which one tickles your fancy better, the traditional style or the modern one?" or "Does that red one look like something that would match your decor?"

76

Entire books have been written on handling objections, so we won't go into much detail here. However, a good plan is to treat an objection as if it were a question. We either supply more evidence to support our case or go back over some point that the prospect may have missed or not understood completely.

In some B2C situations, such as a car sale, we may suspect that if the prospect doesn't buy our product today he or she will probably go somewhere else and buy another one soon after leaving us. So a bit of aggression in closing techniques is appropriate. However, in B2B selling we generally want to avoid being seen as applying pressure to buy right now. Instead, we cultivate a relationship through consultancy in which we try to understand the pressures that our customer faces and find ways to lessen those by helping the customer accomplish goals. Sure, we still want to close the sale. But since we'll be coming back regularly we have to take a bit more time, use a bit more tact, and be a trusted problem-solver.

When we ask for the order, we use a close question that seeks a commitment to buy. Here's an example of an alternate choice close question. "Which one shall I get you the keys for, the orange one or the blue one?" Or we might not even ask a close question. With an assumptive close we simply start filling out the order form. If the prospect has been sold, he or she will let us continue. If not, they won't.

Wrap-Up

Now it's time for the finishing details. We answer any remaining questions and complete the required paperwork. We might show a little service after the sale by taking a minute to explain how things will work from here on out. We might say "congratulations." Our client or customer has made an important decision with this purchase and could certainly be told that we recognize it. And we should always say "thank you" to let our client or customer know that we appreciate his or her business.

Part Three:
Marketing Plans and Media Overview

Chapter Eight: SWOT, Strategic Thinking, and Marketing Plans

Every business can benefit from planning the marketing program effectively and efficiently, so this chapter will look at some of the topics that could be covered in an annual marketing meeting or addressed in a written marketing plan.

Marketing Plan Overview

A marketing plan tells us who'll do what as well as when, where, why and how they'll do it. Forecasting is a big part of planning. We take educated guesses regarding future demand, sales, and costs. This can be based on various methods, such as applying a desired percentage of increase to past or present records or on future estimates of total business volume for our product category. Our marketing plan details our objectives, strategies, and tactics for an upcoming period, typically one year. It also considers the macroeconomic and microeconomic factors that might affect us. These are discussed later in this chapter. Marketing plans vary in formality. As inferred above, it may just involve a meeting in which the management team gets together and talks about the subject every year or so. In larger organizations there may be a dedicated marketing staff that'll put the plan in a written report which then goes to the top executives for their approval.

A good marketing effort involves taking someone through the buyer stages of (a) target (b) lead (c) prospect (d) customer, (e) repeat customer, and hopefully (f) promoter. Here's what we mean by each term. A *target* is a segmented group for which a product is designed. A *lead* has awareness of the product or category. A *prospect* has interest in the product or category and is qualified to buy. A *customer* has made a purchase of our product. A *repeat customer* has purchased our product more than once. A *promoter* is a highly satisfied customer who generates positive word-of-mouth.

One of the most fundamental marketing concepts is the belief that goals for a product can best be met by precisely targeting the right population segments and then satisfying customers through meeting or exceeding their expectations. As detailed in Chapter Three, human *needs* can be described in Maslow's terms and *wants* are desires to fulfill a need in a particular way or with a specific product.

The mental image, or visualization, is one of the most powerful forces in marketing. It's covered in detail in Chapter Ten. Visualization is needed from product conception to consumption. In order to *create* a product or service, we need a clear mental image of it being used. And in order to *sell* the product, we have to transfer such an image to the end user.

SWOT Analysis

A SWOT analysis takes a realistic assessment of our strengths, weaknesses, opportunities, and threats. It's a good first step in formulating a marketing plan. Strengths and weaknesses are generally internal, such as our features and benefits, our pricing, and our unique selling proposition. Opportunities and threats are usually external. Opportunities could include persons who're unhappy with a competitor's product, or who aren't being served well by anyone. Threats could include a new competitor coming in, or some negative situation that might happen which could affect our customers' ability to buy.

Objectives, Strategies, and Tactics

Once we've done our SWOT analysis, strategies can be employed to achieve objectives. In strategic thinking, goal-setting can be thought of as clearly seeing what we want to accomplish, and then placing our visualization on a timeline.

We design a marketing plan to cover objective, strategic, and tactical elements. An objective is a clearly defined goal to be reached. A strategy lays out systematic steps designed to achieve the objective using available resources. Tactics are employed to achieve each step in the strategy. Here's a military analogy from a World War II movie. The objective is to take the hill. The strategy is to knock out a defensive machine gun in a bunker that's in the way. The tactic is to position a soldier to throw a grenade through the bunker's opening.

Mission Statement

A *mission statement* can be thought of as a miniature marketing plan. We could start with it and expand the marketing plan from there. Or we might first develop the marketing plan, and then summarize the mission statement from it. Every company, big or small, can benefit from having a written mission statement because it quickly, succinctly and memorably states the company's purpose in terms of who it serves and why. A good mission statement helps us avoid marketing myopia. As mentioned earlier, this is a natural tendency over time to focus more on our products and internal operations and less on the wants and needs of our customers.

The mission statement should be communicated to everyone employed by the company. That's because whether it's written or spoken, intended or unintended, a marketing message is communicated by anyone involved in contact of any kind with a customer or a prospect. Every employee should also know our intended brand and company personalities, plus our customer service policies regarding warranty work, questions, and complaints. This knowledge comes from internal marketing efforts to keep staff well-informed and properly trained about how they should communicate with prospects and customers.

Two fundamental management methods are *management by objectives* (MBO) and *top-down management*. MBO is a method in which management and employees get together and agree on exactly what should be accomplished in what period of time. It involves some bottom-up planning by considering input from all levels in setting company goals. MBO can encourage employees to take ownership of the marketing plan, and can help keep everyone on the same page of the playbook. In a top-down system management sets the goals, strategies and tactics and then communicates them to employees.

The Annual Marketing Meeting

If ours is a small company and we just have an informal annual marketing meeting with key employees and team members, we still want precision and detail. This meeting can provide our road map for all the marketing activities during the year. One simple method is to discuss the elements of our plan based on the six fundamental questions of a journalist, arranged in the following sequence: what, how, where, who, why, and when. Here's a look at some things we might want to explore with each.

What

This lists the company's objectives for the upcoming period. Here we clearly define our aim or purpose. We could begin with a description of the company's present situation such as a quick SWOT analysis. Next we might discuss our economic position. As mentioned in Chapter Three, macroeconomic factors are beyond our direct control but could affect us and might require some contingency plans. They include national, regional or local inflation, unemployment, income levels, and economic growth. While these are certainly not things we can directly fix, planning for them could minimize their impact on us. Microeconomic conditions are more within our control and include our company's employees, facilities and equipment, financing, suppliers, customers and competitors plus staffing levels, inventory turnover, sales volume, and profitability.

We could also discuss our past and present demand and what we hope it will be in the upcoming year. Demand states were mentioned in Chapter Six and will be discussed in more detail in Chapter Twelve on copywriting. They are negative, non-existent, latent, falling, irregular, full, overfull (excess), and unwholesome demand. If we have negative demand, our promotional strategy might be to try to convert the demand, or simply to abandon or replace the product if it has become outdated or technologically obsolete. Latent demand means that people want the product, but it's not available yet. Maybe we can create it. If we have no demand, little demand, falling demand, or irregular demand, we might be able to create more demand or stabilize it with heavier or more effective promotion. Excess demand exceeds our capacity to fill it. We might need to offer the product in fewer channels or raise the price to get demand and capacity in line. Unwholesome demand is for things we want that aren't good for us.

We can then discuss and define the overall goal to be reached and the timetable for doing so. This could be stated in terms such as gross sales, net revenues, a percentage increase, a market share target, or a return on investment. Each of our products or categories might have different goals.

How

Here, we'll discuss the strategies we'll use to reach our company objectives.

We can begin by looking at our market coverage strategy, which could be one of three basic approaches. *Undifferentiated marketing* means we use the same campaign for all of our target market segments. *Differentiated marketing* (not to be confused with product differentiation) means we use a different campaign for each of our targeted segments, so that we can specialize our message according to the needs of each segment. A *concentrated marketing* strategy means that we're focusing a single campaign on a narrow niche target.

Next we could talk about the details of our marketing mix. For example, one strategy might be to get more revenue out of current products. This could include getting more customers at the present price, selling more units to present customers, or getting a higher price per unit at the same number presently being sold. Strategies might also include things like focusing on a precise niche, or pricing that's significantly different from our competitor. We could cover product awareness, branding, imaging, positioning, differentiation, direct marketing, and personal selling.

We could also discuss our growth strategy. We might want to have better penetration in our existing market for the products we have now, or focus on finding new markets for them. We might decide to modify or replace a current product, or vertically expand the line with related products aimed at our present target segments. Or we could talk about diversifying with a horizontal expansion into entirely new products aimed at new market segments. We should discuss the opportunity costs of investing in various marketing proposals versus using our available capital in other ways.

Where

First we might discuss the physical locations to be covered by our marketing program. We could talk about whether we should be marketing on a neighborhood, citywide, regional or national basis including reviewing any satellite markets near us in which marketing might be done. We might go over any plans for exporting to international or global markets including factors to be considered such as cultures, customs, and politics.

Next we could review the places in which our product is available. We'd look at potential market development, including any possible plans for new facilities that might be opened, or existing ones that might be closed. We could analyze the distribution channels we're presently using, talking about any that we might want to add or delete or increase or reduce emphasis on, such as ecommerce on the Internet. We might explore expanding into or increasing our efforts in institutional markets or the government market at the federal, state or local level.

And of course, we should discuss the tactics to be employed to implement our strategies. These include the specific advertising media to be used plus promotional events such as trade shows. We might talk about public relations and our personal selling efforts.

Who

Now we discuss our target market segments, beginning by talking about the groups of persons that we've identified by demographic and psychographic characteristics. We could also analyze who'll be the decision maker and key influencer in the purchase of our product. We might also discuss who'll be responsible for overseeing which aspects of our marketing plan, and for making any needed adjustments.

Why

Now we try to put ourselves into the customer's perspective, asking why customers want or need our product and how they use it. We try to understand the buying motivations of potential customers in various situations.

We could also discuss how to create customer loyalty, with a view toward the lifetime customer value of all the purchases the customer is projected to make throughout our relationship. We might institute a loyalty program that contains rewards, discounts, or other incentives for repeat purchases or referrals.

We may wish to analyze what could be a customer's perceived risks in purchasing our product. We could also talk about perceived value, and explore ways we could increase it such as with value-added premiums.

We might also discuss message development. We could write a *creative brief* that contains a summary of our target market segments, branding, imaging, positioning, differentiation, and brand personality. It would outline our understanding of the prospects' needs and wants plus our perceptions of the prospect's buying motivations that are logical, emotional, or both.

We'd decide on our desired response to each marketing campaign such as getting the prospect to stop in, call, log on, return a BRM card, sample our product, or remember something. We could define the overall approach we'll take in persuasion and cognitive consistency, with the actual copy to be written later.

When

This defines the time periods during which the product should be promoted in various ways. This can cover seasons, months, weeks, days or hours of the day. For example, promotional strategies might be different during the summer, at tax time, near holidays, the week after payday, on Saturdays, or during the driving hour just before dinnertime.

A Written Marketing Plan

A written marketing plan could contain the information we've compiled from our six basic questions, organized in a report. This can be referenced throughout the year, with projections compared to actual results.

The written document might also include additional topics and supporting evidence, all contained in a nice binder and organized in sections such as those below.

Executive Summary

This is a short overview of the key elements of the plan. The executive summary is similar to a creative brief in that it's longer than the mission statement but is still given in just a few paragraphs.

Its purposes include providing the essence of the combined elements and engaging the interest of the executive who's reading it to delve deeper into more detailed information given elsewhere in the plan.

Mission Statement

Again, this is our clear and concise statement of who the company serves and why. It should be reviewed periodically and revised as needed when new products, geographies, and demographic or psychographic target segments are added.

The Team

This details which company units and individuals are responsible for what elements of the plan.

Present Situation

This section gives the company's current circumstances, including present sales and trends. Target markets could be presented here including our present customers and geographies served, or they might receive their own section. Market share is also important to track, since it gives our company's performance as a percentage of our total category's sales.

Our situational analysis can include the company's product lines and profitability, a unique selling proposition, an industry overview, the regulatory environment, and the present macroeconomic and microeconomic situations. The SWOT analysis could also be presented here, or it might receive its own section.

Competitive Analysis

In the competitive analysis section we discuss our competitors, their positions, their strategies, and our plans to deal with whatever the competitors might be doing or planning.

Objectives

Here we outline the company's specific and measurable goals for the upcoming period. These can include gross sales, profitability, and market share increases.

Strategic Elements

We list the specific actions to be employed in order to reach the objectives. We outline the promotional mix, product improvements or additions, pricing strategy, and improvements in service.

Tactical Details

These are the specifics of how the strategies will be achieved. Here we'd include the advertising media to be used, details of planned public relations and publicity efforts, sales promotions, and any additions to or modifications in channels of distribution.

Controls and Tracking

This states who is responsible for measuring results, how they'll be measured, and how and by whom any required adjustments to the marketing plan will be made during the period.

Chapter Nine: Promotional Planning and Media Selection

A 10,000-page 20-pound book would be both difficult to read and hard to carry, so we're going to keep this chapter relatively brief. Complete books could be and have been written about each of the media topics we'll look at here, so we're not going terribly in-depth on any of these choices. Our objective here is to review their basic features for the purpose of helping us determine the proportion of each medium to use in a particular marketing strategy. Each of the various media has properties that may be a strength or weakness, depending on our goals. Whatever media we choose, we'll have the best chance at an effective campaign if we have ads that are well written, creatively produced, and effectively placed to reach a properly defined target audience at a selling frequency.

Media Options

First we'll review traditional media including broadcast, print, and outdoor. Then we'll look at some options in new media, including web-based and digital mobile media choices. These new media choices are growing exponentially and changing constantly. There's no shortage of suggestions that traditional media are dead. Some say that marketing through web pages, social media, and mobile devices will soon replace all advertising, PR and promotion in broadcast, print, and outdoor media.

The growth of new media is exciting, for sure. Yet we notice that even though they have strong online presences, many big advertisers like Proctor & Gamble, General Motors, and Budweiser are still heavily using traditional media. Companies like these have highly paid professional staffs who study promotional issues every day. Microsoft and Apple are using traditional media to promote their tablet computers and operating systems. Smartphone companies are using traditional media to hawk their models.

So we might conclude that a mix of both traditional and new media is our best bet. Our goals likely involve reaching a variety of people whose environments change and who do different things throughout the day. No single medium reaches everyone everywhere all the time.

Impact and the perceived value of a message through a medium are important considerations in choosing media. While some might argue that an impression is an impression, others say that not all media are created equal for every objective. For instance, a particular advertiser might believe that while an eye on a newspaper page, in a glossy magazine, or on a TV screen may cost more than an outdoor or web ad, its impact makes it *worth* more than an eye on a billboard, computer screen or mobile device. Another with a different goal and target prospect might see it the opposite way. Either view could be valid, depending on the advertiser's goals.

In any case there's little disagreement that an ad on an adult website, or one on a poster above a restroom urinal, carries less prestige than a primetime TV ad. So, in addition to looking at things like rates and cost per thousand when we're buying advertising, we should also assign a value to the impact on our target of a message received through a particular medium. This includes the perception transferred, the attention paid to the ad, and the retention of the message.

Tune-out is another consideration. This term refers to the tendency of a reader, listener or viewer in traditional media to pay less attention to an ad than to regular program or editorial content. *Zipping* means skipping past or fast-forwarding through commercials in a recorded television program. This can be a significant problem for advertisers in shows like sitcoms, but is less of a problem with broadcasts such as sporting events which are almost always watched live. *Banner blindness* refers to the tendency of computer users to ignore ads that are placed around the content they're viewing on the web or their mobile device.

In choosing media, we'll look at our target demographics and geography. Psychographics such as lifestyle, attitudes, and activities also play a part. We'll determine whether our primary goal is reach or frequency, and whether we're after a wide population group or a tightly targeted segment.

In the final analysis, our marketing objectives will always be the biggest factor in deciding what strategies to employ and the proportion of each of the various media to use in a particular campaign. But no matter whether we're using traditional media or new digital ones, certain things remain constant. Let's look at some of those.

Market Research

As mentioned in Chapter Two, market research can be either primary or secondary. Primary is that which is done specifically for us, and it's the most expensive kind. Secondary research was done by others for their purposes, but can be adapted to our needs. Demographic data is the most commonly used secondary research data in marketing campaigns, and national census data is perhaps the easiest to get. It's also free. Other examples of secondary research sources include studies done by the Nielsen TV and Audio divisions, or by Eastlan Ratings for radio listening. These media surveys sometimes include both demographic and psychographic data. Secondary research data is also available from sources such as public libraries and the local Chamber of Commerce.

Unless our product is truly for all ages, lifestyles and incomes, or unless we have more money than sense, we probably need at least some targeting in market segments and media campaigns.

We can target in a number of ways, including geography, demographics, and psychographics. These differ in various media. For example, geographic targeting is easily done with outdoor, but demographic and psychographic targeting are harder there. Demographic and psychographic targeting can be done in radio by using station formats and on TV by selecting cable channels or network programs, but precise geographic targeting can't be done by zip codes or neighborhoods.

As discussed in Chapter Two, quantitative research deals strictly with numbers while qualitative research includes components such as lifestyles, social classes, attitudes and opinions. Here are some examples of quantitative demographic information that we might find in looking at different secondary sources. We can add, subtract, or interpolate based on what we need. Some sample marketing targets are listed in the last column.

Population Segments

U. S. Census	TV	Radio	Common Mktg Targets
0-4	2+	12-17	2-11
5-9	2-11	18-24	12-17
10-14	6-11	18-34	18-24
15-19	12-17	18-49	18-34
20-24	12-34	25-54	18-49
25-29	18+	35-64	25-54
30-34	18-34	65+	35-64
35-39	18-49		55-64
40-44	21-49		65+
45-49	25-49		
50-54	25-54		
55-59	35+		
60-64	35-64		
65-69	65+		
70-74			
75-79			
80-84			
85+			

Other key research terms include variable and validity. A *variable* is a value that changes due to something that affects it in some way. *Validity* is the research term meaning the degree to which a survey has been properly drawn and sampled to accurately represent the population universe that's being analyzed.

Ratings and other surveys seldom query an entire population, but instead use *probability* or *non-probability* sampling. Probability sampling can be random, systematic, or stratified. Again, the group being sampled is referred to as the universe. In a *random sample*, each member of the universe has an equal chance of being selected. In a *systematic sample*, a participant is selected at a predetermined numerical point, such as every 135th person. A *strategic sample* has a representative number of each of the various components of the universe, such as sex and age groups. *Weighting* may be employed to equalize responses, meaning that one respondent's answers may represent more or less persons in the universe than those of another respondent. In a *non-probability sample*, an experienced surveyor uses selective judgment in choosing respondents that he or she believes to be representative of the universe being surveyed.

Understanding Media Audience Estimates

There are many ways to present media audience estimates, with lots of mathematical formulas and sophisticated-sounding comparisons like turnover factors, cost per thousand, cost per click, cost per point and effective reach.

Audience Measurement Types and Terms

In spite of all the fancy formulas, there are really only two basic types of audiences. These are either *unique individuals* reached over the time being analyzed, or the medium's *average users* exposed to a message in a given period. Traditional media terms for unique individuals include *cumulative audience (cume)* and *circulation*. On websites the term is *unique visitors*. In traditional media, terms used to express average users are *average persons* and *exposures*. On websites, the term *stickiness* refers to how well a page holds viewers.

Reach and Frequency

Reach is the term that refers to the number of unique individuals who are exposed to an ad schedule utilizing a particular medium. We also need to know *frequency*, which means how many times the average person is exposed to the ad over its schedule.

Mathematically, frequency equals *gross impressions* divided by reach. To calculate the gross impressions generated by an ad schedule, we multiply the number of ads in the flight by the average persons estimate. For instance, if the average persons estimate for a target audience in a given time period is 5,600 persons, a flight of 10 commercials would generate 56,000 gross impressions.

The term *selling frequency* refers to the minimum number of exposures in a time period that we consider to be necessary to effectively convey our message and have it remembered. While the term *reach* refers to the number of individuals exposed to the message at least once, the term *effective reach* refers to the number of individuals exposed to the message at our defined selling frequency of, say, three or more exposures in a time period such as a week. An integrated marketing campaign might generate some exposures with more expensive media like TV, radio, magazines and newspapers plus "reminder" exposures on less expensive media like outdoor and the Internet. Since more reach generally means less frequency, a major consideration in laying out a media buying plan is to achieve a good balance between impact, reach and frequency within the budget.

Media Rates

Media outlets typically publish a rate card that lists their charges for advertising. It gives unit rates, such as broadcast seconds, newspaper column inches, classified ad lines, or web banner size. Charges are often based partly on frequency discounts, which are the number of ads that the advertiser agrees to run in a contract period.

Some rate cards have vertical or short-term volume discounts for high *share-of-voice* scheduling. This term refers to one advertiser's portion of the commercial space on a particular medium, as compared to that of its competitors. Some campaigns are designed to achieve a high share-of-voice in a short period of time. This might be done with a large print ad, such as a full page. In broadcast media, the approach could be through a saturation campaign, also called vertical placement. This refers to a large number of ads run in a short period of time, such as one radio spot per hour from 6 a.m. to 7 p.m. on a given day or a large number of primetime TV spots in an evening.

Pre-emptible rates may also be available, which is a lower rate for scheduling an ad that may not run if another advertiser agrees to pay a higher price for that spot. Bid rates for web advertising follow a similar principle for ads with search engines, social media, and related sites.

With some media, there may be a *short-rate* policy. This is an upward or downward rate that applies to previous periods in the event that the advertiser runs more or fewer ads than originally contracted. The short rate may result in an additional charge or a credit to the advertiser's account.

Rates can vary widely for various times and placement options. ROS or ROP rates refer to Run of Station, Site, or Publication. This means that the scheduling position for an ad is not fixed, but is at the option of the medium. Prime times, fixed positions and island positions cost more. Published rates are often higher for national advertisers than for local merchants. Many media rates are negotiable to some degree.

An advertising buy with traditional media is often placed by using an *insertion order*. This is a standard form for purchasing and scheduling that's used by an advertising agency, broadcaster, publisher, or other media outlet.

Some media offer a discount to advertising agencies, which is essentially a commission paid to the agency for placing advertising on that medium. The agency bills the client at the regular rate, and the billing to the agency gives the discount, which is generally 15%. Other media use net billing, which means that the rate is the same to either the advertiser or the agency. In this case, the agency typically adds a 15% markup when billing the client. Agencies or media may also charge the client for other services on an hourly, project, or retainer basis. Examples include production, other creative work, and research. Such charges would usually either be listed on the rate card or agreed to up front.

Comparing Media Costs

Three terms used in analyzing media costs are CPM, CPP and CPC. Cost per thousand (CPM) is the cost to generate a thousand advertising exposures, also called impressions. Cost per point (CPP) is the cost to generate impressions equivalent to one exposure each in one percent of a population universe. CPC is the cost for a web user to take a relevant action such as clicking something in the ad like a link to the advertiser's landing page.

Print display ads are typically sold based on circulation and the size of the ad by column-inch. TV ads are often sold based on average rating, which refers to the percentage of television households that are tuned to a given program for at least one minute. In radio, average ratings are calculated by dividing the estimated number of persons listening at a given time by the total population for the demographic cell. A person is counted in a radio average estimate if they listened for at least five minutes in a given quarter-hour.

Broadcast spots are often sold based on the cost per point (CPP). To get this, we simply divide the cost per spot by the average rating. Here's an easy-math example. With a spot cost of $40.00 and an average rating of 2.0, the CPP would be $20.00. Many advertising buys are based on the purchase of a specified number of gross rating points (GRPs). To determine the number of GRPs purchased, we multiply the number of ads by the average rating in the specified time period and demographic cell. Like the CPP cost estimate formula, one GRP is a number of advertising impressions equivalent to one impression each in one percent of the targeted universe.

Ads in both traditional and new media are also often sold based on the estimated impressions (also called persons or exposures) expressed as a number rather than as a percentage. The cost per thousand impressions (CPM) is calculated by dividing the cost per ad in the medium by the average exposures estimate expressed in thousands. With an ad rate of $40.00 and 5,600 impressions, the CPM would be $40 divided by 5.6 thousand, or $7.14.

In addition to CPM, we may also buy Internet advertising on a cost-per-click basis. CPC advertising is generally billed based on our bid amount when a prospect clicks a link to our landing page. Some sites also include as clicks other relevant actions such as leaving a comment or clicking on a photo. With CPC advertising, our click-through rate is better if the ad is effectively written and placed in appropriate web content for our target audience. Social media campaigns and search engines can provide metrics that show us the geography and demographics of our reach.

It's important to remember that on a given medium with a specified CPM, CPP or dollar level, there's an inverse mathematical relationship between reach and frequency. The more reach we get the less frequency there is, and vice versa.

For example, with a $500 weekly flight it might be to the advertiser's advantage to buy a schedule with lower reach in order to achieve higher frequency. For us small-budget advertisers, lower-rated but tightly targeted media are often better buys than top-rated outlets with greater reach and higher rates to match. We'd first look for achieving selling frequency with the target audience, and then decide the media on which this can be done within the budget. Since repetition can help increase message retention, higher frequency is often preferable to greater reach.

CPM is the easiest equalizing tool to put media with varying geographies, audience sizes, and rate structures on level footing for purposes of flight comparison. We're essentially buying prospects by the pound.

Traditional Media

Before we begin, it may be helpful to look at a chronology of new media vs. existing media for the last hundred years or so. When radio came along, people said that it would kill newspapers. That didn't happen. Then came TV, and folks predicted it would kill radio. Nope. FM happened, and funeral plans were in the works for AM. But AM is still thriving, particularly with talk radio. Cable TV came along, complete with predictions about the death of broadcast TV. Wrong. Then came satellite radio and TV, which some said would make terrestrial broadcasting obsolete. That didn't happen, either. Now the web and mobile devices are here, ushering in the interactive marketing era. And plenty of pundits are predicting they'll kill all other forms of media. Maybe. But history tells us it's more likely that existing media *won't* disappear. They'll probably just continue to evolve in the face of new challenges, like they've been doing for over a century now. There's certainly no reason that they can't become more interactive themselves with new technologies of their own. Print publishers, cable companies, outdoor media, radio stations and digital TV broadcasters are working day and night on their own evolutions and revolutions.

So first let's look at broadcast, print, outdoor, and specialty advertising options. To paraphrase Will Rogers, perhaps the news of their death has been greatly exaggerated.

Broadcasting

The term *broadcasting* is sometimes equated with mass marketing. *Narrowcasting* is a term that's sometimes used to refer to the use of stations or programs that target to specific demographic and lifestyle groups. In radio and cable TV, this is the result of programming fragmentation due to a large number of stations in a market. On over-the-air broadcast TV, narrowcasting can be achieved by advertising during specific programs.

A broadcast time slot is called a *spot*. Broadcast advertising can be purchased in different lengths for spots. Common times in radio are 10, 30 and 60 seconds. In TV, the most common times are 15, 30, and 60 seconds. Longer spots can be purchased in both radio and TV. A program-length commercial is called an *infomercial*.

Piggyback ads can be used to qualify for lower rates and for cost-sharing between advertisers. These are two broadcast commercials spliced together to make a single commercial of a specified length, such as two 30-second radio ads for different clients combined into one 60-second spot. TV advertisers sometimes purchase *bookends*. These are two 15-second spots running at the beginning and ending of a commercial break. *Product placement* is occasionally sold in TV, which is the use of a product during the program content. This is more common in film production.

The term *daypart* refers to a standard time period in a broadcast day. Normal radio dayparts are Monday through Friday 6 – 10 a.m. (Morning Drive); 10 a.m. – 3 p.m. (Midday); 3 p.m. – 7 p.m. (Afternoon Drive); 7:00 p.m. – Midnight (Evening); and Midnight – 6 a.m. (Overnight).

In TV, typical U. S. Eastern time zone dayparts are: 5 a.m. – 7 a.m. (Early Morning); 7 a.m. – 9 a.m. (Morning); 9 a.m. – 4:30 p.m. (Daytime); 4:30 – 7:30 p.m. (Early Fringe); 7:30 p.m. – 8:00 p.m. (Prime Access); 8:00 p.m. – 11:00 p.m. (Prime Time); 11:00 p.m. – 11:30 p.m. (Late News); 11:30 p.m. – 1:00 a.m. (Late Fringe); and 1:00 a.m. – 5:00 a.m. (Late Night). These can vary somewhat in the Central, Mountain, and Pacific time zones due to network program scheduling.

Many figures are contained in TV and radio audience estimates, commonly referred to as ratings books. Learning to analyze these requires an understanding of only a few simple terms. The data may be in a printed book or on a computer. Maximi$er, Tapscan, and Strata are examples of computer programs currently used, as of this writing, for in-depth ratings analysis.

One of the first things to look for in broadcast ratings is the population estimates for the market, which are given for two areas. The first is the MSA, which is the city and surrounding area including its suburbs. Ratings firms use the census term mentioned in Chapter Two of *metro* as the short term for Metropolitan Statistical Area. Again, this contains an urban center with a population of at least 50,000 and a total area population of at least 100,000. A Micropolitan Statistical Area contains an urban core of at least 10,000. Both are abbreviated MSA.

The second survey term denotes the larger trade area, which may be called by various terms including the radio term TSA, for Total Survey Area. Nielsen terms for the market outside the urban center include

ADI, for Area of Dominant Influence, and DMA for Designated Market Area. Custom areas can also be built within computer programs. These can be defined geographically using both counties and zip codes.

As detailed in Chapter Two and earlier in this chapter, in demographic targeting population estimates are broken down into standard sex/age groups, called *cells*. These can be grouped together as needed to comprise the target audience. The total of all persons in a group being analyzed is called the *universe*. A rating is simply a station's proportion of the individuals who make up a given universe at a specified time.

We only need to understand five terms to be able to analyze a ratings book. As mentioned earlier in this chapter, media audience estimates talk about one of two estimated audiences, which is either the *unique individuals* reached in a time period or the *average audience* at a given moment. In broadcasting, these two estimates may be expressed in one of three ways: persons, rating, or share. The term *persons* expresses it as a number; *rating* expresses it as a percentage of the population universe; and *share* expresses it as a percentage of the total audience of all stations at a given moment.

Once the above five terms are understood conceptually, we can get fancy. We can calculate various ways that things interact mathematically, including how much it costs to a deliver an advertising message to a given number of people. But no matter how fancy we get, everything comes back to these five basics: individuals reached, average audience, persons, rating, and share.

In looking at radio ratings, a station's cumulative audience could equal its reach. For this to happen, however, the advertiser would have to run one ad in each quarter-hour of the time period in question. For the full radio week of Monday through Sunday from 6 a.m. to midnight, this would require 504 spots weekly. Um, that's probably not practical. So it would be rare that total cume listeners or total viewership would tell us our number of individuals actually reached. Therefore, broadcast ratings computer programs like Stratus and Maximi$er are able to adjust cume figures to estimate reach according to the size of the ad schedule purchased during a time period. If we don't have a computer program to do it for us, we can get a quick-and-dirty estimate of the individuals reached by calculating the number of quarter-hours in which we're running a spot as a percentage of the total number of quarter-hours in the program or time period. We can then apply this percentage to the cume figure to estimate our schedule's reach. We could apply similar math to get quick-and-dirty reach estimates in other media.

In TV ratings, the term share refers to a program's audience at a given time, expressed as a percentage of either Households Using Television (HUT) or Persons Viewing Television (PVT). To calculate average radio share, we take the average persons estimate for a given station and divide it by the estimated total listening audience to all stations combined.

Broadcast reach and frequency plans can be (1) *horizontal*, which involves high frequency within a select audience (low reach) over a long period. (2) *diagonal*, which involves low frequency with a broad audience (high reach) over a long period; or (3) *vertical*, which involves high frequency with high reach occurring over a short period of time.

Production for TV, cable and video is generally more complex than for radio or audio, and therefore the cost is usually higher.

Print

Print advertising can mean everything from business cards and letterhead to flyers, classified and display ads or advertorials in newspapers and magazines, or inserts distributed along with them. Printed materials can also be delivered via direct mail.

Collateral materials are consumable printed items including business cards, letterhead, billing forms, and appointment cards. A *flyer* may be included in a direct mail campaign, used as a print insertion, or distributed as a handout. It's usually a standard-size sheet of paper printed on one or both sides, and may be folded.

Display advertising refers to that placed in the regular portions of a print publication, as opposed to the classified section. It's usually purchased by the column inch, which is an area one inch deep by one column wide. *Classified advertising* is organized by topic and usually appears at the rear of the publication. It's typically purchased by the word. An *advertorial* is a display ad that simulates editorial content. Publications generally require that advertorials be marked as "Advertisement" at the top of the copy. In addition to display and classified ads, newspapers may be used to deliver pre-printed inserts. Magazines may be used to deliver *bound-in cards* or *blow-ins*, which are pre-printed advertising cards inserted in the magazine by machine.

As mentioned earlier in this chapter, a display ad can be purchased *run of publication*. This ROP ad can appear anywhere in the editorial content. A *fixed position* ad can be bought by the section, page, or position on the page. An *island position* is the term for a premium-priced print ad, store display, or broadcast spot separated from all other advertising by editorial matter, floor space, or program material.

The main components of the layout for a print ad include the headline or header, subhead, body copy, image and white space. The purpose of the *headline* is to grab attention and get the viewer to read more. The *subhead* gives additional information designed to lead the reader to the *body copy*, which contains the main text. The *image* can be a photograph, an illustration, a chart or a table. Color is often a key component of a print ad, particularly in conveying emotion. A print ad is often designed to convey a mental picture or emotional image as well as the information in the text.

Direct mail is, of course, promotional material sent by using the postal service. A mailing list is compiled from an in-house database or rented from a list company. Direct mail is often used as a form of direct response advertising, and typically includes a BRM card. A test mailing is sometimes done to measure results using a particular package before funds are committed to a larger mailing campaign. For statistical validity the *Rule of 300* is often employed for test mailings. This means that it's sent to enough households to generate at least 300 responses.

Outdoor and Out-of-Home

The term *outdoor advertising* generally refers to the use of billboards. Location is one key consideration in selecting a billboard, and another is size. The most common size of billboard is the 30-sheet or poster size, which is roughly 12' x 25'. Another popular size is the junior panel. It's much smaller than the 30-sheet poster, and is sometimes called an 8-sheet or 6-sheet. It can cost a lot less, but often sits closer to the road so that it actually appears about the same size when viewed. Another factor in selecting a billboard is illumination. Although the length of ad message is limited, billboards are often used as a primary medium or for low-cost frequency reinforcement to advertising in other media, and for location positioning.

The term *out-of-home advertising* includes both billboards and *transit* advertising. Transit media include buses and taxicabs. Out-of-home advertising can be purchased on a single board or vehicle, and is often scheduled in a *showing*, which is a concept similar to GRPs. It refers to the number of advertising impressions created over a given period of time by the total of all the billboards or transit vehicles used in the campaign. A 100 showing generates impressions equivalent to 100% of the target population, a 50 showing equals impressions equivalent to half the target population, and so forth.

Specialty and Premium Advertising

Specialty advertising items have the business name, logo and perhaps a slogan or advertising message imprinted on them. This includes things such as decals, bumper stickers, door knob hangers, signs, posters, banners, T-shirts, jackets, sweats, caps, hats, mugs, pens, calendars, inflatables, time planners, key tags, refrigerator magnets, license plate holders, magnetic auto signs, and loyalty cards. The items may be sold, given away individually, or included as premiums with a purchase.

Trade Shows, Exhibitions, and Events

Trade shows and *exhibitions* are usually held in large venues, where a number of vendors in related industries display their wares. They typically feature meetings, training sessions and seminars held outside the exhibition hall. *Events* may be designed to draw the general public, such as fairs and festivals. Trade shows, events, and exhibitions all typically feature space for rent, which involves a display promoting the products of a company.

Point-of-Purchase

Point-of-purchase advertising is generally done in the form of printed display materials at a retail purchase location, although other media such as video displays are sometimes used. POP items include banners, window decals, floor decals, posters, shelf talkers, table tents, coasters, and menus. A bar or restaurant might be decorated with a holiday theme. Good point-of-purchase advertising can add atmosphere and excitement, and reach prospects at the exact time they're ready to buy something.

New Media: The Internet, Mobile Devices, and Digital Advertising

Traditional media depend on interruption advertising. That is, they sneak an advertising message to someone who's engaged in some other activity like watching a football game on TV. Digital advertising, on the other hand, can put a precisely targeted message in front of someone at the exact time they're searching for it, or based on their previous activity on the web, with precise metrics provided to measure results. These ads can work like the Yellow Pages on steroids, so a digital component utilizing the Internet and mobile devices can be an important part of a marketing campaign.

At the most basic level, people use the Internet and mobile devices to do one of three things: to search, to browse, or to interact with others in some way such as in social media or ecommerce. The Internet is amazing. Someone actually figured out how to connect all the computers in the world together. It uses *hypertext transfer protocol* (http) commands that enable all of the connected computers to communicate with each other. Today's Internet is sometimes called Web 2.0,

106

because some had called web marketing dead following the dot-com crash that occurred from 1999 - 2001. The worldwide web (www) was created by Tim Berners-Lee in 1991. It allows browsers such as Internet Explorer, Firefox, and Google Chrome to index and share information among users. This has led to today's trend which many see as a new marketing era that they're calling *interactive marketing*. This term fundamentally refers to the use of a two-way channel such as the Internet or a digital telephone for making direct purchases and for conducting other transactions such as online banking. Since customers' and sellers' computers are directly connected to each other, prospects, customers and other stakeholders can be segmented down to the individual level through sophisticated databases.

The term *digital marketing* can be used to refer to all marketing on the Internet using a desktop computer or on a mobile device with either the Internet or a digital phone connection. The term *mobile marketing* refers to campaigns designed specifically for display on tablet computers and smartphones. Smartphones can be set to automatically search for a web connection prior to accessing data over a potentially more expensive phone connection. It seems that smartphones are always with us, and texting has replaced much verbal conversation these days. All social media and about every other site you can think of now either has an app or is at least viewable on mobile devices. Smartphone apps can be used as a calculator or a metronome and can tell us the weather forecast, the current news, or the latest sports scores. We can check the stock market, use our GPS map to tell us how to get where we're going, or we can find the location of the nearest campground or highway rest area. And on and on. Google's ranking algorithm prioritizes sites that are optimized for mobile devices.

A website's content can create immediate action, so some say that the worldwide web is a direct marketer's dream come true. Used effectively, the web can be a low-cost sales vehicle that has database information, response rates, and consumer feedback instantly available.

We may want to do database marketing with email campaigns, and perhaps use some pay-per-click promotions on search engines and social media. We might distribute an e-zine or a podcast. Our options in new media are exciting and constantly growing. Let's look a bit more deeply at some.

Our Website

Websites are simply groups of related webpages. A *universal resource locator* (URL) is an address on the worldwide web, and every webpage has its own URL. A hyperlink is often placed somewhere on a given page so that the user can click the link to move to another section, webpage, or website. Hyperlinks from other relevant websites are an important factor in search engine rankings. The last part of the web address, such as .com or .net, is called the *top level domain* (TLD). Internet content is written using the computer programming language called *hypertext markup language* (HTML).

To be effective, our website must have well-presented content that's appropriate to the needs of the visitor. In order to promote our services or sell products on our website, we have to get traffic to it. We can advertise offline in traditional media to build website traffic, or we can do it in other places on the Internet. Perhaps the oldest and most irritating way of advertising one website on another is the use of *banner ads* and *pop-ups*. These typically contain a click-through link. A *trick banner* generally has little positive effect for most businesses since it generates low quality web traffic by attempting to fool people into clicking through to another website. *Incentivized traffic* is another example of low-quality web traffic. It consists of visitors who went to a website purely to receive something such as a premium. As mentioned earlier, the term banner blindness refers to the fact that people tend to ignore banner ads when they can, and try to close them when they can't. Pop-up blockers on web browsers are designed to keep them from appearing in the first place.

Web ads using hyperlinks to the advertiser's site are usually purchased on a CPM or CPC basis, but they're sometimes contracted for based upon pay-per-lead or pay-per-sale. Compared to traditional media, costs are low in using most forms of new media. However, web activities like social media can be both important and time consuming, so the time investment must also be considered along with other expenses like content preparation, writing, and production costs.

People go on the web for lots of reasons. Sometimes they're looking for entertainment. Other times they're researching something, interacting on social media, or doing ecommerce. In all these cases, up-to-date, relevant, informative, engaging and entertaining content helps bring in website traffic and keep visitors there longer. Entertaining and engaging can mean lots of things, including good music, cute, fashionable, funny, interesting, or compelling. In addition to entertaining, advertising and selling, a website can serve other functions such as research, customer service, or public relations. Many websites utilize cookies, which store information regarding a visitor's activity on the site, and these cookies can be used in highly targeted web advertising campaigns.

If a company has multiple products in deep or wide lines, advertising probably should take the visitor to a relevant landing page instead of sending them to a generic home page. On the landing page, an offer may be made to provide something of value in return for getting an email address and perhaps other data from the visitor. A company may have dozens or even hundreds of different landing pages, each relevant to a particular product, offer, or advertising campaign. Less frequently, a *splash page* is used, which is a landing page containing branding graphics that's shown prior to the site's home page. However, relevance is generally considered to be more important that flashiness.

As with promotion using other media, two fundamentals are important in converting website traffic into sales. First, we want to get them there. Second, we want to keep them there. As mentioned earlier, *unique user* and *unique visitor* are web terms for unduplicated individuals who visit a site. This is roughly equivalent to the term cumulative audience that's used in broadcast media and the term circulation used in print media. And again, website *stickiness* refers to the ability to keep users on the site for longer periods of time, visiting more pages while they're there. Stickiness is equivalent to getting subscribers to spend more time actually reading a print publication, and to broadcast media efforts to get those who tune in to watch or listen longer. A site's *bounce rate* gives the percentage of its viewers who don't spend much time on the site or who don't visit multiple pages. *User friendliness* of the site is very important in keeping stickiness up and the bounce rate down.

In addition to their primary website that can be accessed by prospects and customers, some companies also have an *intranet* which functions only on the company's computer network. Others utilize an *extranet* that has been set up on the Internet for use only by those with passwords.

Many sites incorporate a *blog*, which is short for *weblog*. The term *blogosphere* refers to those who write or comment on blogs. A blog can be a good way to help establish us a thought leader. We can do this by commenting on our own blog, or by using a *backlink strategy* in which we comment on other blogs and give a link back to our own site. Many blogs are designed using the free software WordPress, which can also be used to build a full website. WordPress does not require html programming knowledge. For those of us who wish to design, build, and maintain our own custom site using WordPress, many service providers can host it.

There are local firms almost everywhere that design custom websites using html. Additionally, many companies sell such services on the web in a variety of price ranges. Custom design and maintenance can be expensive but is often well worth it depending on our needs. Again, once a site has been built it might be hosted locally or by one of many hosting services available on the Internet.

Some companies may not need custom website design and maintenance. They might sell few or no products on the Internet, and only have a need for a website that's essentially just an online brochure or a place to be used by a visitor for a specific purpose such as watching a training video, getting more product information, checking prices, or placing relatively few orders. Its content may only need to be updated rarely. In these cases, one inexpensive way to build and maintain a website is to use a pre-built template that requires no programming. These are designed for those who need a web presence, prefer to do it themselves, and don't want to spend much money. The goal is to provide tools that help individuals and businesses have a good web presence even if they don't know the first thing about html programming. Typically, this can be done for an entire year for about the price of a business lunch or two.

With these types of services, a business or individual can search for and secure a domain name, and then build and update content on their own site by choosing from hundreds of pre-built website templates in many categories, with email accounts available. Persons just add text and graphics to the design, pretty much like using a simple word processing program. Plain-language metadata can easily be added to each page which is automatically converted to html to help search engines find it (SEO is covered later in this chapter). And for those who need them, ecommerce products can be added to the site including a shopping cart, email marketing, and search engine optimization.

There are a number of these website services that can be found online. Many have staff onsite around the clock, with tech support available 24 hours a day, 7 days a week, every day of the year. Our service is available at www.michaelmayweb.com.

It's important to list goals, decide on a budget, and compare options before selecting an approach to a website.

Content Marketing for the Web and Mobile Devices

Content marketing means providing relevant material on a site to meet some need such as public relations, training, or promotion. It should be designed so that it works well for someone who may be using a traditional desktop or laptop computer, or who's on a mobile device. The specific content for any website obviously depends on its purpose. Content often involves not only text and graphics, but also video materials such as product demonstrations and training. If we want people to come back to our website often, we need to keep this regularly updated.

Social Media and Sharing Sites

We can do content marketing on our own website or through outside avenues including social media and web video sharing. At the time of this writing, the biggest social media sites are Facebook, Twitter, Google+, LinkedIn, Pinterest, and Tumblr. All have advantages and disadvantages. Facebook is the giant, with over a billion users worldwide, followed by the half billion or so at Twitter and Google+. LinkedIn is the best choice for making B2B connections. Tumblr is popular with teens and younger adults. Pinterest is a sharing site for images, and YouTube and Vimeo are the top video sharing sites. Facebook and YouTube are great places to start, and perhaps we'll also use Twitter, LinkedIn and others depending on our target audience. Of course, many of us don't have the time to try to develop online personal relationships with a lot of our customers, but it's not all that time-consuming to at least maintain a presence on relevant social media and sharing sites. We'll put pertinent content in our profiles, on our pages, and in our posts. And we'll upload appropriate pictures and videos.

Paid advertising is also available on social media and sharing sites. A pay-per-click or CPM-based arrangement can be used. Because users are there for personal interaction, ad content on social media is often used more like PR than traditional advertising. So in many cases social media are used to augment our traditional media efforts rather than to replace them.

In his book *The New Rules of Marketing and PR* (John Wiley & Sons, Hoboken, NJ, 2013), David Meerman Scott says that on the web we really don't advertise in the traditional sense. Rather, he asserts, we try to understand our buyers and tell stories that connect with their problems. Instead of concentrating on what we want to say, we focus on what they want to hear.

Search Engine Marketing

We certainly want to make sure that people can find us when they're searching for what we're selling. For that, we use *search engine optimization (SEO)*. Search engine ranking criteria change all the time. However, a few factors are consistently important. To rank better in search engines, a website must be optimized for displaying well on mobile devices. Relevant content should be updated regularly. Content should be written so that it's "keyword rich", meaning that search engine spiders can easily index the page according to what potential visitors are searching for. And links to it from other relevant sites are also an important factor.

The top three search engines are Google, Bing, and Yahoo. The most popular by far is Google, so let's look more deeply at that. The others work in a similar way. In addition to their normal or "organic" search results based on queries, search engines have paid advertising services. On Google, these include Google AdWords, the Google Display Network, and AdSense. *Google AdWords* is for those who want to advertise in relevant search results and on other websites that have related content. The *Google Display Network* puts up display rather than text-only ads, and *Google AdSense* is for content publishers who want advertising to appear on their own websites and get paid for it.

Google AdWords is a quick, easy and effective way to get started with new media advertising on the web and mobile devices. A company or individual opens an account with Google, writes an ad that contains words, a link, and no graphics. Then the advertiser decides on whether to pay for the ad on a CPC or CPM basis, selects keywords and phrases to bid on, decides on a bid amount to pay for the ads, and sets a daily budget.

The Google Display Network allows *interest-based advertising*, which uses text-plus-graphics ads similar to those found in traditional media. It lets advertisers specify demographic targets plus psychographics in the form of interests. The advertiser lists its interest categories, and ads are placed based on an individual's previous visits to websites with content in categories related to the interests that have been listed.

Targeting is as essential in new media as it is in traditional media. Google can target AdWords ads from keywords used in a search by a user, by placing the ad on a site relative to the keyword targets of the ad, or based on the specific target audience segments that the advertiser has identified by geography, demographics, and interests. They're sold on an auction basis and run according to two main criteria: the advertiser's bid price based on impressions or clicks, and the ad's quality score. Quality score factors include the ad's predicted CTR based on its past performance, the relevance of the ad's content to the search or site's content, and the quality of the advertiser's landing page.

Search Results Ads are those based on the keywords listed with Google by the advertiser. A click-through has essentially given us permission-based advertising. The prospect was looking for the topic on the search engine and is now intentionally going to our website specifically looking for the content.

Contextual advertising refers to that placed by Google on a web page based on the site's similarity to the ad's content. Google uses factors including keyword analysis, keyword frequency, and relevant hyperlinks in choosing web pages on which to display contextual advertising.

With *placement targeting*, the advertiser decides where ads will be placed. The advertiser can choose the specific pages on websites where ads are desired, based on the advertiser's own determination of its relevance to what the advertiser has to offer.

In addition to basic search results and paid advertising, Google provides a variety of other tools. *Google Analytics* is a website statistics service that is available free or in a premium version to anyone with a Google account. A user can have up to 50 free website profiles, each of which can generate detailed statistics about who visits a website and where they come from both in terms of geography and the referrer, such as social networks, social media, and direct visits. It can be integrated with AdWords to track conversions such as sales and lead generation. *Google Alerts* can help with reputation management by monitoring feedback and comments and alerting a business or individual when something comes up. *Google Reader* can be used for RSS (Really Simple Syndication) for updates on material posted on user-selected websites. For example, a company's website might use RSS capability to automatically update information such as the current weather on the company website.

Online Auctions

Another Internet ecommerce vehicle is online auctions. Lots of brick-and-mortar businesses sell merchandise through auctions on eBay and other auction sites. Many have a storefront such as an eBay store listing both deep and wide inventories that can be purchased outright or at auction. In a no-reserve auction, the individual customer decides the price to be paid. An item may have a reserve price below which it will not be sold, and many items have a Buy-It-Now price.

Email Marketing

Email marketing can be a cost-effective way to reach people, particularly those on an in-house database, as an alternative to or in addition to postal mail. Email marketing should be *permission-based*. This requires that the recipient *opt-in* by giving permission to receive information and offers, and be given the ability to *opt-out* of future promotional efforts. Without an opt-in, such promotional email offers are considered to be spam. One thing that can often be emailed effectively is a periodic newsletter. An expanded version of this is called an *e-zine*, or electronic magazine. Many people are wary of opening emails from parties that they don't know, since an email may contain spyware or other harmful programs that are designed to be secretly installed on their computer to steal information, or to maliciously cause harm to the computer.

Multimedia, Streaming, and Webcasting

Multimedia promotion involves some combination of text, audio, video, and graphics. It might be distributed on DVD, a Blu-ray disc, or CD. This is generally called *electronic promotion*. It can also be webcast using streaming media, essentially broadcasting over the Internet. A podcast is a multimedia presentation sent to interested parties by subscription. *Viral marketing* occurs when someone views something on the web, receives it in their email, or gets a podcast, and then forwards that material to others.

Part Four:
Creativity Tools

Chapter Ten: Visualization

In just about any kind of communication, creativity is a good thing. Copywriters and performers often incorporate humor and wit, because these things are important parts of our lives. We learn to be succinct in getting to the point, generally utilizing as few words and as little time as possible, and we incorporate the unexpected with the element of surprise. In addition to ideas and feelings, we often need to transfer images. Visualization can spur creativity by tapping the power of the subconscious mind and by providing us with a unique point of view that brings perspective to our wit.

The Craft of Mental Imagery

Visualization is a craft that's one of our most useful creative skills. We use it to come up with vivid mental images, and then we transfer those pictures to others through skillful communication.

We can do "mental pushups" in order to keep our mind's eye in shape. One tactic is to learn to look at something like a pair of coffee cups, and ask *"What else could this be?"* When we look at a word, we can ask *"What else could this mean?"* We try to see a clear mental picture in full color and motion. Then we use words to describe what we see in detail.

Another good exercise in visualization and word description is *captioning.* We might add some text to an odd photo. We could look at a cartoon, cover up the artist's caption, and make up our own.

We can tap some of our subconscious mental power by consciously letting our mind's eye roam wherever it will. Ernest Hemmingway used to say that he achieved his life's accomplishments by the simple act of forcing himself to think for one hour a day. Some say that our conscious and subconscious minds are most closely connected in near-sleep states. So we might try closing our eyes for thirty minutes in the morning and thirty minutes in the evening, letting the mind wander in free association. We could keep a notepad by the bed so that when we get something good, we can immediately write it down.

According to Sigmund Freud, dreams are the mind's eye at play. He contended that the mental processes in dreams are virtually identical to those we use in wit. With practice, we can expand our skill at using the mind's eye to conjure up vivid pictures. We can look at an everyday thing and come up with something unusual about it, another thing with which we can merge it, or a secondary meaning. A chief talent of creative people is the ability to look around and see something that others don't. Poets, songwriters, novelists, commercial copywriters, and humorists develop their own slants on looking at things and their own ways of describing them.

We may find something that's either more or less truthful than the obvious. We might see something a little bit bigger or smaller than it should be. If we exaggerate by overstatement, that means it becomes larger than reality, and if we understate it we make it smaller. We could take a stocky person and make him the size of a tractor-trailer rig. Or we could exaggerate the height of a tall person. In our practice, it doesn't have to be poetic, dramatic, or funny. We're just exercising the visualization process. We ask "How tall are they?" As tall as the Empire State Building? We see it in our mind's eye. We make them *become* the Empire State Building. Then, once we have a good beginning visualization we can work on polishing the image, tweaking it to just the way we want to see it.

Some might think of this as daydreaming. As mentioned in Chapter Three, daydreaming is sometimes an escape mechanism called mental flight. Our creative use of it is like the difference in throwing wood chips in the trash or putting them in the fireplace to create heat. We channel the energy in some useful way. So when we let our mind wander in free association, we should also practice the art of assigning word descriptions to the images we find. Then we write them down for use now or later, or they're probably lost forever.

A Method for Visualization

We can use a simple three-step process to create a visualization.

1. We see a mental picture.
2. We add an unusual association. We ask *"What else could this be?"* or *"What else could this mean?"*
3. We describe our visualization using active verbs.

For example: *"Big Ears? He looked like a taxicab coming down the street with both doors open."* Here we've visualized two different things or meanings and stated them as being one. And our image moves. If we take our mental pictures and have them doing something, it makes the image both more visual and more memorable. Action tends to create greater clarity in communicating visualization.

We write with perspective. For example Agatha Christie, who ranks near the top in the list of all-time best-selling authors, takes a different look at things than, say, J. K. Rowling or Shakespeare. This is called the voice, slant, or point of view. As creative communicators, we have to define the perspectives used by the characters in our scripts. Developing the slant means defining our characters both physically and mentally. With a slant, they'll be much more effective than if we're simply feeding them disconnected lines. For characters that we use regularly, we can come up with a format which will help us plan by telling us how much material we need to prepare.

For example, let's take a four-hour disc jockey show. We may decide that we need to prepare, for instance, 32 minutes of material each day. Now we need slants so that we can customize the material for each character. How does our DJ approach the weather? Is he or she a cynic who believes the weather service doesn't actually have any equipment except a dartboard? If so, then we may have a little sound effect that's heard when the weather dart is thrown. "Well, let's see what the weather is going to be today..." Then there's the sound of the dart hitting the board. "OK, that's what the official forecasters say." Then the newsperson could say "It's not like that." And the DJ might respond with, "The next thing you're going to tell me is that we've really sent men to the moon, right? Naaah...it's just trick photography." A drop-in character on the show might be a guy who goes into a bar and meets these great women, but they just leave with somebody else and he always has a story about it. We develop a slant for each character and then write or compile lines which create visual scenes that fit them.

A good communicator is a both wordsmith and a language merchant, meaning that we know our words well and can use them to transfer ideas and images. We develop both a good vocabulary and performance skills. We learn to find creative associations and visualizations by looking at everyday life and trying to see things that other people might not. Then we point them out by transferring these associations and visualizations with descriptive words and psychophysical techniques. In the next chapter we'll look at humor and wit as creative tools.

Chapter Eleven: Elements of Wit and Humor

Creative communication involves more than just a little psychology. And when we talk psychology, the conversation often turns to Dr. Sigmund Freud (1856-1939), the founder of psychoanalysis. He wrote what's generally considered to be his most important work, *The Interpretation of Dreams,* in the year 1900. People seem to either love or hate Freud. Personally, I think we should give a high-five to someone who single-handedly founded an entire field of healthcare, but that's just me.

Apart from the controversial Freud, many people are unaware that he conveniently classified the elements of wit for us over a century ago. In 1905, Freud wrote a study titled *Wit and Its Relation to the Unconscious,* first translated and presented in the U. S. in 1938 by Dr. A. A. Brill, who was the first to practice psychoanalysis in the United States. Brill's original book was *The Basic Writings of Sigmund Freud (*1938, 1966, Brill, Modern Library, New York), and it included Freud's research on wit. That study has recently been republished as a standalone book. It is *Wit and Its Relation to the Unconscious* (Freud and Brill, Dover Publications, 2011). Although the examples of humor contained in the text are obviously very dated, both the reasons why people laugh and the thought processes that are described are timeless. Anyone in marketing would be well advised to get this book, read it, and keep it in the library as a reference on creative writing. In our text's brief study of the creative aspects of wit, humor, and comedy we'll refer to Freud as our authority on some key elements.

The Psychology of Wit

So why did the founder of psychoanalysis study joke writing? Freud explored wit as a means of interpreting dreams. He said that, like wit, "indirect expression, the substitution for the dream-thought by an allusion, by a trifle or by a symbolism analogous to comparison, is just exactly what distinguishes the manner of expression of the dream from our waking thoughts." Freud differentiated dreams from wit by pointing out that dreams serve to protect against pain, while wit seeks to acquire pleasure. He said that "in these two aims all our psychic activities meet."

Freud described wit in a number of interesting ways. These include "playful judgment, the union of dissimilarities, contrasting ideas, sense in nonsense, the succession of confusion and cleverness, the sudden emergence of the hidden, and the peculiar brevity of wit." He went on to say "…wit is the voluntary combination or linking of two ideas which in some way are contrasted with each other, usually through the medium of speech association." Freud added that the contrast may not always be between ideas, but instead may show "a contrast or contradiction in the meaning and lack of meaning of the words", as in word play. He noted that wit could be conveyed in the way that words are written, or in the way that they are spoken, including what he referred to as "sound-wit, play on words, the wit of caricature, characterization wit, and witty repartee."

Wit, Humor and Comedy Compared

Freud drew distinctions between wit, humor, and comedy. He said that a chief distinguishing factor of all wit, humor, and comedy is its peculiar economy, defining wit as *economy in inhibition*, humor as *economy of expenditure in feeling*, and comedy as *economy of expenditure in thought*. Freud contended that "wit is made, while the comical is found." However, he also stated that we can "expect to learn nothing else about the nature of the comic other than that which we have already become aware of in wit." He noted that intellectual wit, in order to be enjoyed, must be shared with another. He said that both humor and comedy can be enjoyed alone, without the necessity of sharing.

According to Freud "we can make a person comical at will by putting him into situations in which the conditions necessary for the comical are bound up with his actions." In what Freud called *comic of situation*, we laugh when we admit to ourselves that, had we been placed in the

124

same circumstances, we probably would have done the same thing. Enter TV situation comedies.

Freud discussed the *comic of motion*. We find it funny when the actions of someone else are immoderate or inappropriate. He said that "we laugh because we compare the motions observed in others with those which we ourselves should produce if we were in their place."

He also explored the concept of the *comic of ideation*. According to this concept, human beings are in the habit of believing that things are in certain proportions. The comic element occurs when they're out of proportion to the ideational concept. For our purposes in this book, we will call this phenomenon *exaggeration*, through either overstatement or understatement.

He explored *parody*. Freud described this as a means to "destroy the uniformity between the attributes of persons familiar to us, and their speech and actions, by replacing either the illustrious persons or their utterances by lowly ones."

Freud also described the *comic of imitation*, saying "the attitudes, gestures, and movements of the human body are laughable in exact proportion as that body reminds us of a mere machine." This would include the art of pantomime and robot-like movements. He characterized this as the degradation of the human to the mechanical or inanimate.

In differentiating humor from comedy, Freud described humor as emotionally based. He called it "a means to gain pleasure despite the painful affects which disturb it; (humor) acts as a substitute for this affective development, and takes its place." He noted *gallows humor* as its coarsest form. In this text, we include gallows humor under the general heading of *darkside* humor.

Freud also refers to *economy of sympathy* in humor, using a story by Mark Twain as an example. In the story, Twain's brother is injured in a construction accident, being hurled through the air in a premature explosion of dynamite. While the listener would expect sympathy, Twain speaks instead of his having lost a half-day's pay.

Other emotional feelings that Freud says can be economized in favor of humor include anger, pain, and compassion. In this text, we refer to this technique as *minimization,* with an inadequate response. Freud went on to assert that humor is often used as a defense mechanism in the face of stressful, sorrowful or painful situations. He also talked of using nonsense as a device of wit. In our study, this technique of inanity and playful fancy is called *whimsy.*

Freud said that some wit exhibits a "tendency", advocating a particular viewpoint or position. People tend to tune out that with which they inherently disagree or view as untrue. *Tendency wit,* though more risky, has more potential to generate a specified response, including laughter. So tendency wit has more potential on both the upside and the downside.

He described the other type of wit as *harmless* or *abstract* wit. This is wit just for the sake of it. Freud said that the most harmless of all jests are word witticisms, making this important point: *only wit with a tendency runs the risk of offending people who do not wish to hear it.* He said that tendency wit usually requires three persons. These are the wit maker, the object, and a third person (our prospect) in whom the purpose of the wit is to produce pleasure. Freud also pointed out that, while safer, abstract wit is likely to bring only a smile. He states that the terms "harmless" or "abstract" should not be confused as meaning "shallow" or "poor" wit. The terms harmless and abstract simply refer to wit that shows no tendency toward an underlying philosophy.

Freud said that wit, humor, and comedy are all attempts to regain the feelings of a bygone time, "the state of our childhood in which we did not know the comic, were incapable of wit, and did not need humor to make us happy."

Why People Laugh

For our purposes in analyzing joke structures, we'll break these down into four main reasons why people laugh at something written or spoken. These are surprise, victory, superiority, and as a defense or escape mechanism. Let's look briefly at each.

Surprise

Freud's *comic of expectation* dealt with the supposition that things should be a certain way. The sudden realization that they're not can produce laughter. This is surprise at the unexpected.

Victory

One use of wit described by Freud is *verbal invective*. Freud says that "by belittling and humbling our enemy, by scorning and ridiculing him, we directly obtain the pleasure of his defeat by the laughter of the third person, the inactive spectator." For our purposes, we'll refer to this use of wit as *victory* that can be felt in tough circumstances with a peer.

Superiority

Freud described the use of tendency wit as a weapon with which we can attack or criticize what he described as "those who claim to be in authority." He told us that this is what makes caricature funny, saying that "we laugh even if it is badly done, simply because we consider resistance to authority a great merit." We'll refer to this as *superiority*, a breakdown of authority as is done in satire.

Defense or Escape Mechanism

Freud points out that wit can be used to express criticism, skepticism, and cynicism, and is also valuable as a defense mechanism for protecting the psyche under difficult circumstances that are beyond our control. This is used when facing powerful opponents or mentally disturbing situations.

Analyzing Jokes as Building Blocks for Creativity

For those who want to study comedy writing in depth, here are two excellent books. The first is written by Joe Toplyn, head writer on both "The Tonight Show with Jay Leno" and "The Late Show with David Letterman." It is *Comedy Writing for Late-Night TV: How to Write Monologue Jokes, Desk Pieces, Sketches, Parodies, Audience Pieces, Remotes, and Other Short-Form Comedy* (Twenty Lane Media, Westchester, NY, 2014). The second is written by the husband and wife comedy writing team of Gene and Linda Perret. Their writing credits include "Three's Company", "The New Bill Cosby Show", "The Carol Burnett Show," and "The Tim Conway Show." They've also written for numerous stand-up comics, including Yakov Smirnoff, Phyllis Diller and Joan Rivers. Gene was Bob Hope's head writer and worked on all his personal appearances and TV specials for 38 years. Their book is *Comedy Writing Self-Taught Workbook: More than 100 Practical Writing Exercises to Develop Your Comedy Writing Skills* (Quill Driver Books, Sanger, CA, 2015).

In this book, we'll present a brief overview of some fundamentals for those who just want a quick and easy reference that provides a few basics to help them utilize a bit of wit and humor in applications like writing ads and other marketing materials, designing web content, preparing spoken presentations, and performing in local broadcasting.

As mentioned earlier, for the purposes of this text we separate wit, humor, and comedy by degree. We define *wit* as intellectual creativity, *humor* as being designed to bring a smile, and *comedy* as having the purpose of producing laughter. Most of what we create for marketing purposes is based in the intellect, and therefore likely to be classified as wit or humor. But sometimes we might want to establish a spirit of fun, and this could very well include material that's designed to generate laughter. Comedy can be based in lots of things, including the script, the delivery, its timing, the bizarre, sound or visual gags, and even shock.

An old saying in the recording industry is that country music is three chords and the truth. Truth is also an essential element of wit. Freud stated that the psychological process evoked in us by the witty expression "depends in every case on the immediate transition from the borrowed feeling of truth and conviction, to the impression or consciousness of relative nullity." In layman's terms, what we once saw as true becomes suspect, or truth is pointed out where we didn't previously see it.

Like poetry and drama, wit, humor and comedy can be considered to occur in either long form or short form depending on our needs and the time available. In a commercial, we'd use shorter forms such as individual jokes or witty dialog. We might also incorporate produced bits that often last just a few seconds and are analogous to blackouts in classic live comedy. A blackout is a short scene onstage, typically involving two characters. A setup leads to a quick punchline, and then the lights go down. Its equivalent in a commercial could be that the punchline ends and we quickly move to the next scene or topic. On A DJ radio show, our bit could end and we immediately hit the station jingle.

If we have the time and really think that we can hold our prospect's interest, a personal presentation or a YouTube video used in content marketing might emulate a sketch. A sketch is longer than a blackout and may have multiple setups and punchlines.

Jokes are devices used to build humor, but they don't *define* humor any more than hammers define the construction industry. Both are simply tools used in their crafts. We study joke structures because if we're going to build witty or humorous situations, it's helpful to study ways that others have put such ideas together in the past.

Characterization, vocal techniques, facial expressions, and bodily movements are also elements of humor and comedy that are just as important as words, if not more so. A zany character like Jim Carey often does things that are hilarious without saying anything at all. And the wit should fit the setting with the intended message driving the humor rather than vice versa.

The Value of Humor

Humor is valuable because it's an important part of peoples' lives. The law of supply and demand says that humor, or anything else for that matter, is valuable to the extent that we want it and don't have it.

Humor is good for those of us who see or hear it because it makes our daily lives more pleasurable.

For those who write, working the wit has definite advantages. We all know the value of physical exercise to the health of our bodies. In the same way, exercising the wit is good for the brain. It's like doing mental push-ups.

Dreams are not readily programmable in the conscious mind, but stem only from the subconscious while the conscious mind sleeps. Wit, however, is said by Freud to be a *consciously stimulated* but *essentially identical* activity. Some psychologists refer to the subconscious mind as the *superconscious*, since it's generally recognized to hold somewhere around 90 - 95% of our mental power. According to Freud, developing our wit can help us harness more of this.

Everyone probably wants to believe that they have a good sense of humor, and this would certainly include our target audience and our customers. But they probably have neither the time nor the training to sit down, analyze what's happening around them and write witty things. However, they do recognize good wit when they hear or see it. So it's up to us to determine who they are, how they view the world, what message we're trying to get to them, and what they'd think is witty if they could sit down and write the script themselves. We relieve them of that pressure.

Premise of the Joke: Situational Humor

When we write for marketing purposes, we're trying to communicate something. We have a *premise*. So once we've selected a topic and have broken it down into sub-topics, the next thing we decide is what we want to say. A joke can be a creative way of stating something or making a point. This tendency wit can be political. More often though, it's something such as humorously illustrating a situation in which, for example, having casualty insurance, a new set of tires, or a particular brand of beer can keep us protected from potentially big problems.

The humor is conveyed in the joke itself, the delivery, and in the way it's built into the situation. If we start out with a bunch of jokes and try to build the situation around the jokes, it might work and sound witty. But if we start out with the situation and then create jokes to fit, we probably have a better chance. If, for instance, the ad copy calls for us to be humorous about someone doing their job, we first need to determine exactly what point we want to make about that. Then once we have the message we want to convey, we can rephrase it. We ask ourselves how we could imply that in a creative, humorous way.

Switching

The term *switching* means changing a joke to fit our needs. The two parts of a joke are the setup and the punchline, so therefore there are three ways to switch. We can change the setup, change the punchline, or change both.

For long-form comedy, television and movie producers employ highly skilled writers. Professional comedians also use writers on a contract, per-project, or even a per-joke basis. We small business marketers don't have that luxury. But we can sure look for jokes on the Internet (respecting copyrights, of course). We can also build a library of humorous books with jokes organized by topics. There are many good ones out there, and new ones come out all the time.

Here are some suggestions for beginning a reference humor library. The first is compiled by Pat Williams, who is Senior Vice President of the Orland Magic and is one of America's top motivational speakers. His book is *Winning with One-Liners* (HCI Books, Deerfield Beach, FL, 2002). The second is written by Garrison Keillor, the host of the long-running radio series *A Prairie Home Companion*. The title is *Pretty Good Joke Book* (HighBridge Company, Prince Frederick, MD, 2009). The third is a book specializing in insult humor. It's written by Louis Safian, and is titled *The Gargantuan Book of Insult, Offense, and Effrontery* (Skyhorse Publishing, New York, 2014). Next is an anthology compiled by Grant Tucker, titled *5,000 Sidesplitting Jokes and One-Liners* (Skyhorse Publishing, New York, 2013). Another anthology edited by Geoff Tibbals is *The Mammoth Book of Jokes* (Running Press,

Philadelphia, 2006). And for a nice reference library of over 20,000 jokes in about a thousand categories plus tutorials on writing and performing, here's a great two-book series. The first is: Milton Berle, *Milton Berle's Private Joke File: Over 10,000 of His Best Gags, Anecdotes, and One-Liners* (Three Rivers Press, New York, 1992). The second contains different jokes and categories. It is: Milton Berle, *More of the Best of Milton Berle's Private Joke File: 10,000 of His Best Gags, Anecdotes, and One-Liners* (Three Rivers Press, New York, 1992).

When we do a web search or use reference books as tools, we can look up humor related to our topic and use it for inspiration, switching it to fit our needs. As we build our humor library we shouldn't just categorize the books for reference. We should read them and study their jokes' structures. We'll be learning a lot of humor, which is great for meeting the daily demands of copy and script writing. We'll also begin to emulate creative styles used by others. Writing can mean constructing new material entirely from scratch, but quite often it's the skill of remembering or looking up something and switching it to fit the present situation.

For example, let's use an existing joke to get our core visualization. Then let's switch it to fit our needs. *It rained so long, I saw an ad in the paper for an ark salesman.*

First we'll switch the setup. Let's make the bad weather snow instead of rain. Now let's also look for a new punchline. *It snowed so hard, I saw a guy loading two of every kind of animal onto a giant snowmobile…Snoah's ark.*

Let's change the setup again. After it had been snowing so long, it warmed up. OK, then what happened? Let's do some general word associations: suntan, brightness, polar bear, sled dogs, warmth, UV rays, snow melting, sunglasses, hats, miserable, nakedness, and happiness. Let's also list some *people* related to the warm weather: sunbathers, swimmers, rednecks, tennis players, baseball players, body builders, lifeguards, surfers, and nudists. Now let's make some comparisons and write some "roughs", which are core descriptions of visualizations that could be polished later if we decide to use them. After snowing so long, when the sun came out everyone took off some of their clothes. So here's a setup and punchline we might use.

Everything is getting back to normal since it warmed up after the big snowstorm. Now I just have to get the polar bear off the air mattress in the swimming pool.

What happened to the baseball players or the tennis players? Here's a thought. *I'm glad the sun came back. Last week I watched Wimbledon, and Serena Williams was wearing snowshoes.*

How about ice skates? Who wears ice skates? Hockey players. If the ice melted, what would they do? *Instead of hockey sticks, the players were hitting the puck with snorkels.*

How about *places* that relate to snow, or the sun? Hawaii, beach, swimming pool, Montana, Alaska, Tahiti, Panama. Now let's list some *ideas* that relate to snow and the sun: warm feeling, freezing, sweating, sunburn, riding a bike, sipping on a margarita, summer, and unusual heat. What are the Alaskan sled dogs doing? *It's warmer than it's been in a long time. My sled dogs are sipping on margaritas.*

So switching does involve writing from scratch. We're just using an existing joke to prime our visualization pump. Our situation might dictate half of the joke, which is either the setup or the punchline. Then we come up with the other half to fit our needs, or we switch both the setup and the punchline after using the other humorous idea to get our own creative juices flowing.

Polishing

As mentioned earlier, the first thing we have to do is write down our initial thought. Again, this is called a rough because like a diamond, it's going to need polishing. Shakespeare said that brevity is the soul of wit. Freud stressed it, too. The term *polishing* refers to the art of removing all unnecessary words, and structuring those remaining so that the surprise element comes as close as possible to the very end. Ray Worsely at the Hollywood School of Comedy Writing in Hollywood, California used to say that a good joke is like a bee. The stinger is in the tail.

133

A one-liner contains the setup and the punchline in the same sentence. While not all jokes can be true one-liners, the setup should be the minimum words required to get to the punchline. For illustration purposes, here's a one-liner written by Milton Berle: *A female deer is always trying to make a buck.*

K-Words

An old device in humor is the *Rule of K's*. Words with a "K" sound in them just seem to be funnier than other words. No one really knows why, they just are. The "k" in the word buck makes the above one-liner funnier. A chicken is funnier than a hen. A check or cash is funnier than money. A tourniquet is funnier than a bandage. So when we can, we use words with a "K" sound in them.

Rule of Threes

Another generally accepted rule with humor is that lots of times things work better in threes. Using three items in a setup establishes a pattern that can be broken in the punchline to create surprise. Here's an example from Joe Hickman: *I went to a tough school. The cheerleaders had brutal tryouts. They had to do a kick, a turn, a jump, and a drive-by shooting.* Here's another example using the rule of threes: *The flight attendant says, "You can have veal, sausage or chicken." The passenger says, "Will we have turbulence?" The flight attendant replies, "Nope. Just veal, sausage, or chicken."*

Monologue

A commercial or content video can mimic a monologue. A humorous monologue is made up of a series of chunks held together by blend lines. If we wanted to do a brief monologue on snow, with about five subtopics, we would probably need between fifteen and twenty jokes.

A blend line contains an element of the joke that came before it and the joke that will come after it. Sometimes the subtopics can be segued smoothly without blending. Once again, let's say that our subject is the weather. We're talking about how sick we are of the snow falling. Our subtopics include shoveling it, and how we hate to drive on it. A blend

134

line between subtopic chunks would contain a mention of shoveling it, plus something about driving to work on it. The blend could talk about getting our car out of the driveway, from shoveling to when the rubber meets the rink.

Also, we often structure some toppers. These are a series where the punchline of one joke acts as the setup for the next.

Straight Character vs. Comic

We could structure a commercial or content marketing video in a two-person format with one person doing the setups, called the *straight*. The *comic* is the one who throws out the punchlines. For variety and surprise, occasionally they switch roles.

Topical Setups

Topical humor involves current events and other things that might be on the mind of our prospect at a given moment. Setups can be taken right out of the newspaper. We just grab a line of news copy and away we go.

Here's a tax-filing topical setup line from the news. *"Late hours are in effect for local postal workers."* We could then add, *"Meanwhile, local sporting goods stores are reporting increased sales of ammunition."* This, of course, makes reference to news stories in which postal workers went berserk and shot up the place. Here's another one from a newspaper setup, combined using the rule of threes. The straight says *Wow! I just read an article that says fresh coffee acts as a cancer inhibiter. It also says that if you drink wine or beer every day, it's good for your heart...and that marijuana can treat glaucoma. What's it all mean?"* For the punchline, the comic says *"It means that you'll live forever and never need glasses."*

Other commercials can sometimes be good places to look for topical setups, but we generally want to make our point without roughing up a specific competitor. This is too brutal and would probably get us sued: *(Competitive taco place) is selling a Macho Nacho. It's a tortilla chip with hair on it.*

Our Basic Writing Formula

We'll use this fundamental strategy for systematic writing.
Associate
Visualize
Write Rough
Polish

We can mix the following ingredients in each of our jokes. For our exercises, each should contain both of the first two elements and may also have one or more of the last three.
Truth
Surprise
Combining
Exaggeration
Word Play

Joke Structures

Now we'll look at some joke structures that can be used to address Freud's reasons why people laugh. These are presented for purposes of analysis only. Remember that a structure is nothing but a frame on which we can wrap our own creativity. We can think of them as aids to visualization. They're not mutually exclusive, so one joke often contains elements of two or more. This kind of classification is merely a learning tool that we can use in dissecting humor written by others, and which can also be of tactical use in writing our own. The bottom line, however, is that if it's good we just use it and don't worry too much about how it was built.

Laughter Reason #1: Surprise

Surprise is an essential ingredient of humor. Below are some formulas designed to address surprise not just as an element of wit, but also as a structural design. We twist as near as possible to the very end, revealing a surprising association, a combination, or a secondary meaning in the words spoken.

Shock can be described as extreme surprise. This kind of humor tends to deal heavily in the risqué. In varying degrees it often moves from the library to the locker room. The following structures can be useful techniques for constructing jokes specifically designed to surprise.

Reverse

When we put things exactly backward to the norm, the form is called a reverse. We get somebody's thinking going in one direction, and do a quick 180.

For example, here's one from Pat Williams: *I'm writing a book that'll be in a class by itself. It's for people who want to be unpopular, maladjusted, unsuccessful and fat with low self-esteem.* Here's an example with the reverse on the very last word. *I was a millionaire once. But I spent half my money on women and drinking. The rest I just wasted.* Or this one-liner: *An ex-wife is a lifetime commitment.* Here's another: *"You are very bad to criticize other people."* Here are some even faster ones: *"Metamorphosis hasn't changed."* And: *"Nobody cares about apathy."* Or *"I've been meaning to procrastinate, but I can't seem to get around to it."* And finally, here's one from my former student, longtime friend, and ex-brother-in-law Dan Fuchs: *"I've been trying to make up my mind whether or not to be indecisive."*

Word Play

Word play is probably the most-used element of humor. Word plays are often used as adlibs. Obviously, the more we read and write jokes the more quickly we can think of adlibs when called upon to do so.

An association list can be used in looking for word play possibilities on a topic. One way to organize the search is to think of some major parts of speech associated with it. We just start listing nouns, verbs, adjectives, and adverbs. For example, let's use the topic of television. We'll list some nouns: *remote control, channel, volume, screen, and tube.* The primary meaning of each of these, as related to TV, is obvious.

137

Remember that our basic question for combining-type humor is *"What else could this be?"* And for word play it's *"What else could this mean?"* So let's analyze these words for alternate meanings. Again, we'll just look for unusual associations and write down rough ideas. If we think we might have something, we can polish it later.

What else could remote control mean, besides the device that changes the channel? Someone's life could be out of control. Maybe this person is controlled by aliens. He's a couch potato, so maybe the remote is controlling *him.* Our significant other could have us under remote control.

What else could tube mean? It could mean a tire tube, or something from anatomy class. The term "boob tube" refers to TV, but it could also relate to body parts. *My girlfriend called and said her boob tube went out. So I sent over some silicone.* What else could tube mean? *I bought a boob tube on eBay. It seemed like a great deal until I opened the mail and found a brassiere.*

Let's change word play subjects. *I went to an unfinished furniture store. They sold me a tree.* Here's another: *Did you know that you can legally throw hundred-dollar bills out of your car? I saw a sign that said "$100 fine for littering".* Or: *What do you call the gym at the Miami Dolphins' training facility? The multi-porpoise room.* Here's a closing thought from Pat Williams: *Our business school had a baseball team. We never stole second. We embezzled it.*

Misunderstanding

Now let's take a look at misunderstanding jokes. Either a clever or a dumb character can deliver this form. A clever character can say something that's intentionally misused, in order to demonstrate his wit. A dumb character says or does something that enables the audience to feel superior. The clever character will speak tongue-in-cheek, while the dumb character will simply not understand what he's saying. In one of my favorite Leslie Nielsen scenes, his *Police Squad* character walks in for an interrogation and talks to a well-endowed blonde. She says, "Okay, Copper...is this some kind of bust?" He says, *"Yes ma'm, it's very impressive. But I'd just like to ask you a few questions."* Here's another example: *I just read that in Los Angeles a pedestrian is run over every*

36 minutes. You'd think he'd leave town. Or this one: *I heard that Garth Brooks just sold his 2 millionth concert ticket. How in the world does Garth Brooks find the time to go to 2 million concerts?* Here's one from Pat Williams: *I asked him which is worse, ignorance or apathy. He said "I don't know, and I don't care."* Here's another: *My boss says I'm inconsistent. Well, maybe once in a while. But not all the time.* And one more: *The job application question said "length of residence at present address." The prospective employee wrote "about 40 feet, not counting the garage."*

Definition

The definition form of humor simply states a word and then defines it in a humorous way. Here are some examples.

> *Life? That's work, women, and football...adjusted seasonally.*
> *Humvee: That's a Chevy on steroids.*
> *Diagnosis: that's when the doctor charges you two hundred bucks to ask you what's wrong.*

Here's a variation: *I asked the bookstore clerk to show me the self-help section. She said "If I did, that would defeat the whole purpose."*

Crossing

This joke form can be a good mental exercise in practicing the skill of combining unrelated ideas. The words combine to connect, couple, link, fuse, merge, blend, or mix. Remember that Freud refers to this process as the very definition of wit itself.

The crossing joke form is the humor equivalent of the blocking sled in football practice. It's not necessarily something we're going to use during the game, but if we push it around the field long enough it'll help us build strength during our wit workout.

The crossing joke, as with some other things we write, begins with an association list. In one column, we put words related to the topic. In the next column we list totally unrelated words, using literally anything that pops into our head.

Like puns, or the use of a cliché in the punchline rather than the setup of a joke, the crossing joke often comes out sounding corny. Sometimes crossing jokes result in perfectly usable material. Other times, they make weaker lines that can be used as adlibs, as setups for stronger punchlines in a topper structure, or as cornball humor for establishing a spirit of fun.

Once we've listed our related and unrelated columns, it's time to analyze each word. Then, we combine the qualities of two unrelated items. Who uses it? How? What are the functions of this thing? How does it work? When do we use it? Why? Here's the formula for the joke. *I crossed my blank with a blank, and got a blank.*

Let's put together some lists. For example, we'll do a related list of control room items for a disc jockey. Since this is for illustration purposes we'll keep it short. Items in the control room: *microphone, CD player, telephone, computer, mixing console, speakers, DJ, headphones, music library, newsperson, and commercials.*

Now let's make an unrelated list. We'll start with *trees, food, soup, cheeseburger, and Harley Davidson.* Of course, we want to use funny sounding words whenever possible, so let's list some words that have the "k" sound in them: *car, desk, candy bar, Popsicle, bike, cabbage, cockatiel, Chrysler, credit card, cat, carburetor, cake, kids, Klondike, shellac, breakfast, books, rectal thermometer.*

There's an idea. What would we get if we crossed our newsperson with a rectal thermometer? Well, what does a rectal thermometer do? It shows our temperature, from the aft baggage compartment. So we say to the newsperson *"I think I'll cross you with a rectal thermometer. That way, the next time you make an ass of me, at least I'll get the current temperature."* Here are some other roughs made from crossings using the lists.

I crossed the station's music library with a cheeseburger. Now we have songs that you can really sink your teeth into.
I crossed the station's computer with my old Chrysler. I thought, why not? The computer could use a big hard drive.
I crossed my headphones with a candy bar and got a sweet sound.
I crossed my newsperson with a Popsicle. Now I get the cold facts.

140

Whimsy

Whimsy is a playful fantasy or just plain nonsense. This one is from Woody Allen: *I'm so mad I could crush a grape with my bare hands.* Here's one that just couldn't be. It was written by a former student of mine, the late Andy Jones: *It takes an awfully tall man to hunt ducks with a rake.*

Exaggeration

Exaggeration is an element of humor that's found in many jokes in the form of overstatement or understatement. Here's an example of exaggeration by maximization. *A tall, beautiful brunette waved at me through the window. She had to be tall; I was flying on a jet.* Here's another: *I found a way to make relationships work faster. Instead of getting married you just find somebody you already hate and buy them a house.* This understatement from Milton Berle uses a number. *At my age sex is sensational. Especially the one in the winter.* How cold was it? *It was so cold that instead of crawling under the electric blanket I set the bedroom on fire.* Here's one from Pat Williams on a sports team. *At the beginning of the year we had a booster club. By the end of the season it had turned into a terrorist group.*

If we state something *less* strongly than should exist, that means that we exaggerate by minimization. This form of understatement is a totally inadequate response to something. *Bob walked into the reception area with an Uzi, shot all the pictures off the walls, went into the manager's office with a chainsaw, and cut the legs off his desk. Then he stormed into his own office and set fire to all the paperwork. So Mary went in and said, "Is something bothering you?"*

Risqué

The word risqué means risky. Freud defines smutty wit as being "that which brings sexual facts or relations into prominence through speech." He says that the obscene goes beyond that which is common to both sexes, and is connected with things that cause shame. He adds that obscenity includes the "excrementitious", a term he uses to refer to bodily functions.

For our purposes then, we'll define risqué humor to include human anatomy, sexual relations, and bodily functions.

Politics, religion and foul language should be considered risqué as well. Target audience and context will guide us in using it for our specific purposes. Since all readers of this text probably know plenty of dirty jokes, we won't get graphic here.

Implication is often used to lighten references to risqué topics. Here's an example of that. *"I love the beaches in France. Some women there wear really sexy bikinis. Others don't."* The double entendre lets everyone know that we enjoy looking at naked women on the nude beaches of France, without us coming right out and saying it.

Here's an example with anatomy. *Last night, I let it all hang out. But the cops made me put it back in.* Here's another: *My math is so bad that I have to drop my pants to count to eleven. (Pause) And then I have to round up.*

Here's an example dealing with bodily functions. *Today, I feel mean enough to lock the bathroom at a kegger.*

Here's a groaner, using a cliché in the punchline instead of its normal position in the setup. *My neighbor thinks my wife does the weather on my radio show. He's always calling her to see if the coast is clear.*

Laughter Reason #2: Defense or Escape Mechanism

We've all heard stories of successful entertainers who rose from tough childhood circumstances, such as growing up in the ghetto. They used humor or some other form of mental flight as a defense mechanism. The comedian may have escaped by writing thousands of jokes while the actor practiced roles in front of a mirror and the musician got lost in the fingerboard of a guitar.

Darkside Humor

Freud referred to the peculiar economy of wit and its use in what he called gallows humor. For our purposes in this text, we broaden the concept somewhat and use the term darkside humor in describing those jokes that deal with death, pain, discomfort, and other negative aspects of life. Darkside humor is often mixed with elements of the risqué.

Understatement, also referred to as inadequacy or minimization, is the opposite of overstatement and is often used in writing darkside humor in a way similar to that in which implication is applied with the risqué.

Like the risqué, darkside humor can easily generate negative audience reaction. Since religion deals with death by its very nature, for our purposes we include it here. Religious humor deals with our innermost convictions and most deeply held beliefs. It can be very easy to offend someone with religious humor. Here's one that satirizes some recent problems with priests in the news: *I'm not going to confession anymore. I couldn't get a word in edge-ways.* Here's another dealing with religion, combined with the risqué. *My religion is different. We don't sacrifice virgins. We developed a cure.*

Let's look at some criteria for determining whether a joke is in good taste and for disqualifying the use of a darkside joke in our marketing material.

First of all, we probably shouldn't use humor dealing with recent events that led to someone's actual suffering, pain, or death. A general rule-of-thumb is to ask whether sufficient time has passed. What constitutes "sufficient time" is a judgment call. We might do a joke about Mrs. Kennedy at the parade, but for some that could still be a touchy subject.

Secondly, we probably shouldn't use humor that could cause emotional pain or discomfort to someone. A "fat" joke is an example. In extreme cases, the use of inappropriate humor can even lead to legal action for personal injury. Woody Allen once said that his ex-wife sued him over a monologue. Upon his reading in the news that she had been "violated", he joked onstage during a show that *"Knowing my ex-wife, it was probably not a moving violation."*

Third, even if we don't think either of the first two things could happen, we must determine whether our darkside humor might cause someone to see us as being inappropriately irreverent, cruel, cold, or unfeeling.

Here's one that probably shouldn't be used. *It's Pearl Harbor Day. Let's go get bombed.* Even though a lot of time has passed since this tragedy, the joke would fail the second and third of our disqualification criteria. Here are some examples of darkside humor that would probably be usable in most situations:

The disc jockey's boss says, *"Have a good time this weekend. But on Monday, we need to have a talk about your ratings."*

At a restaurant, the waitress says this: *"Call me over when you've finished your meatloaf. I can't wait to tell you what the cook found in the hamburger."*

This one deals with illness: *Today's healthcare tip: never put salt on your blood pressure pills.* Here's one from Pat Williams: *Never trust a doctor who stores his hypodermic needles on a dartboard.*

Here's a story from a co-worker: *"I overheard the boss talking to the owners about my paycheck. And I don't think it's anatomically possible to stick my raise where they said."*

Laughter Reason #3: Victory

Our term victory, referred to as verbal invective by Freud, refers to winning a battle of wits against someone who is generally our equal. We could score a victory against a spouse, a significant other, or a co-worker who has somehow taken the upper hand against us. We could also achieve it against someone who has insulted us. Here are some joke structures that can help us get a victory.

Insult

Like risqué and darkside humor, insult jokes can be dangerous. Typically we want our product and company to be seen as likeable and our persona as clever. If an insult is unprovoked, it could cause the audience to see us as an attacker.

Of course there are times in marketing such as a political campaign when we may *want* to be seen as bold and even as an outright aggressor. But otherwise an insult generally needs a provocation in order to be funny. Ours is more likely to seem clever if it's given some reason to exist. Using this in the setup is called a *raison d'etre*, which is French for reason-to-be. On a program or in a commercial, we might have multiple characters with good-natured conflict. The straight might insult the way the comic is dressed and that becomes the provoking setup. Now both can fire off insults, each topping the one preceding it.

Sometimes a local personality is called upon to do a "roast" of a well-known local figure, such as the mayor. A roast, of course, involves insult humor. If we are the roaster, our insults probably have little or no provocation. For the roastee, of course, our remarks in the introduction give him or her every reason to use insults as a weapon again us. One good rule to follow is to insult the roastee only on things that have little significance in real life. While we'd probably want to avoid insulting the mayor's political decisions, we might chide her about other things that have been brought to the attention of the public. Perhaps she has a well-known fondness for fast food, or likes to play tennis. Here's a Pat Williams roast line: *Our guest of honor is living proof that having a dream, a goal, and struggling hard to attain it doesn't always work.*

Self-Insult

Like the insult, the self-insult often benefits from provocation. It can also be used to establish or reinforce the traits of a character. Bob Hope once said *"A penguin is a bird that has wings but can't fly. I know the feeling. I have golf clubs."* Here are some other examples of self-insults.

My ship finally came in. It's a plywood duck boat with a rotten transom.

Your memory is the second thing to go when you get old. I can't recall what the first one is.

Hey, I'm not dumb. I started driving a car when I was in second grade. I was 16.

145

Here's one that I heard my friend Betsy Harris tell. *Last night I was out with an older man and someone asked me if he was my dad. I said "Give me a break. My dad isn't that old!"*

I went to a psychologist. After running some quick tests, he said "Don't worry about it, Michael. You don't have a complex. You really are inferior."

Savers

Both insults and self-insults can be used as savers. A saver is a punchline that gets its setup from the inadequacy or inappropriateness of a response to whatever preceded it. For example, *"I'm sorry. Am I keeping you awake?"* Here's an example from a dialog when hosting an event. The host might say something to the co-host and get an insufficient reaction. Then the host could add *"I don't know what to say. I've never had an undertaker as my co-host before."* Here's another one. *"Is this a live performance or jury selection?"* Or *"Is this an audience or an oil painting?"*

If someone in the audience heckles us or sounds unenthusiastic in response to the punchline we just gave, we could throw out a saver such as *"Check your medication. I think you might be getting low."* And there's Steve Martin's immortal line to a heckler: *Yeah, I remember my first beer.* Here's one from Pat Williams: *Your train of thought, sir. Does it have a caboose?* And another: *Look buddy, pretend I'm your wife and ignore me for a while, ok?* Whenever we do a live event or a recorded program that we can't edit, it's often a good idea to prepare and have ready a number of memorized savers, just in case.

Laughter Reason #4: Superiority

As human beings, there are basically two ways we can achieve superiority over the powerful, the rich, and the famous. The first, of course, is to go out and make ourselves even more powerful, rich, and famous. The second way is easier. We can say something that brings our target person down to or even below our level.

When we mock the structure of something that has been written, spoken, or sung, the process is called *parody*. And when we consider

146

someone to be in some superior position in relation to us, such as having supervisory, political, or economic power, they become a target for *satire*. The IRS is a good example. We can say almost anything about the IRS because few endear it. Other examples include the courts, the president, congress, the governor, the police, movie stars, the super-rich, body builders, supermodels, novelists, and recording artists.

While there certainly are exceptions, we typically want to avoid being up on a soap box all of the time. Unless we're promoting a candidate or issue, it's often best to avoid taking political sides. Also, as a general rule we don't to say things that are designed to try to harm the reputation of someone. More often we're simply teasing by pointing out foibles. We can do parody and satire not only about rich, powerful, and famous people but also about well-known places, ideas, and things. Let's take a closer look at each.

Parody

With parody we take a familiar structure and mimic it, changing the words. We might parody a phrase just spoken to us, mimicking its length and phrasing while changing the words and/or adding sarcasm. Here's a parody of an author's cliché: *This book is dedicated to my wife, without whose credit cards it would not have been necessary.* Songs can be parodied with a MIDI sequencer or a helpful musician or two. Some musical artists such as Weird Al Yankovic and Cletus T. Judd get excellent royalty checks from their parodies of hit songs. We might parody a competitor's commercial or one that's unrelated but creatively combined. Parodies are often considered fair use under U. S. and other countries' copyright laws, but we're not offering legal advice in this book. Check with an attorney before using a parody in marketing.

Satire

Satire pokes fun at the status quo. It's usually considered fair game to satirize those who are powerful, such as persons who are politically, socially, or economically above us. But we generally don't pick on minorities, the unfortunate, or the handicapped. Here's some satire from Joe Hickman on politics: *What's black and brown and looks good on a politician? A Doberman.* This is from Pat Williams on a game official: *That ref called so many penalties that the pea in his whistle caught fire.* Here's one on a product: *I'm on the Jose Cuervo diet. You still get fat, but you don't care.*

Chapter Twelve: Copywriting - Selling Ideas, Feelings, Images, and Action

The creative aspect of advertising and promotion is its most important foundation, and good copywriting is its first fundamental. Unless our message is creatively written, effectively produced and skillfully performed, it's just not going to have good impact, regardless of the media or venue we choose for its placement. Copywriting applications include scripts for public relations speeches, business correspondence, employee training materials, and sales presentations just to name a few. We could be writing for a display ad in a newspaper or magazine layout. We might author an email, a website landing page, or a web content video. Our material could be for a 30-second TV ad. We might be trying to convince other company personnel to accept an idea that we have. We could be writing emotional copy to create feelings related to our company or product. We might be establishing an image. Or we might be trying to generate an immediate sale of our product.

Whether we're writing advertising or any other sort of script, we need to engage, inform, and influence. And whether we're using a personal presentation, traditional media, or new media including the web and mobile devices, the fundamentals of communication and human behavior are the same. In this chapter, we'll focus on copywriting for advertising, with the understanding that many of the concepts also apply to other copywriting applications.

Before we look at copywriting methods, let's first look at how advertising fits into the total marketing effort. In writing and producing commercials we attempt to create and transfer information, imagery and emotions to influence consumer behavior. We shouldn't confuse advertising with marketing. Advertising is a component of promotion, which is just one of the four major elements of marketing.

Where does advertising fit into the marketing process? Let's again briefly review the 4-P's. The first is product, which refers to our physical widget, service, person, feeling, image, or idea. The second is pricing, which refers to its cost relative to its benefits and those of its competitors, plus its position on the price/quality continuum. The third is place, which means where and when the product can be acquired. The fourth is promotion, which is designed to make consumers aware of the other three.

Promotion is made up of four components. The first of these is *sales promotion.* This includes all incentives and discounts from the maker, distributor, or dealer. The second is *personal selling.* This is person-to-person contact regarding product sales. The third is *publicity.* This is non-paid and often uncontrolled promotion such as news coverage, public relations, social media, and word of mouth. The fourth is *advertising,* which is an attempt to influence consumer behavior with the use of a controlled message through paid media.

So to put it in simple terms, advertising is 25% of the promotional element, which is 25% of the marketing effort. Keeping the math easy, advertising makes up about $6\frac{1}{4}\%$ of the marketing program. It's certainly not the only thing in marketing, but it's a good and important component.

When writing commercial copy, we often start with a feature/benefit analysis. This involves writing down the key features of the product, then listing their associated product benefits and customer benefits. When talking about a hot tub, for instance, we might list the following feature: it has a custom-fit, insulated cover. The product benefit is that the cover forms a tight seal. The customer benefit is that this helps keep heating costs low. In the order analyzed, we could state the feature/benefit relationship this way: *This hot tub has a custom-fit, insulated cover. It forms a tight seal, which saves money in heating costs.*

However, in commercial copy and personal selling, it's often best to state them in a different order. By leading with the customer benefit, we're often more effective at building conviction with the prospect. This could be stated as follows: *This hot tub saves money on utility bills. Its custom-fit, insulated cover seals heat in.* This method first states the point and then uses the other information as evidence to prove it.

Ads need to be refreshed periodically due to the advertisement life cycle during which the ad is noticed by prospects and is effective. Other times the ad is changed due to a revision of its goal. Sometimes an ad's objective is product awareness, also called ATR for awareness, trial, and repeat. Other times the goal might be to encourage brand switching, to differentiate the brand from its competitors, to position the brand relative to another, to build brand loyalty, to instill an image, or to seek an immediate response to an offer. Whatever the case, a good advertising campaign through any medium is integrated with all the other elements of marketing in an IMC.

Targeting and Consumer Behavior for Copywriting

Before we can start writing copy, we need to define exactly who it is that we want to address. Our approach could be very different if we're B2B with trade advertising designed to reach distributors and retailers than with B2C advertising aimed at consumers. Are we speaking to the end user? Who else might be involved in the buying decision? We may need to keep in mind that the influencer or the final consumer of our product may not always be the purchaser.

Targeting is covered in detail in Chapter Two. Undifferentiated marketing, also called mass marketing, uses a single approach to promote a product to all of the persons in a broadly-defined marketing group. Targeted marketing identifies likely prospects by placing them in segments according to criteria including demographics, psychographics, lifestyles, and other factors including income and buying habits.

Once we know who we're speaking to, in order to write our copy we have to know what motivates them. As detailed in Chapter Three, consumer behavior is the tendency of consumers to acquire products and services for reasons and in ways that address their needs and desires.

One popular consumer behavior model breaks buying into eight steps. These are need recognition, need description, product specification, seller identification, proposal solicitation, proposal evaluation and selection, order procedures and order route specifications, plus performance review. Another lists six buyer readiness states: awareness, knowledge, liking, preference, conviction, and purchase. For our purposes in this book, we keep it consistent by sticking with the AIDA formula.

Some Commercial Types and Formulas

A commercial is, of course, designed to influence the prospect to do something. To produce the result we want, it must be effectively written, performed, and produced. In this chapter we discuss copywriting. Producing and performing are covered in later chapters.

Commercial Types

First we'll look at some types of commercials. *Institutional advertising* is designed to build and maintain goodwill for the client. It's often done on behalf of banks, stockbrokers, car dealers, and for other businesses that depend on customer trust. *Image advertising* is designed to create our idealized picture of the business or product in the mind of a prospective buyer. The image could be of high quality, fast service, reliability, or any other attribute that the company wants the prospect to associate with the product. *Direct response advertising* is designed to generate an immediate action such as placing an order on the telephone, on a website, or by returning a business reply mail card. *Impact advertising* focuses on high ad volume, or placing ads in media that have been shown in the past to generate superior responses for the business. *Reminder advertising* consists of brief messages such as those found on billboards and transit ads, and is often used in conjunction with longer ads in other media. These help achieve frequency.

Political advertising happens during election cycles, and is designed to influence opinions regarding candidates. It generally presents facts selectively, and is sometimes called by the unflattering name *propaganda.* A dictionary definition of propaganda is *the use of only selected facts with deliberate omission of conflicting information, repeated across various media, in order to promote a political agenda.* OK, that's pretty much what we do in political advertising. But since we have democracies in the U. S. and other free nations, it's much different than state-controlled propaganda. Each side presents its own selected facts, and then the voter gets to sort it all out. Rules governing election advertising change periodically, and are available for the U. S. at fec.gov and at fcc.gov. Our crack legal team wants me to point out once again that this summary is not intended as legal advice, but only as a broad definition of terms in use at the time of this writing.

For a U. S. broadcast media buyer, there are three major FCC rules that we'll summarize. These are lowest unit charge, reasonable access, and equal opportunity. The *lowest unit charge* basically means that a station must charge a candidate for any office the lowest unit charge for any unit of the same class and type that has been sold for any contract that has any part of it running during the political window. This window is 45 days prior to a primary election and 60 days prior to a general election. *Reasonable access* means that the station must sell advertising to candidates for federal offices. For non-federal candidates, broadcasters can limit the class, type, and number of spots available. The *equal opportunity* provision indicates that if a candidate for an office uses a station, competitive candidates must be able to obtain time on the station in which to reach a similar sized audience at a similar rate.

A related type of advertising that's done during campaign cycles is *advocacy advertising.* With this type, a political action committee (PAC), labor union or other group runs ads designed to promote a point of view on a topic on behalf of one side.

Negative advertising that draws attention to flaws and deficiencies, real or imagined, is often used against political candidates and against opponents on issues. Negative advertising may also be employed against other types of competitors, but the burden of proof for claims may be greater and the risk of lawsuits may be higher than in political and advocacy campaigns.

Negative appeal advertising is sometimes used for political or advocacy campaigns, or for products such as insurance or medications. It attempts to show how miserable life could be without the product, candidate, or the issue solution that's being advocated.

Public Service Advertising (PSA) is that which is done on issues of interest to the public, generally on behalf of non-profit organizations or civic groups. These announcements are sometimes run for free by media when they emphasize community welfare or service. They may also be mentioned by a business during regular paid advertising, such as: *Acorn Plumbing reminds you that school is out, so when you're driving be sure to look out for kids playing. They may not be watching for you.*

Some types of advertising are designed to directly attack our competitors' ads or products. *Inoculation Advertising* uses an approach similar to getting a vaccination against an illness. It employs an ineffective presentation for something that a competitor uses in their advertising, in an attempt to make that competitor's own advertising less effective. For example, some competitors to GEICO Insurance have run ads attempting to make GEICO's claim that "15 minutes could save you 15% or more on car insurance" seem old-fashioned or excessive in the time required. *Me-Too Advertising* lets prospects know that our company also does what a competitor's advertising says that the competitor does, and often points out how we do it better or for less money. In *Non-Price Competition Advertising*, we show how our product is a better choice than our competitor's even though it costs more. We stress things such as how our product is easier to use, has superior quality, or performs a task better or more easily.

As mentioned earlier, some media allow *Advertorial Advertising*, which is a commercial presented as editorial or program content. This often appears as display advertising in a print publication, which typically requires that the advertorial be marked "Advertisement" at the top of the copy. Similarly, in broadcasting a product may simply be talked about in the program portion rather than during an advertising break.

154

Sometimes suppliers or trade association groups participate with retailers in advertising campaigns. With *Co-op Advertising*, a manufacturer or distributor of a product contributes a given percentage or dollar amount toward an advertising campaign on behalf of a retailer or other reseller, based on factors including the volume of product sold by the reseller and the percentage of space that's given to the product in a particular ad. With *General Appeal Advertising*, a trade group or association presents advertising promoting a product category rather than a specific brand. One example is the Radio Advertising Bureau's campaigns promoting the idea that "radio advertising works". Other examples include "Beef…it's what's for dinner" and "Got milk?"

One type of campaign that's generally considered unethical or even illegal is *Ambush Marketing*. This attempts to piggyback onto an event such as the Super Bowl without becoming an official sponsor. A related type of advertising is a *Tie-In Promotion* that relates to another advertising campaign that's presently running or has recently run. This is often a local advertising campaign that's piggybacking on a national campaign with which the local retailer is legally affiliated in some way.

Professional Advertising is done for the likes of accountants, doctors, lawyers, and some institutions. These ads may have special rules for mandatory copy that must be included to meet ethical standards or legal requirements, such as "member FDIC" for a bank.

Commercial Formulas

Here are some examples of structures that can be useful as starting points when sitting down to formulate our own ideas for ads or campaigns. As with learning joke forms, knowing some formulas that others have used can be helpful in getting our own creative juices flowing. Here are some of the most common.

Analogy, Metaphor and Simile Advertising: This is advertising copy that compares something to another seemingly unrelated thing. In general, a metaphor uses one thing to mean another, an analogy uses a direct comparison and argues how the two are similar, and a simile includes "like" or "as". For example, here's a metaphor: *Liars are snakes.*

Here's an analogy: *That man is a mountain. It would take an earthquake to move him out of the way.* And here's a simile: *Chevy trucks. Like a rock.*

Announcement Advertising: This type of advertising gives information regarding some important occurrence or a significant change such as a new location.

Before and After Advertising: This ad shows what things were like before the product was used, and how things improved with the product.

Comparative Advertising: This is a type of positioning or differentiation ad that directly compares a product to its competitors.

Descriptive Advertising: This ad focuses on detailing the product's features and benefits.

Emotional Situation Advertising: This type emphasizes the feelings associated with the use of the product rather than the features of the product itself. It presents the product as a means of getting the feelings that are showcased in the ad. For example, a jewelry or toothpaste ad might speak of love.

Fake Interview Advertising: This is a simulated person-on-the-street or guest-on-the-show interview.

Fake Remote Advertising: This is a recorded ad that simulates a live broadcast from a given location.

Free Information Advertising: This type of ad stresses a report, booklet, or pamphlet available by request. This type of advertising is typically done to generate leads for a multi-step sales process.

Invitational Advertising: In this type of ad, the prospect is invited to attend a special event as a guest. For example, a mailer could be sent out inviting leads to a seminar on investments as a means of acquiring and qualifying them for later follow-up.

Personality Advertising: People like to buy from folks that they know, like and trust. When a businessperson performs his or her own radio or

156

TV ad or Internet content marketing video, the prospect can get the feeling of knowing them personally.

Price-Item Advertising: This provides a list of low prices for certain items, generally either as evidence to support a claim of everyday low pricing or of low prices at a sales event. The prices listed often include leader pricing for some items.

Question-Based Advertising: This type of copy poses rhetorical or leading questions, and presents the product as a solution.

Reason-Why Advertising: This begins by making a statement regarding some situation and then explains how it can be improved or overcome with the use of the advertised product. For example, membership in a health club or following a given diet could be used as a solution to being overweight. This is sometimes also called *Problem-Solution Advertising.*

Rebate Advertising: This type of promotion features a return to the buyer of some portion of a product's price. Rebate advertising might be done by a manufacturer, distributor, or retailer.

Slice of Life Advertising: This type of advertising presents a scenario that's recognizable to the target audience, with the product featured. This is sometimes also called *Dramatization Advertising.*

Teaser Advertising: This ad does not reveal the product itself but instead offers small bits of information concerning features and benefits. A teaser ad campaign is designed to generate curiosity, and is immediately followed by an ad campaign that promotes the brand.

Testimonial Advertising: Testimonial ads can be pure gold. These employ an endorsement of a product by someone who has used it. They can transfer the perception of an image involving how another customer has used a product, and thus convey feelings which can be much more powerful and influential than facts such as features and benefits. The testimonial could come from a well-known personality such as a broadcaster, an actor, a coach, or an athlete. Or it might come from an ordinary customer.

Topical Advertising: This links the product in some way to one or more events that have recently happened or are presently occurring. For example, many non-political ads parody campaign commercials during an election period, and many mimic football or baseball scenes during their respective seasons.

Branding, Imaging, Positioning, Differentiation, the Offer, and Action

As in any form of creativity, there's no such thing as a rigid, bulletproof formula for writing effective advertising. However, it can be helpful to remember a few fundamentals.

Advertising action goals can be either direct or indirect. *Direct action* ads seek a response such as to stop in, call, sample, log on, or return a BRM card. *Indirect action* ads seek the goal to remember something. Product awareness, branding and imaging are closely related types of campaigns that seek to create something that sticks in the mind of the prospective buyer so that they'll remember it when buying time comes. For our purposes, we'll define *branding* as seeking to have a logo, jingle, or some statement remembered. These could stress a product's uses, price, quality, and any particular buying motivations that might be focused on in a given campaign. *Imaging* seeks to have a mental picture or a feeling remembered and associated with our product.

Positioning and differentiation are similar strategies that tell how we're unique, or how we're a better choice than a competitor. *Positioning* stresses how a business occupies either or both of a relative position and a unique position. With *relative positioning*, a business focuses on carving out a niche in the consumer's mind. This is sometimes visualized as a ladder, with each business that the prospective consumer thinks of in a category occupying a given rung. *Unique positioning* is also sometimes referred to as a unique selling proposition, or USP. This idea refers to some selling point a company or product has that is, hopefully, unavailable with the competition. *Differentiation* means telling how our product differs from its competitors and how it's better or more desirable.

Hopefully some combination of our advertiser's branding, relative and unique positioning, and differentiation will have led to a slogan, also sometimes called a positioning statement. This memorable phrase can then be featured in all of the client's advertising. Simply put, the most important words in advertising are the ones that people remember when they think of the product. Done well, slogans can stick for decades. If we're old enough we still know the rental car place where they try harder. We remember what to do if we absolutely, positively have to get it there overnight. And there's still no doubt what goes plop, plop, fizz, fizz. In copywriting, we need to tell our client's customers and prospects something that's relevant, catchy, and memorable.

Perhaps most importantly, there should be a strong offer or other compelling reason why someone should stop in, call, sample, log on, return our BRM card, or remember our product or service. We often mix direct and indirect action goals in the same ad. For example, we could do some product awareness, branding, positioning, differentiation and imaging at the same time we're promotion a sales event that asks customers to come in now for immediate savings. Whether our action goal is direct, indirect or both, we should ask them to actually do something.

Marketing Vehicle Selection

A communication vehicle is a channel through which a message is carried. Copywriting requirements vary widely by the medium to be used and the marketing goal. Generally speaking, whenever we use words we want to paint pictures. And when we use pictures we want to suggest or reinforce words. It all goes together to deliver the intended message through whatever advertising vehicle we're driving. Here are some examples of the differences in the approach to copy written for use in various media.

A *display ad* in a newspaper or magazine needs a headline and possibly a subhead to serve as the opening hook. The headline features large, bold type above the body copy. A subhead is a secondary heading between the headline and body copy. The purpose of a headline and a subhead is to entice the viewer to read more. A meaningful image is often included, which might be a photo, an illustration, a chart, or a table. The body copy is the main text. At the end of the layout is a call-to-action along with the required contact information. An Internet display ad works in a similar way.

A *classified ad* uses very brief copy. It's typically part of a two or three step selling process. In the first step, the classified ad generates an inquiry. In the second and possibly third steps, the product is sold in a follow-up such as through an information pamphlet, expanded information on a website, or with personal selling. For example, the actual sale may occur in the second step. In some cases, more information or a qualification step might be needed in the second step, with the actual sale happening in the third. Google AdWords ads, and those placed in social media newsfeeds, work in a similar way. The copy is usually short, conversational, and is designed to grab attention quickly. It often entices the reader to click through for more detail on a landing page of a website. Banner ads also generally have short copy plus a link, and often include an image or Flash animation.

When a *brochure* is used in a multistep selling process, it might be sent following a response to a classified ad or left behind after an initial personal selling contact. It could be sent in a direct mail piece or picked up as point-of-purchase advertising material. The brochure's front cover generally has a strong headline and image to entice the prospect to read the body copy inside. It should have a call-to-action at the end, asking the reader to take the next step in the selling process.

A *direct mail piece* is highly measurable and targetable, and the ad material can be as long as is needed to detail the message. It typically contains copy on the envelope itself that's designed to catch attention, plus a letter inside that uses a conversational, personal approach. A brochure is also often included along with a business reply mail card or other contact information.

A *billboard* needs to get the pertinent information across with a glance at an image such as a photo or other graphic plus very brief copy that can convey the message in about 7 words, with the whole billboard exposure lasting around 6 seconds or less. As mentioned in Chapter Nine, one of the best uses of a billboard is for location positioning. This tells prospects where a business is and how to get there. Billboards can also be used as a primary medium or for low-cost frequency reinforcement to support messages in other media.

Broadcast TV spots need to tell the story in 30 seconds with graphics, words, sound and video. Network programs can vary widely in terms of their target audiences, so selection is often done by individual programs. *Cable TV networks* tend to target select audiences in terms of demographics and lifestyles, and selection can be more easily done by channel. A *radio spot* usually contains 30 or 60 seconds in which to communicate the message with words, sound effects, and music. Selection can be done by format.

A content marketing video posted on our own website, social media, or a video sharing site might run for two minutes or more, depending on the interest level of the content itself. Production quality is also important. These videos should be kept to the minimum length that's required to tell the story. Videos that are too long can lose attention before the point is made.

Copy could also be written for a printed or emailed newsletter, or for an expanded email newsletter called an e-zine. These are generally offered for free in order to collect email addresses. To be read, the newsletter or e-zine must contain content that's of real value to the recipients, and it then becomes a marketing vehicle in itself. These are used to maintain awareness, for PR, and for other uses including promotion of our own products plus ads sold to others. Email marketing campaigns should include both opt-in and opt-out methods and take into account factors such as deliverability due to ISP blocking and spam filters. The *From* and *Subject* fields affect whether an email is actually read, in a way similar to how the copy on a direct mail envelope affects whether or not the direct mail piece is opened.

Copy also needs to be written for the various pages of a website, including the landing pages designed for specific products and offers. Search Engine Optimization (SEO) becomes a consideration in the way we write copy for our websites and landing pages. Search engine spiders look for things including a site's optimization for mobile media plus keywords in the copy, regularly updated content, and links from other sites. If we do any ecommerce on our website, we should make an ongoing effort to keep our SEO program up-to-date. A blog (weblog) can help with SEO as well as providing regular and relevant contact with customers and other interested parties. A blog requires regularly-written new copy, and it can be updated not only by us but by our readers as well.

Demand States

These were mentioned in Chapters Six and Eight. Here we'll discuss them in more detail since we obviously need to understand the demand state for our product when writing copy. Here are the eight that are generally recognized to exist, and how we might address them in marketing.

Negative Demand: This means the customer not only doesn't want something, but may even be willing to pay in order to avoid it. Examples of products with negative demand include outdated technology, medical and dental services, and life insurance. This requires counterpoint marketing that overcomes the negative thoughts and mental images. For outdated technology, our best bet may be to try to liquidate it by slashing the price. For medical and dental services, the procedure itself might be uncomfortable or even painful, but we can sell the positive feelings of being healthy. A life insurance policy reminds us of our mortality, so we could try to create an offsetting image of the negative consequences of *not* having life insurance, such as a spouse and children being forced to live in poverty in the event of the prospect's death.

No Demand: Yep, this means that demand simply doesn't exist. Consumers are either not aware of the product or just have no interest in it. Obviously, this requires stimulation marketing designed to create the missing awareness or interest.

Latent Demand: This occurs when a consumer has a need that's not satisfied by an existing product. When we finally have some widget to meet the latent demand, we give the prospect reasons to act now and upgrade to our new goodie.

Declining Demand: This happens when consumers buy the product less frequently or have stopped buying it all together. Reminder advertising could be appropriate here.

Irregular Demand: This is periodic demand based on factors including seasons, holidays, months, or even the time of day (such as having breakfast at a hamburger place or lunch at a nightclub). Promotions such as discounts, sales events, special financing and rebates can be used to counter irregular demand.

Full Demand: This is the situation when supply and demand are in equilibrium, and consumers are buying all the products put into the marketplace. Advertising focuses on maintaining or building market share. Since the category is not growing, any new business that we get has to come from our competitors.

Overfull Demand: This occurs when the demand is greater than the supply. This situation might require de-marketing or counter-marketing to help bring supply and demand together. For example, a product might be offered at a higher price or in fewer locations.

Unwholesome Demand: This happens when consumers know that a product is not good for them but they want it anyway. Examples include cigarettes, alcohol, gambling, and other things that people enjoy while ignoring their harmful side. Advertising emphasizes fun, excitement, and other positive feelings that might be attached to whatever it is that we know better than to be doing in the first place.

Strategy and Intent

Once we know who we're targeting, our demand state, and the advertising vehicle for which we're writing, we can define our intent and develop a strategy for what we want the copy to accomplish.

For both ethical and legal reasons, we want to avoid deceptive and unfair advertising. *Deceptive* advertising makes false or misleading claims through statement, inference, or omission. *Unfair* advertising involves unethical or illegal promotional activity that may harm our customers or that's designed purely to hurt competitors rather than to help consumers.

Let's summarize some strategies used in copywriting. We'll consider whether we're mass marketing or targeting a niche. If we have a direct action objective, we want the prospect to stop in, call, log on, or return our BRM card. With an indirect action goal, we want the prospect to remember something. Perhaps we'll focus on product awareness, branding with our logo or slogan, or on imaging that's designed to build top-of-mind-awareness so that our product comes to mind when the prospect has a need for something in our category. We might stress positioning or differentiation, and we could employ a pricing strategy that's either significantly higher or lower than our competitors. Whether our action goal is direct, indirect, or a combination of the two, we always want to give the prospect a strong offer or other compelling reason to do what we're asking.

Hook, Body, Hook

One way to visualize how to make our advertising point is to think like an educator by giving an opening summary, presenting the body of our information with a strong offer or compelling reason to do something plus supporting evidence, and then ending with a closing summary of what's been covered and giving the "assignment" in our call-to-action. We can put that in the language of a prize fighter: *hook, body, hook.* Let's explore each in a bit more detail.

Opening Hook

The opening hook, also called a headline or grabber, varies according to the purpose of the ad and the medium being used. Our purpose may be to create product awareness, position or differentiate our product from competitors, build our image, generate web traffic, gather leads, or make an immediate sale. In a radio ad, the hook is the opening statement. In a TV ad, it's that plus the first shot or two. In a print ad, it's the headline and subhead plus the photo or other graphic. In direct mail, it's the envelope. In a brochure or catalog, it's the cover.

On a website, it's the landing page. In an email campaign, it's the "from" and "subject" fields.

Whatever our marketing goal and communication vehicle, the opening hook accomplishes the attention step of the AIDA model. It may do this by arousing curiosity, stressing urgency, promising a benefit such as value or savings, making a comparison, issuing a challenge, giving a guarantee, raising a question, or creating an interesting scenario.

Whatever grabber we use, we need to keep in mind that our prospects pay selective attention. This means that a listener, viewer, or reader tends to see or hear only messages that are consistent with his or her current desires, needs, beliefs, attitudes, or opinions.

Body Copy

In the body copy, we create perceived value to accomplish the interest and desire steps. If necessary, we build the need for a product in our category. We present our case using personal, conversational language with simple words and short sentences. We provide factual and/or emotional evidence to back up our claims as to why the prospect should want our product to fill the established need.

We may focus on our product's features and benefits. If so, we'd first translate the product's features into customer benefits. In a 2-step analysis we'll look at the feature followed by the benefit to the customer. *This car has a 4-cylinder engine, which saves you gas.* We might use a 3-step analysis listing the feature, the product benefit, and the customer benefit. *This engine has an aluminum block. That makes it lightweight, which saves you money on fuel.* As mentioned earlier, in our copy we'd typically state them in reverse order with the customer benefit stated first and the other information acting as evidence. The ones above would be: *This car saves you gas with its 4-cylinder engine*, and *This car save you money on fuel with its lightweight aluminum block.*

We might ask leading or rhetorical questions to make a point. We could repeat a slogan which is a hopefully memorable phrase that identifies our product or company, what we do and why. This helps create top-of-mind awareness. We may focus on our image in a campaign to help build or reinforce our reputation. With positioning and differentiation, we remember *Weber's Law,* which asserts that consumers are more likely to buy a product based on its perceived differences from similar products than they are to buy the product based on its features and benefits in isolation.

If we've identified a unique selling proposition, we might want to emphasize this reason to buy since it separates our business or brand from its competitors. According to *Marketing (Sandhusen, Barron's Business Review Books, 4th Edition)* the USP is a concept that was first advanced by Rosser Reeves of the Ted Bates Advertising Agency. Reeves proposed that all advertisements meet three criteria regarding the USP. (1) Each ad should offer a special benefit to the customer. (2) The benefit must be unique to the brand being promoted. (3) The benefit must be strong enough to pull customers toward the brand.

We want to stress value, emphasizing the product's benefits relative to its cost. In a highly competitive situation we might stress value added in the form of an extra benefit in addition to our core benefit, such as a premium being offered. And of course we need to make a strong offer to stimulate a buy, or give a compelling reason for the prospect to do something such as remember an idea or image.

Closing Hook

This accomplishes the action step by summarizing our product, its benefits, our offer or other compelling reason to do something, and the proposed action that we want prospects to take. We might ask them to stop in, call us, sample our product, log on to our website, mail back our BRM card, or remember some idea or image we've been stressing. We also include our address or other contact information.

Example

Here's an example for a radio or TV spot, with each section identified in boldface type: If this were TV copy it would contain two columns.

166

The script would be in the right column, with video instructions on the left. Either written shot descriptions or a storyboard could be used.

> **Opening Hook:** *It's easy to spot a lady who's fashionable and thrifty. Just look at her shopping bag.*
> **Body:** *When the bag says "Smith Clothing", you know that it contains the latest fashions, all reasonably priced. Want big savings? Fall coats and dresses are marked at 30% discounts right now, just in time for back-to-school buying. And summer blouses are half price. Smith Clothing puts it all together for today's fashion-conscious woman...at unbeatable prices!*
> **Closing Hook:** *Stop in now for fall savings, and see why the best-dressed ladies carry packages from Smith Clothing, 1350 North Main.*

Note the branding slogan: *the best-dressed ladies carry packages from Smith Clothing.* Also note the offer: *Fall coats and dresses are marked at 30% discounts right now.*

Use of Narrative

We need to determine the best narrative for our intended point of view or perspective. The first person is the person speaking ("I"). The second person is the one being spoken to ("you"), and the third person is the one being spoken about ("they"). Following is an example of an idea written in the first person, and then restated using the second person.

> *First Person:* "I love great pancakes, so I'm having breakfast at Perkins."
> *Second Person:* "When you want great pancakes, try having breakfast at Perkins."

Here's another example showing first person and third person narrative:

> *First Person:* "At Sears, *we're* having a sale."
> *Third Person:* "Sears is having a sale."

The use of a concept that we'll refer to as the "first place" in ad copy is similar to the first person narrative. However, instead of sounding like a representative for the firm, we give the impression that we're at that place of business.

> *First Place*: "For great savings on flooring, *come to* Carpet World, downtown."
>
> *Third Place*: "For great savings on flooring, *stop in* at Carpet World, downtown."

In copywriting, brevity rhymes with levity just like it does with humor. We want to eliminate unnecessary words. For example, let's look at this line: *"You can get great deals on flooring at Carpet World."* The words *you can* are probably unnecessary to the meaning and therefore could be left out. Additionally, the message is often stronger when "iffy-ness" is eliminated. Sometimes use of the word "if" subconsciously limits the message to those who might happen to be doing what the copy has suggested they might be, and could contribute to mental tune-out of the message by others. For example:

> *Weak:* "If you're going to be traveling this summer, get your car tuned up now."
>
> *Stronger:* "Before you do your summer driving, get a tune-up for your car."

Idea Sources

Ideas for good scripts, including commercials, can come from virtually anywhere: a book, a popular movie, a personal friend, a song, a sight, a sound, a smell, or anything else the creative mind can perceive. We might use brainstorming, a team approach to copywriting, to generate ideas.

Or, as in writing humor, we could use the fast and simple method of writing out a word association list. We just take the basic idea about which we want to write and start listing all the words that pop into our mind. Sometimes, an idea will come after writing only a few words. Other times, the list may become quite extensive. An expanded example of a word association list is provided later in this chapter, but for now we'll use a short one. Let's assume that the challenge is to write 30 seconds of copy to sell new guitar strings priced at 40% off at a local music store. The initial association list yields the following:

New strings
Play your best
Old strings

Then we sub-associate some ideas with the word "old":

Cheese
Wine
Grandmother
Gold

And voila! Here's a script written by simply stringing together the ideas taken from our short word association list.

(Grandmother voice)

"This is Granny Goodstrings for Music Villa, with a few words about aging. Now personally, the older I get, the better I get. But old age can be murder on some things. For instance, take your guitar strings. They just can't give you the best music if they're not quite up to snuff! So remember: old is gold when it comes to great cheese, fine wine, and your dear old Granny. But you need new guitar strings. Pick some up today, and save forty percent. Head for Music Villa...a full step higher. Music Villa, 1325 Main Street. And tell 'em Granny sent you."

The offer is 40% savings on guitar strings, and the branding slogan is *"Music Villa, a full step higher."*

Commercial Creativity, Wit and Humor

For our purposes in planning scripts, the term *creativity* means originality of thought and execution in transferring ideas, images and feelings in order to engage, entertain, inform, and influence.

Wit is engaging intellectual creativity that can be used in virtually any commercial. *Humor* makes some sort of fun revolve around the product. It can be a good vehicle to carry a marketing message and is more than just the use of jokes. Much of humor is derived from the effective use of characters. An old joke says that your audience will tell

169

you what it was. *If they laugh uproariously, it was comedy. If they smile, it was humor. If they just sit there and stare, it was drama.* Expanded sections on humor and characterization are included in Chapters Eleven and Sixteen.

Engagement, Entertainment, Education, Persuasion, and Action

Let's recap some things that our copy needs to do. It should engage or entertain, inform, influence and create action. Engagement and entertainment help accomplish the attention and interest steps of the consumer behavior model. We also need to teach prospects what we want them to remember, give a strong offer or compelling reason to do something, and then make a call-to-action. To create an engaging message, we have to initially figure out the features and benefits of the product or service that we wish to reveal, and define our target prospect in terms of demographics. Then, we determine our target's point of view and create a message that expresses the value of our product or service according to the truth as our prospect sees it. Next, we try to understand the circumstances that he or she is in, and mentally put ourselves there. This engagement or entertainment aspect, of course, must be creatively merged with teaching prospects our desired marketing message and, finally, persuading them to do something. As mentioned previously, six commitments often sought in advertising copy are:

> Go somewhere
> Call
> Log on to a website
> Return our BRM card
> Sample
> Remember

Logical or intellectual motivating factors are typically addressed in our copy. These are also called stated motivations, since the prospect is likely to say that a purchase is based on logic, even when the buy is emotionally driven. Logical motivating factors include:

> Money (Profit or Save)

Urgency (Fear of Losing Out)
Efficiency (Saving Time or Effort)

Emotional motivating factors are also sometimes addressed in advertising copy. Often, these are not spoken outright and are therefore referred to as unstated motivations. These may just be alluded to in ad copy through such things as the acting, the vocal interpretation, the music, the editing style, or in the images used. Emotional motivating factors commonly include:

Pleasure
Love
Dissatisfaction
Sentiment
Self-Improvement
Thrills
Inspiration
Sympathy
Concern
Pride of Ownership
Survival
Escape from Pain or Discomfort
Need to Prove Something
Guilt

Topical Observations

Commercials, speeches, and other presentations can often benefit from topicality. If the demand is to be creative with twenty pieces of commercial copy each day, we may want to check the related material in a humor anthology book for some good visualizations and switching possibilities. We might also subscribe to a topical creative service such as American Comedy Network, Funny Firm, or Tom's Lake Humor Company, but it may lack in terms of localization. So here are some techniques for writing original material, and for adapting that gleaned from our books and creative services.

As we've said before, an important element of creativity is observation. We need to be in the habit of using creative visualization, and we should know what's going on around us. An observation book is an excellent way to regularly watch our world. We simply get a notebook, tab it, and then write down at least one observation each day for each category listed.

For example, as we drive along the street we may notice that everybody is walking a dog. We write down that observation. We don't need to make it witty. At some point later, the thought may indeed become useful in a commercial, or as the setup or punchline of a joke. It may simply become a topic of conversation. Or it may just sit there for months or longer before we find a use for it, if ever. But if we don't write it down, we'll forget it and it'll be lost.

We should check the local broadcast stations, newspaper and the Internet each day to research relevant world, national, statewide and local stories and events. We might also subscribe to publications such as magazines like *People* or *Entertainment Weekly* to keep up-to-date on the hot music and movies and what's happening in the lives of the stars. We could also get subscriptions to other publications that our client's customers might read.

Phrases and clichés can establish familiarity, and thus are particularly helpful.. A phrase becomes a cliché through repeated use. These can be found in virtually any area of our life's contacts, from news and sports to advertising slogans. It's also a good idea to keep up on current slang for use with characterizations.

Listed below are some categories for our initial observation notebook. Again, we try to write something in each category every day. This forces us to think about a variety of topics, and could help keep us from missing something interesting that occurs in an area that we might otherwise have given no thought to that day.

> Atmospheres/Environments
> Attitudes/Emotions
> Characters (Communicator/Audience)
> Clichés/Phrases/Quotations
> Doctors/Lawyers/Professionals
> Economics/Finance
> Entertainment: Music/TV/Movies

Everyday Life
Family/Kids
Friends/Friendship
Getting Up & Going/Traffic
Government/Politics
Internet & Social Media
Jobs/Employers
News/Current Events
Objectives/Obstacles
Promotions/Holidays/Events
Slang
Sports/Fitness/Hobbies
Weather

Word Association

As mentioned in Chapter 11 and earlier in this chapter, one of the most effective methods for systematizing creativity is the word association list. So we'll close this chapter with an expanded look at that subject. Once a list has been written down it can be reviewed for commercial copy ideas, client positioning statements, word-play possibilities, and for other purposes. Lists should be saved by topic for future use. A word processing or spreadsheet program can be used for this.

In combining ideas using the word association list we often use what Freud referred to as *allusion*, also called *implication*. We associate our topic with something seemingly unrelated from our word association list(s). Then we imply a comparison, rather than stating it outright. For instance, let's say that our subject is summer vacations, and we decide to talk about a trip to the city of Orlando and all the entertainment that's there. We could imply that by saying *"Orlando is a great place. You don't need a TV. 'N Sync, Shamu, and Mickey Mouse all live there."* Again, we're not necessarily looking for funny. We're looking for wit through creative implication.

There are six columns across the enclosed sample page. The first column is *phrases and clichés*, our second is *free association*, the third is *people*, the fourth is *places*, the fifth is *ideas*, and the sixth is *things*. The phrases and cliché column is leftmost for convenience in writing, because these are often best used as setups to establish familiarity.

First, we list our topic. In this example, it's snow. We begin with free association, writing down any word or phrase that pops into our head. This is often all we have to do to get our creative juices flowing. But in order to look for more possibilities it can be helpful to also list unrelated or opposite words for combining the incongruous. We do this on the bottom half of our attached sample sheet. We could even break our main topic down into subtopics. So we might do shoveling the driveway, driving to work, and weather forecasters. We would then do word associations under each subtopic as well, so we could have pages and pages. For our illustration purposes in this chapter, we're only doing these six columns on one main topic. Under the first column, phrases and clichés, we list the following:

> I need antifreeze in my blood.
> It's colder than hell.
> It's a ninety proof day.
> The roads are slick.
> Slow as molasses.
> I'm sick of seeing snow.
> Shoveling snow sucks.
> I can't wait until spring.
> This weather gets me down.
> I hate driving in the snow.
> I love to ski.
> It's a quiet winter morning.
> It's a snowmobiler's dream.
> It's snowing an inch an hour.
> It's so cold that I can see my breath.
> Water freezes before it hits the ground.
> My nose is frozen.

Under the second column, free associations, we list these:

> Cold
> White
> Wet

174

Wild
Frostbite
Snow-cones
Fire
Christmas
Stuck vehicles
Snowmobiling
Skiing
Layers of clothes
White dress
Cuddling
Cabin fever

When we've listed our free word associations, we then list people, places, ideas, and things.

Under our people column:

Highway department
Snowplow operators
Ambulance drivers
Fire department
Little kids
Old people with snow blowers
Homeless people
Skiers
Truck drivers
People with small animals
Hockey players
Evan Lysachek

Under the places column:

Mountains
Alaska
Tundra
Antarctica
North Pole
Billings

South Pole
Russia
Sweden
Greenland
Iceland
Canada
Ski resorts
Driveways
Sidewalks
Roads

Under ideas:

Freezing
Shivering and shaking
Drinking hot chocolate
Hot toddies with the neighbors
Hot-tubbing with some friends
My girlfriend came over to keep me warm
Warm house
Curling up under a down comforter
Fireplace is crackling
Rescue mission
Electric blanket
Running the heater in the car

Under things:

Sunglasses
Mittens, gloves & hats
Snowsuits
Warm thermal underwear
Snow boots
Snow blower
Snow shovel
Coats
Socks
Icicles
Ice sculptures

Hot chocolate
Marshmallows
Whipped cream
Carrots
Broomstick

Here's a sample radio spot for XXYZ Insurance, written using the above word association list.

You wake up on a crisp, quiet winter morning. It's snowing an inch an hour, and that's a snowmobiler's dream. The problem is, you don't <u>have</u> a snowmobile. You have a car. And you have to drive to work. You're sick of seeing snow. You're sick of shoveling snow. Your nose is frozen. You're putting antifreeze in your coffee, and the roads are slicker than waxed glass. That's when you're glad that your auto policy is with XXYZ Insurance. Because if Evan Lysacek slides by your car doing pirouettes and clips your front quarter panel on the way, you just make one quick call. They'll send a wrecker to tow your car to a preferred body shop that will get started on repairs right away. And your policy provides you with a quality rental car, until yours is back in tip-top shape. A snowstorm can be peaceful and beautiful when you're on the mountain skiing. But when you're driving...well, that may be a different story. Stop shivering and shaking when it snows. Call 999-9000, and winterize your car insurance. XXYZ Insurance...a warm fuzzy feeling for Montana winter drivers.

Word Association
Idea Search List

Topic: _____   Date: _____

Phrases and Cliches	Free Association	Related People	Places	Ideas	Things

Unrelated and Opposing Thoughts

Phrases and Cliches	Free Association	People	Places	Ideas	Things

178

Chapter Thirteen: Principles of Video and Audio

      This summary is designed to cover video and audio basics that can be helpful whether we're recording on our smartphone to create Internet and mobile media marketing materials or utilizing local radio and TV ads. Knowing a few essentials can be helpful even if some or most of these are recorded and edited by others such as a media outlet or advertising agency. Good quality is absolutely essential if we're doing something that'll run on local TV or radio. Other types of production can sometimes get by with a bit less effort, but our video and audio should still be high quality if we want to get the best effect from it.

Video for Marketing

When we make a video for our business, it might be for internal or external marketing purposes. An internal business video might be used for things including selling-in for those in our distribution channels, for new employee orientation, or for staff training on matters like customer service or product knowledge. An external business video could be designed for promoting our product with a local TV spot or in a web content video, or for training customers through a DVD in how to assemble or use our product.

Video Hosting

If we're going to use our video on the Internet we need some sort of *video hosting*. We might put it solely on our own website, or we might send it elsewhere to expand our reach, such as posting it on our Facebook page. Of course the biggest video hosting site, by a long shot, is YouTube. Since it's owned by Google, YouTube has excellent search capabilities, so finding a video hosted there is easy. As of this writing, YouTube and some other video sharing sites can host and play videos in resolutions up to 4K. We can upload relevant videos to our YouTube channel for hosting, and we can even have them post automatically from there to our Facebook page. There are also numerous other video hosting options. In second place is Vimeo, with both free hosting like YouTube or a commercial plan called Vimeo Pro. A third hosting possibility is Wistia, which can do cool things like collect the email addresses of the viewers of our videos. Like Vimeo, Wistia has both free and paid plans available. And there are plenty of other hosting options. Whichever we choose, better production quality means more effectiveness in getting our marketing or training message across. It also creates a better image for our business.

Creative Video Production on a Budget

Creative production means using the imagination to come up with a good marketing or training message and then applying the required technical skills. Pretty much anything that can be imagined can be produced, subject to time and budget limitations. And with today's technology, very little specialized equipment is necessary to do a pretty good job. The biggest requirements are knowledge, skill, and time.

Producing for Content Marketing and Local Media

A number of very good books are available that go into much detail for both video and audio production. For a comprehensive college-level text, try *Video Production Handbook* (Owens & Millerson, Focal Press, New York, 2013). Here are two good books that cover the basics. The first is *How to Shoot Video That Doesn't Suck* (Stockman, Workman Publishing, 2011). It focuses on the storytelling aspect of video, and at this writing it's the top-selling book in the category on Amazon. The second is *Videopia* (Franks, Lulu Publishing, 2009). It zeroes in on the fundamental equipment and techniques needed for producing video content for the web and electronic distribution. Complete books are also available on subtopics such as shot composition, lighting for video, and possibly for whatever editing software is being used. It's also a good idea to study a camcorder's manual to learn all of its capabilities. And a great resource for anyone who works with video is *Videomaker* magazine.

Production Phases

Production can be done in either an analog or a digital environment. The two are often utilized together, such as when using an analog audio mixer and mic with a digital camcorder.

The term *analog* means "analogous to", and refers to an electrical representation of the original waveform. Analog storage media include magnetic tape and vinyl phonograph records. Each time an analog recording is dubbed through rerecording it, the waveform representation becomes less accurate. This causes a progressive loss of quality after each instance of copying or dubbing, which is called a *generation*.

Most recording, storage, and editing is done in digital. This is a process in which the video or audio is converted to digits and stored as numbers. This results in very little loss of quality throughout numerous generations of transfers and reproductions.

What we generically refer to as "production" actually involves three phases: preproduction, production, and postproduction. We plan, write and organize in preproduction, record in production, and then polish and edit in postproduction. Let's look a little more closely at each phase.

Preproduction

This is the planning stage in which budgets are set, the story is conceived and made into a script, and casting is done. The first step in preproduction is to set a goal for our marketing video. We need to decide exactly what we want to say and to whom. We lay out shooting and editing plans that list our overall style and approach to the video and audio we'll use. This could include our story, the characters, our shots, their composition, the camera angles, our point-of-view, the editing style and any video effects (VFX) that we might employ in postproduction. And we determine how and where this video will be seen. For example, it might be a 30-second TV spot designed to promote our product awareness, branding, imaging, differentiation or positioning. Or we might have a four-minute video explaining how to set up or use our product that will be included on a DVD in its package, available on YouTube or Vimeo, or uploaded to our own website.

Once we've defined the video's goal, our budget, the shooting style, the venue, the length, and the general editing approach we'll take in postproduction, we can set about writing the copy, planning our video shots, and selecting our talent.

D. Eric Franks advises us to follow the old adage of *"plan the shoot and shoot the plan."* He says that video instructions included with our script can be as simple as a shot list on an index card, written alongside the copy, or illustrated in a drawn storyboard that gives visuals for each shot.

And Steve Stockman points out that "great video comes from thinking humans, not equipment." That's why I recommend that a person read his book on video storytelling before beginning to think about things like cameras, lighting equipment, and editing software. He reminds us to think in terms of shots, and that every story "has four elements: a hero, a beginning, a middle, and an end."

Stockman says that we should think of our shots like a sentence with a noun and a verb. In other words, a subject plus action equals a shot. He says that the description "a dog walks past the house" is a complete story in one shot, but that the description "a dog" all by itself is not. He adds that our video should be as short as possible to accomplish its purpose, and that in general each shot should be no more than 10 seconds in length. Stockman reminds us that the complete video story is made up of a series of sequences, that each sequence is made up of scenes, and that each scene is made up of shots.

Production

Let's begin by defining some basic terms. The *story* is the combination of all the scenes that make up the full video. A *scene* is the combination of everything that's happening at one time or place with the same character(s). A *shot* is a single camera event in a scene, and a *take* is an attempted video shot or audio recording. A *shoot* is the event at which we record video in a studio or on location. Now let's discuss some equipment that's used in production. For most shoots, we'll need a minimum of a camera, an external microphone, a tripod and some lights.

Cameras

Smartphones and tablets have put a video camera in our hands everywhere we go. Smartphone video quality is good and getting better all the time. But for producing media marketing materials and web content videos, camcorders still rule.

For production we need a decent camera with a headphone jack and an external mic jack. Even if we're shooting our video with just a smartphone, we can get a cable like the one available at Sescom that enables the use of both an external mic and headphones while recording video with an iPhone or iPad. It features a 1/8" (3.5mm) TRRS plug that connects to a jack on the iPhone or iPad. The cable is available in various lengths. For example, the Sesco iPhone-Mic-6 comes with a 6' cable.

One critical factor in the production phase is the proper selection and placement of an external microphone. Whether we're using a smartphone or a camcorder, we generally don't want to use the camera's built-in or camera-mounted mic. That's good for reference audio or background sound, and not much more. A wired or wireless lapel mic, a handheld mic or a good shotgun mic will work much better. For most shoots, a lapel mic is probably the best-sounding and best-looking choice. We want to use headphones so that we can monitor the audio as we're recording it. We also need a tripod and a lighting kit.

183

Our *aspect ratio* means our shot's width compared to its height. Sometimes we may use an aspect ratio of 4:3, such as for SD video on a DVD. Mostly, though, we'll want an aspect ratio of 16:9 for widescreen HD. Our frame rate should be chosen based on the desired output, such as 24, 25, or 30 frames per second (fps). If our camera will let us, we want to shoot progressive rather than interlaced video. Progressive scanning is the format used by computers and the Internet. Interlaced scanning is a format that was developed for TV in the days when CRT monitors were the standard. We'll set our software to render the finished video in the format that we want.

For example, our HD camera might shoot 720p, 1080i, 1080p, or 4K. A good rule to follow is that we can reduce but not increase to get to our desired output number without losing quality. So if we shot 1080i, we can down-convert it to 720p and be just fine. But quality suffers if we try to up-convert by going, say, from 720p to 1080p. Quality also suffers a bit when we convert interlaced video to progressive, such as going from 1080i to 1080p. When we upload our video, we should do so in the format in which we want it viewed.

At the time of this writing, a good rule of thumb for anyone who's looking to buy a new camcorder is to get one that shoots at least in 1080p. Even better is a 4K camera, which shoots at the ultra-high-definition TV standard (UHDTV) of 3840 x 2160p at a 16:9 aspect ratio. Our camera should have either a large CMOS chip or 3CCDs.

It doesn't need lots of bells and whistles. If auto mode is all we have for shooting, it will probably do an acceptable job if our lighting and composition are good. However, having manual exposure, focus, and white balance will give us much better image control, though they require a little more knowledge, skill, and work. With manual focus and exposure control, we can control perspective in terms of *depth of field*, which determines what elements of a picture are in the camera's plane of focus. Optical image stabilization is also nice. And to get good sound, we definitely want an external mic input (XLR is best) plus a headphone jack.

184

Basically, here's the sequence. We light the scene, set our focus, white balance, and then we shoot. A zebra stripes feature in the camera helps in setting the camera's exposure with the lighting of our scene. We set the zebra stripes to show at a given level, such as 100%. We can use it to set the camera by opening the aperture until we see the stripes, and then reducing the aperture slightly until they're gone. We can also use the stripes to help make adjustments in the intensity and placement of our lighting instruments. Once the lights are set, we should use manual focus so that subject movement doesn't cause our auto-focus mode to reset during a shot and cause momentary blurs.

After we have the lights set, the exposure determined and the image in focus, we use our white balance. The camera sees pure white as the combination of all colors. So once the camera sees white correctly, it then sees all other colors accurately. We just turn on the white balance mode, focus on a pure white card, a sheet of white paper, a white wall or a white shirt, and then press the white balance button.

Tripods, Dollies, Sliders, and Jibs

Whenever possible, we want to avoid shooting hand-held. Video looks way more professional if the camera is stabilized when we shoot. Basically, any tripod or even a monopod will work, but if we want to do camera moves with a tripod, we need one with a fluid head. This makes pans and tilts look nice and smooth. A *pan* is a side-to-side camera move, and a *tilt* is an up-and-down camera move. It's great to have a tripod with locking legs and a spreader, and a bubble level is nice, too. Adapters are available that make smartphones mountable on tripods. For quick mobility, there are shoulder-mount camera steadying devices that can help stabilize the camera in place of a tripod.

Other devices can also be used for shooting stable video with differing movements and angles. Various shots can be done with a *dolly* on which a tripod can be mounted. A *dolly in* shot moves toward the subject, while a *dolly out* shot moves away. A *truck* shot moves the dolly to the left or right, and a *tracking* shot has the dolly follow the subject's movement.

Instead of a dolly, camera track slider rails can be used. These might be attached between two tripods or floor mounted. A *crane* or *jib* can be used for shooting angle shots from above or below. These use the terms *boom up* or *boom down*. A jib is generally mounted to a tripod with the camera on one end and a counterweight on the other.

Lighting

Audio is sound waves. Video is light waves. So if we want good video, we need good lighting. If we insist on the best video lighting equipment, we'll get expense pro-level gear by the likes of Lowell. But inexpensive and adequate lighting kits are available at video and photo specialty stores as well as on Amazon and eBay. These can include light stands, bulbs, reflectors, and carrying cases. They use cool, power-saving CFL or LED bulbs. Even if we just use clamp lights from Walmart or Home Depot, good CFLs are available there that have the color temperature of daylight, which is in the 4600K to 6500K range.

In setting our lights, shadows can be used to create mood. *Hard lighting* creates darker, more defined shadows. But hey, we're not doing Dracula movies. *Soft lighting* is diffused light like that from LEDs, CFLs or a *soft box* that creates fewer and softer shadows. It's easier and will work well for most training and demonstration videos. Diffused light is used on many TV sitcoms and news sets.

The standard lighting scheme is a 3-point lighting setup. This utilizes a key light, a fill light, and a back light. The *key light* is the main instrument lighting the subject. It will either have the brightest lamps or be closest to the subject. It's positioned according to how bright the subject is to be and how the shadows need to fall. The *fill light* mitigates shadows on the subject caused by the key light. The *back light* shines from the top rear and separates the subject from the background by providing a rim of light on the head and shoulders. A good rule of thumb is to start with enough capacity in our kit for the equivalent of at least 1,000 watts for our key light plus 500 each for our fill and back lights.

A light's intensity changes at the square of the distance. So a key or fill light can be moved forward or back to adjust the amount of shadow it creates or removes. Reflectors often function as fill lights, bouncing back some of the key light. When shooting outdoors the sun may function as the key light, with reflectors used for fill and backlight.

We may use the existing scene as our background, or we might put up a *backdrop*. If we're going to do compositing in postproduction, we'll shoot the scene in front of a chroma key screen or wall. This is used for electronically layering images. It's typically either a bright green or blue screen, although any color can be keyed. If we use a chroma key background, we have to separately light it very evenly and move the talent away from the background far enough to keep shadows off of it.

As we shoot, our video and audio are recorded to a storage medium inside the camera. This might be an internal hard drive or something removable such as a media card, DVD or digital tape. Files may be uploaded directly to YouTube or another website from a smartphone or tablet, or they might be transferred to a desktop computer for editing.

Shot Types, Perspective, Composition, and Continuity

Shots are often described by their distance from the subject. These include a *close-up* (CU), *extra* or *extreme close-up* (XCU), *medium shot* (MS), and *long* or *wide shot* (WS).

And sometimes shots are described by their intended use. We often open with an *establishing shot* that sets the location of our scene, which might be a wide shot of a building's exterior. Then we could move to shots of our performers indoors. A *beauty shot* is a CU of our product. A *time lapse* shot can show our subject moving faster than normal by shooting at a slow speed and playing it back at the regular rate. Conversely, we can create *slow motion* video by recording at a high speed and playing back at the regular rate. An *over-the-shoulder shot* is sometimes used in interviews, shot from behind the interviewer or subject. We might also shoot some *reaction shots* of the interviewer, the subject and the audience. These types of shots can be used to provide variety and to cover audio edits. Ambient sound from the scene, called nat sound (natural), should also be recorded for use in editing or enhancing audio tracks.

As mentioned earlier, the most important aspect of our video production is the story, which is broken up into scenes. *Perspective* is how the audience experiences a shot through our camera lens. Our viewer obviously sees what the camera sees. Our *point of view* (POV) can be varied according to the needs of a scene. We might, for example, want to make our subject seem more authoritative or powerful by shooting from a low angle rather than the standard eye-level angle. We could add imbalance or uneasiness by shooting from a *Dutch angle* in which the camera is off-level. Or we could place the camera in such a way that the viewer is seeing a scene from the eyes of our hero, which is called *Lead POV*. Our *field of view* is determined by how close our camera is to our subject, and by the focal length of our lens. This might be macro, wide angle, or zoom.

A big part of telling our story is in the *composition* of our shots during production. This is determined by factors including how the shot is framed, the camera angle, and where we've positioned the camera relative to our subject. In general, we want a shot to have a foreground, a middle ground, and a background. We might also employ *leading lines* in scenery that guide the eye to our subject, and we might have items in the picture that *balance* other things in the shot.

Our *framing* is often determined by context. In some cases, such as talking heads shots in a training video, we might use a TV news style in which our subject is in the middle of the screen looking straight at the camera. If we want to be a bit more cinematic, we might have our subject looking somewhere other than directly at the camera and our composition following the *rule of thirds*. In this case, we divide our screen into 9 segments by mentally drawing tic-tac-toe lines on it and placing our most important elements at the intersecting lines, avoiding the center square. Some cameras have a feature to turn on a rule-of-thirds grid that shows in the viewfinder. If a shot has our talent gazing to the side or being on the move, we want to leave room in front of them to be looking or moving into.

Color is another important consideration in how we compose our shots. In video, we use the RGB color model, which stands for red, green, and blue. These three primary colors can be mixed to create any other color. We should study the color wheel and know what colors are complementary, meaning that they're opposite each other on the wheel. Colors can help our subject stand out from a background, they can convey emotion, and can add meaning to a scene such as a dark blue tint to denote night in the video.

Scenes are often shot at different times, days, and camera angles. Maintaining *continuity* means that we pay attention from shot to shot to things like keeping the lighting consistent and to having our characters style their hair the same, wear the same clothes, and appear on the same left or right side of the screen as in the other shots in the scene.

Postproduction

Postproduction involves correcting, enhancing, mixing, copying, cutting, pasting, and trimming in our editing software.   We'll assemble the various events in order on the timeline, trim them, and then add transitions.

In some cases, we might be able to shoot an entire sequence so that it's ready for an upload to Facebook or YouTube right out of the camera without any editing at all. Or maybe the camera's pause button is all the editing we'll need for a given project. In any case, we should always shoot with the end product in mind. If we're going to edit later, that means we plan our shots in a way that makes editing more efficient. And realistically, if our project is going to look and sound its best it's going to require at least some trimming or tweaking before we send it out on a disc, through our website, or on a video sharing site.

For postproduction we may just use a simple editing app available for our smartphone. Or we might get fancy and use a desktop computer with a fast processor and lots of memory. If so, we want at least two big hard drives. Our program will be on one, with our video and audio files on the other. We'll also need good editing software, and there are lots of options out there. Here we'll just mention the present top four. If our computer is a Mac, we probably want Final Cut or Avid Media Composer. If we're using a PC, the top two are Adobe Premiere and Sony Vegas, which come in both professional and consumer versions.

The consumer versions of today are pretty much as powerful as their professional counterparts were just a few years ago. Effects such as transitions, color processing, brightness, and titles can be added to video clips, and audio effects including equalization (EQ), reverb, and compression can be added to audio tracks.

The three main areas of a typical video editing software screen are the docking windows, the preview window, and the timeline. *Docking windows* include the one that contains the video, audio, and graphic files that we'll use in our project plus windows for various menus, tools and effects. These can be moved around on the screen, and the layout can be customized by the user according to where the windows work best for the current editing project. The *preview window* shows the present state of a selected file. The *timeline* shows our events in the order they'll appear with a reference to the amount of time in each event and in the overall project.

The basic sequence in editing is to set the project properties for the video and audio to match the media we're using, import our clips and graphics, place them on the timeline in their intended order, trim them, and then add transitions to bring them together.

Once a rough edit has been done, we refine it to our liking and then export it to whatever file type we want for the finished production. Depending on the file size, this final rendering of the project can take a while.

Editing Events

An *event* is something that has been placed on the timeline. This might be a video clip, an audio file, a graphic, or a title. Events can be edited either on the timeline or in the preview window, but for our overview purposes the timeline is the fastest and most intuitive way.

There are two basic types of edits. A *split edit* separates a clip into two sections so that the unwanted material can be deleted. A *ripple edit* closes any gaps on the timeline by moving all clips to the left that are to the right of a gap that's removed.

After our events are in order and edited, we add *transitions*. Our software may have a gazillion transitions available, but we'll mostly use just three. These are cuts, crossfades, and fades to black. D. Eric Franks points out in *Videopia* that these can help tell our story by denoting time and place. He says that a *cut* means the same time and place, a *crossfade* means there's a minor to moderate change, and a *fade to black* and back means the change is a big one. If we're going to use any transitions that require fading or cross-fading of clips, we'll want to leave some frames at the front and/or rear of the clips. These are necessary so that we don't create the fade over the program material that we want featured before or after the transition. Once we've positioned our clips, we just drag the transition into place on the timeline.

Effects and Filters

Effects such as color correction and brightness are our next order of business. These are also sometimes called *filters*. When we've decided what effect we want to use on a video file or a graphic event, we simply drag it into place on the timeline just as we do with transitions.

Good video editing programs contain a number of very useful effects and filters for correcting or enhancing our video in postproduction. *Color correction* filters are probably the ones used most often. A *3-way color corrector* enables shadows, midtones and highlights to be adjusted separately. A *tint filter* lets us add an overlay of some color to a clip, such as a blue tint for night shots, and an *RGB Curves* filter lets us adjust the hue and saturation in each of our three primary colors. *Blur effects* are often used to soften backgrounds. We can *crop* a clip, layer images using the *chroma key* filter, and use *transform* filters to change a clip's properties such as its position or size.

Motion Graphics, Compositing, and Effects Plug-Ins

If we really want to get fancy we can add motion graphics, compositing, and expanded digital visual effects. Adobe Flash can be used for simple animations. The number one program for motion graphics and video effects is Adobe After Effects. It's a layer-based application that can import and manipulate many different image formats. These can be overlaid and combined in a way similar to the way that layers work in Photoshop. We can go all-out Hollywood with effects like 2D and 3D animation, compositing using chroma key, tracking, rotoscoping, and a particle system for generating multiple animated elements. Other motion graphics and VFX programs with capabilities similar to After Effects include 3D Studio Max, Nuke Studio and HitFilm Pro. Expanded effects capabilities are also available with plug-in software from third-party developers including Boris FX, FX Factory, and Red Giant.

Once a clip or image has been processed in an application like After Effects, it's generally sent back to the primary editing program for completion of the final project.

Audio Effects, Voice-Overs, and Titles

Sound effects and music are often added in the postproduction phase, and existing sound can be edited or enhanced. Audio effects are added in pretty much the same way as video effects. Audio volume control can be done by numerically changing the volume in a box to the left of the track, or by using the *rubber band* on an audio track. This is simply a line that can be dragged down to reduce the volume of the track or clip. Audio effects that can be added typically include EQ, delay effects, and compression. There's more on those later in this chapter.

A *voice-over* may be added or enhanced in post, which is an announcer who is heard but not seen.

Titles are usually the final thing added to our rough edit. These can include static titles, lower thirds, and credit rolls plus other options. In some programs titles can move around with crawls, rolls, and basic animation like spinning in or out. Titles and graphics are sometimes created in programs like Adobe Photoshop or Illustrator and then imported into the editing software

Editing Style

Perhaps the first rule of editing is that we avoid *jump cuts*, which are cuts to the same shot. Jump cuts result in an unnatural-looking movement in the video, and typically happen due to a needed edit in the audio. One way to avoid a jump cut is to insert a cutaway shot. This is called an *insert edit*. This could be a reaction shot showing someone else such as the interviewer or the crowd, or some related item such as a beauty shot of the product. Another way around jump cuts is to have a second camera shooting a different type of shot. For example, if the main camera is shooting a straight-on CU the secondary camera could be shooting from a significantly different angle or might be shooting a MS or a WS. Then, when the audio cut is made, a shot from the second camera is inserted. The main video shot is called the *A-roll* and the secondary camera and cutaway shots are called the *B-roll*.

Another important consideration is the time between edits. This varies according to the action in a scene. If the pace is frantic there may be an edit every couple of seconds. If it's more relaxed, there may be 10 seconds or even more between edits.

Basics of Audio and Acoustics

In a large percentage of the content seen on the web, the video is good but the audio absolutely reeks. A significant part of the perception that a video leaves with a viewer...some say most...comes from the quality of the audio. So please bear with us. We'll cover some fairly technical stuff in this section, but it provides a good background for making sure that our audio is of sufficient quality for radio production, and that it's at least as good as the pictures in our video. We'll begin our discussion of audio with some basics about the way sound behaves.

The term *acoustics* refers to the branch of physics that deals with the behavior of sound including its production, transmission, and reception.

A *sound wave* has a peak and a trough plus a wavelength and a period. The *peak* is the wave's highest point and the *trough* is its lowest. The

193

wavelength, or cycle, is the physical distance for one complete pulse from crest to crest. The *period* is the time that the wave takes to make one complete cycle. *Mechanical waves* are either transverse or longitudinal waves that travel through a solid, liquid, or gas. A *transverse wave* forms an up and down pattern that's perpendicular to the direction that the wave is moving, like a weighted fisherman's cork bobbing up and down when a water wave passes. Sound is carried in *longitudinal waves* (also called *pressure waves*) which oscillate in the same direction that the sound is going. Molecules move with the wave only as far as their positions of equilibrium will allow. They're pushed forward by the crest and then stretched backward by the trough. These changes cause vibrations in the human ear and other receptors such as microphone diaphragms.

We graphically represent a single sound using a sine wave. This has a zero reference point and shows the positive and negative peaks of the sound over time. In our audio productions we work with complex sounds that combine numerous sine waves into a waveform. We see frequency and amplitude displayed on a timeline.

Sound waves can be reflected, bent, compressed, and stretched. *Refraction, reflection, interference, diffraction, and masking* alter sound, so these are important considerations. Let's look at each.

Refraction is the bending of a sound wave. Sound waves travel in a straight line when whatever they're moving through stays constant. But changes in things like density, wind and temperature can bend the sound. When the sound source itself is moving, a sound wave can get either compressed or stretched. This is called the *Doppler Effect*. The sound wave *compresses* as the sound source approaches, and then *stretches* as it moves further away. For example, the compression of the sound of a train's horn causes perceived pitch to get higher as the locomotive gets closer, followed by falling pitch caused by the stretching of the sound wave after the train has passed us.

Reflection is the bouncing of sound or light. The angle of incidence equals the angle of reflectance. Echo is a single sound reflection, and reverberation involves multiple sound reflections.

Interference can occur when two or more sounds reach a listener from different sources. They could even be the same sound, in which one source is the direct sound while the other is a reflection of it. These can either reinforce or interfere with each other.

Phase cancellation occurs when a delayed or reflected wave is 180 degrees out of phase with the original. The crests and troughs of the waves can literally crash into one another and cancel each other out. Phase shifting and cancellation are bad when uncontrolled, but are useful in digital delay devices for producing such effects as phasing and chorusing. To mitigate unwanted sound reflections, recording studios and concert halls are sometimes designed so that no two dimensions are doubles of each other. Hard, reflective surfaces are avoided, being replaced by softer, more absorptive materials like carpeting, curtains, and acoustical ceiling tiles. And some studios have no parallel surfaces.

Diffraction occurs when sound is partially cut off by an obstacle or when it passes through a constricted opening. One simple example of diffraction is talking while several fingers of the hand cover most of the lips. Another is to speak through a cardboard tube. Placing a finger or thumb over any part of the microphone pickup element, or cupping the hands around it, have similar effects. They restrict or compress the sound wave, diffracting that which reaches the pickup element and altering the characteristics of the sound.

Masking is the inability to hear some sounds because of the presence of others. For example, high frequency notes may be hard to hear if intense low frequency sounds are present. Unintended masking is a bad thing. But masking can be a useful tool in covering recorded noise with, for example, a sound effect or music during postproduction.

Sound Effects

Sound effects (sfx) can be used to cover audio edits, for the masking of noise, or they can be an important part of the story. They can reinforce an idea, create an atmosphere or mood, or help build a scene such as howling winds, rushing water, or a noisy crowd. A *Foley stage* is a part of a studio which is designed for creating live sound effects that can be synchronized to film or video.

We probably won't have a full Foley in our production facility, but we can certainly improvise and create a number of good, believable effects using common materials and objects. For example, thunder sheets are commercially available from some cymbal makers. But we can use almost any thin and relatively large sheet of metal to create the sound of thunder. We can also make sfx using a synthesizer. We can record a clock ticking, a cell phone ringing, or our own sound swallowing water. You get the idea.

Production Music

First, here's the bad news. We can't use copyrighted music in a production unless we license it from its owner. The good news is that we can inexpensively get licensed, royalty-free music for use in our productions both on physical discs and online. These libraries contain a wide variety of music specifically written for videos and commercials, and are often timed to standard commercial lengths.

Also, synthesizers, drum machines and computer programs can be used to create original production music. One computer example is a loop-based musical composition program, such as Sony Acid Pro. An ever-increasing library of loops is available to create music in every style imaginable. MIDI-generated music sequences can also be created for use in commercial production, and we can always bring in some live musicians.

Music and sounds can sometimes be sampled, looped or otherwise edited, remixed, and revised to create original compositions. Copyright law regarding sampling is not as clear in its requirements as are the rules regarding the use of compositions themselves.

Recording and Editing Audio

Some means for recording, editing and enhancing audio is included in video editing software. Powerful standalone programs can also be obtained separately, including Adobe Audition®, Sony Sound Forge®, and Audacity®. Audition is included with a subscription to Adobe Creative Suite ®. Sound Forge is included with Sony Vegas Pro®. Audacity is available on the Internet as a free download.

These programs allow us to play voice, sound effects or music from one or more tracks while simultaneously recording on others. This is called *full-duplex recording*. Most sound cards have this capability, although some older ones may only offer half-duplex recording.

A recorded audio clip is called a *soundfile*. A pictorial representation of a soundfile's waveform shows its frequency and amplitude along a timeline. The view can be zoomed in or out to magnify or reduce the size of the waveform on the screen.

Digital audio is edited with a mouse by pointing and clicking on the waveform. Audio clips can be edited using standard commands including cut, copy, delete, and paste. Unless we save and replace the original soundfile, it's not affected when these commands are executed or when effects are added. So to preserve our original, we should save our edited soundfile with a different name. This type of digital editing is called *non-destructive*. Undo and redo commands allow mistakes to be fixed quickly and easily while we edit. After all the soundfiles have been edited, they're placed in order on various tracks for final *mixdown*.

File attributes include the sample rate, bit depth, and channel output settings (for mono, stereo, or surround sound). Obviously, stereo is the channel output that's used most often. One standard setting for the master *sample rate* is that used for CD audio, which is 44.1 kilohertz, and others are also available. *Bit depth* is also set in the software. Higher sample rates and bit depth mean more sound quality but bigger files that require more memory and processor speed.

For our purposes in this book, we list seven qualities of sound using the acronym FATQINS. Here they are, along with sample signal control and processing devices.

1. *Frequency*:   Equalizers, Pitch Shifters
2. *Amplitude*:   Unity Gain Amplifiers
3. *Time*:   Delay, Echo, Reverb, Phasing
4. *Quality*:   Harmonizers, Chorusing
5. *Intensity*:   Variable Gain Amplifiers
6. *Noise*:   Gates, Filters, Phase Inverters
7. *Stereo*:   Pan Pots, Volume

Now let's discuss each in more detail.

Frequency

The *frequency* of a sound wave is its number of cycles per second, which is given in Hertz (Hz). The human ear can perceive frequencies ranging from about 20 Hz to 20,000 Hz, depending on the individual. Humans perceive the audible frequency of a sound wave as *pitch*, which refers to a tone on the musical scale.

A pure tone involves only one pitch, and harmonics are additional tones added to the fundamental one. Frequencies below the human hearing range are called *infrasound*. For example, subwoofer speakers can produce low frequencies that can be felt but not heard. Frequencies above the human range of hearing are called *ultrasound*.

A normal human singing or speaking range is about 2 octaves, with professional speakers, actors, and singers sometimes using 3 octaves or more. Altogether, human vocal ranges cover about 5 octaves. Looking at a piano keyboard, the approximate singing ranges are: Bass: E2 to C4; Baritone: G2 to E4; Tenor: B2 to G4; Alto, G3 to D5; Mezzo-soprano: A3 to F5; and Soprano: C4 to C6. Your mileage may vary.

The pitches we hear in the sound frequency spectrum are divided into *octaves*. These represent the interval between any two frequencies that have a tonal ratio of 2 to 1. There are 12 unduplicated half steps, or individual pitches, in an octave. This is called the *chromatic scale*.

Beginning with the note of A and counting up using sharps, these would be A, A#, B, C, C#, D, D#, E, F, F#, G, and G#. The next half step, of course, would be the pitch of A, one octave higher than the first tone of A, at exactly double the frequency of the original A-note. A major scale has 7 unduplicated positions, sung in the familiar "doe, ray, me, fah, so, lah, ti, doe, with the second "doe" being the eighth position or octave.

Comb filtering occurs when varying reflections occur at the same frequencies. Time differences can cause the frequencies to add to each other, to phase cancel, or to do something in between. *Flanging* and *phase shifting* are digital effects that utilize this process. We want to be in control of this, so we try to record our audio in a way that reduces it. Then any desired amount can be added in post. Acoustical treatments and mic placement can reduce comb filtering. We can avoid hard, reflective surfaces or cover them when recording, and position mics to pick up more primary sound and fewer reflections.

Frequency is shown graphically by the tightness of the waveform. *Equalizer* (EQ) devices are used to cut or boost various sound frequencies. The two basic types are the *graphic equalizer* and the *parametric equalizer*. Equalizers are adjusted according to factors including room acoustics, the microphone(s) in use, the distance at which a mic is worked, and other things that may affect the sound such as how a handheld mic is positioned and gripped. *Pitch shifters* are devices that can change the position of a sound on the musical scale.

Amplitude

In human hearing the term *amplitude* refers to the degree of motion of air molecules within a sound wave and is perceived as differences in volume. Graphically, amplitude is the height of the wave from its peak to its trough. Greater amplitude means that the sound wave contains more energy. *Unity Gain Amplifiers* don't alter the shape of the original waveform. They simply make the waveform bigger and the sound louder.

Time

The *time* element of sound refers to the velocity at which it travels. Sound must have a medium in order to travel, which is called propagation. Sound waves can be propagated through a gas, liquid, or solid. Obviously, most of what we hear comes through the air. The speed of sound is not a fixed value like the speed of light. It varies with a number of factors. Moisture in the air slightly increases the speed of sound. Altitude decreases the speed of sound, since air becomes thinner. Sound travels faster in liquids and solids than in air.

When working with digital devices, we generally consider sound to travel at one foot per millisecond, which equals 1,000 feet per second. Therefore, a sound wave with a frequency of 1,000 cycles per second has a wavelength of 1 foot. Time processing effects devices are sometimes generically referred to as *digital delay* devices. They record a sound and then delay its return in varying ways to create different effects. The simplest delay effect is echo. *Echo* is a single reflection of sound. It repeats and decays, like what you'd hear if you yelled "hello" in a box canyon. *Reverb* has multiple reflections coming from surfaces like walls, floors, and ceilings and simulates sound occurring in various indoor spaces. *Flanging, chorusing,* and *phasing* are similar-sounding effects that can be used for a variety of purposes such as to add a surrealistic quality to a sound, to "fatten" it, or to make it "swoosh".

Quality

Quality can generally be considered to be the combination of timbre plus reflection, refraction, diffraction, reinforcement, and interference. Quality, like frequency, can be seen in the thickness of the waveform.

The original quality of the sound is called *timbre* (pronounced TAM-bur). It's the result of the combination of a primary tone plus its *harmonics*, which occur in multiples of the original frequency. Every person has a unique voice because of the timbre created by factors including the size, shape, and relative positions of the chest, larynx, mouth, sinus cavities, teeth and tongue.

We shouldn't confuse harmonics with harmony. *Harmony* is the combination of musical tones that will produce either euphony or dissonance. *Euphony* is a pleasant, agreeable combination. It occurs when the frequencies of the combined sound, expressed in Hz, equal the ratios of small, whole numbers. Most vocal harmonies are octaves, thirds, or fifths. As mentioned previously, an octave combination produces the ratio of 2 to 1. A major third interval produces a relationship of 5 to 4, and a major fifth produces a ratio of 3 to 2. *Dissonance* occurs in relative degrees with some other combinations, such as intervals of major and minor seconds.

The quality element of sound is first dealt with during the production process. Microphone selection is an important consideration. The one we'll use for a specific sound depends on a number of factors. For instance, a ribbon mic is sensitive and so is not appropriate for recording plosive sounds like a kick drum.

Budget is also a consideration. If we don't happen to have a $4,000 Neumann U87 microphone lying around we may have to work with another, such as a great-sounding $100 Shure SM-58 dynamic or a $250 Shure Beta 87A condenser handheld or stand-mounted mic. An industry-standard wired lapel microphone is the Sony ECM-44B, which at the time of this writing carries a street price of around $175. A popular shotgun mic is the Audio-Technica AT897, which is presently available for around $200.

Placement is the next big consideration, and again depends on the sound to be recorded plus the characteristics of the microphone to be used. Distance and angle of incidence are also set. For example, plosives can be reduced by varying the angle of the diaphragm relative to the sound wave, but off-axis coloration can become a factor. There's more on microphones later in this chapter.

Intensity

Intensity refers to the ability of sound to be heard at a distance. Increasing the intensity of a sound raises its perceived volume and lowers its dynamic range.

We can make changes to the original amplitude, such as limiting its peaks or expanding its low points. A *variable gain amplifier* (VGA) limits, compresses, boosts or "gates" the waveform. A *compressor/limiter* is a VGA in which the output level rises at a gentler rate as the input level is increased. Compressors have a number of parameters that can be adjusted individually, including attack and release times. Some compressors have an interactive knee function that automatically adjusts these. For voice, compression is typically transparent, meaning inaudible to the human ear, at settings equal to or less than 4:1. This means that 4 dB of input creates 1 dB of output. A limiter can be set so that a given level is never exceeded. An *expander/gate* is a type of VGA in which the output level decreases as the input level decreases. This is often used for eliminating unwanted transient sounds, such as when recording a voice in a room where an air conditioner is running. An *automatic gain control* (AGC) boosts the level of low signals. Audio editing programs generally have either a *normalize* or a *hard limiting* function to increase the intensity of an audio track.

Volume as heard by the human ear is measured in watts per square meter, notated as W/m^2. As with light, the inverse square law states that the intensity of sound varies as the square of the distance. Of course, the law works perfectly only in a perfect environment.

Still, we need to understand that this is why we need to *get our microphone close to our subject*. In theory, a dynamic mic hears our subject 9 times louder at a distance of 1" from the mouth than it does at a distance of 4" from the mouth. (Remember, it's the distance *squared*. $4 - 1 = 3$, and $3 \times 3 = 9$). The reproduced target sound is more accurate when the mic is relatively close, and the further that either a dynamic or condenser mic is located from our subject, the more background audio it picks up in relation to the target sound.

While we're recording and editing, we want to protect our hearing. We use the decibel scale of sound pressure level (dB SPL) to measure sound as experienced by the human ear. This scale begins at the threshold of hearing, represented by 0 dB, and is logarithmic. 120 dB is about one trillion times louder than the threshold of hearing, and represents the maximum safe hearing level. 140 dB is twenty times the safe hearing level. At 160 dB, we get instant and permanent ear damage. Electronic amplification can easily boost intensity beyond safe hearing levels, so headphone volume and proximity to loudspeakers are important considerations.

Noise

Noise is our sixth property of sound. Our goal, of course, is clean, noise-free sound. However, noise can creep into our project from all sorts of different sources. Our first line of defense is to try to position our audio source in a noise-free area and to place microphones effectively. We have a number of weapons available to fight *environmental noise*. These include carpet, acoustical ceiling tiles, sound absorbers like curtains, plus the sound insulation like fiberglass that's inside walls and floors. *Electronic noise*, including radio frequency (RF) and hum, sometimes creeps into audio cables. *Unbalanced* audio connectors use just two wires in the cable, which are signal and ground. *Balanced* audio connectors use three wires in the cable and reduce electronic noise.

Noise filters are sometimes used in both production and postproduction. These are selective equalizers that are designed to keep specific frequency ranges from passing. AC hum can come through electrical outlets, and can be fought with 60-cycle filters. Ground loop isolators are another type of filter to fight hum at the source. Some amplifiers and mixers have *phase inverter switches* that can also be used to reduce or eliminate noise at its source. Some software programs, such as Adobe Audition, have noise sampling and reduction features to reduce or eliminate recorded noise. This should be our last line of defense. Again, it's best to keep noise out in the first place rather than to try to get it out once it has become part of the recorded signal.

Stereo

Binaural human hearing comes from two ears that are, on average, about 7 inches (18cm) apart. So when we hear most frequencies we can sense differences in arrival times. This creates a stereo field that, depending on the medium in which the sound will be heard, might be considered. So this is the final element in our FATQINS formula, referring to each sound's placement in the stereo field. We consider five basic stereo placement regions: front, back, left, right, and center. A sound can be moved perceptually to the left, right, or center with *pan pots*. It can be moved perceptually forward or toward the rear with volume changes, since relative loudness creates prominence.

Microphones

Microphones and speakers are *transducers*, meaning that they convert acoustic energy either to or from electrical energy. Mics are selected according to what is being amplified or recorded, and under what conditions. The three major characteristics of a microphone are its type of element, its pickup pattern, and its physical form. All microphone elements have a *diaphragm* which vibrates when struck by a sound wave. The two most-used types of microphone elements are dynamic and condenser mics.

The *dynamic microphone* is the most popular element design. There are two kinds of dynamic microphones: the moving coil and the ribbon. The most common is the moving coil, in which the diaphragm vibrates, causing an electromagnetic induction of current as a coil of wire on a plunger moves inside a magnetic field. The magnetic disturbances are converted into electrical impulses. This type of dynamic mic is rugged and can survive the rigors of on-location use and abuse. The ribbon microphone is a type of dynamic mike that has a warm sound but has a very sensitive transducer element, so it's usually restricted to use in a studio.

The element in a *condenser microphone* operates on capacitance rather than a moving coil. The diaphragm acts as the topside of the capacitor, with a voltage stored between the diaphragm and the capacitor's rear plate. As the diaphragm moves, the voltage varies between the plates. Since the vibrations are reproduced by a capacitor and thus need voltage, a regular condenser microphone requires a power source. This may be a battery, or *phantom power* supplied through the mic cable by a mixing console using its XLR connection. The *electret condenser* microphone uses a special type of condenser that has a permanent electrical charge.

The term *electret* combines the words *electrostatic* and *magnet*. Electrets are used in portable recording devices like smartphones and tablets as built-in microphones.

Other types of microphones exist but are rarely used in our applications. These include crystal, carbon, piezo, laser, and speaker microphones. They won't be discussed here.

Impedance and Frequency Response

Impedance is important in selecting a mic. This refers to a microphone's resistance to the flow of electrical current in its signal path. Professional microphones are low impedance, usually at 200 ohms. Another consideration is its *frequency response curve*. This is a graph showing response in decibels over the range of frequencies reproduced by the mic. The *noise floor* is important when recording quiet sounds. This is the sound level that creates the same output level as the noise inherent in the mic itself. The maximum *sound pressure level* (SPL) is the level of sound the mic can accept without audible distortion. A mic's dynamic range is the difference between the max SPL and the noise floor. The *clipping level* describes when the diaphragm reaches its physical limit.

Microphone Pickup Patterns

Both the volume and the frequency response of a mic can be affected by a sound wave's angle of incidence, which is the angle at which the sound wave strikes the diaphragm.

A *polar pattern* is a two-dimensional representation of a microphone's pickup pattern, showing the mic's diaphragm in the center. This is normally included in literature provided by the manufacturer. The standard pickup patterns are omnidirectional; half-omni or hemispherical; bi-directional or figure eight; and unidirectional: cardioid, supercardioid, and hypercardioid. A sound wave directly striking the diaphragm from the center of the pickup pattern is said to be *on-axis*. When sound strikes the microphone *off-axis*, but still within the pickup pattern, some frequencies will be reproduced differently than they would be if the sound waves were on-axis. This is called *off-axis coloration*. Higher frequencies are more susceptible than lower frequencies to this effect, which typically becomes more noticeable as the angle of incidence increases.

Omindirectional mics pick up in a full circle of 360 degrees. Omnis are sometimes the pickup pattern for lapel mics. They have little or no proximity effect, and low sensitivity to plosive sounds.

Hemispherical microphones pick up in a semicircle of 180 degrees. This is the pattern used for surface mics such as pressure zone microphones. PZMs are attached to a surface such as the top of a conference table, using the tabletop as a sort of diaphragm extension. They pick up the sound from everyone sitting there as the waves propagate through the tabletop. *Bi-directional* or *figure eight* mics pick up sound from the front and rear but not from the sides.

Cardioid, supercardioid, and *hypercardioid* pickup patterns are also known as *unidirectional* patterns because they pick up mostly from the front of the mic. Cardioid and supercardioid are the standard for handheld mics.

Of the three, the cardioid mic is the most accommodating for off-axis vocals. It has a heart-shaped pickup pattern with good side pickup and almost total rear sound rejection, so it has good control for feedback.

The supercardioid pattern features a narrower front pickup with less from the side but more from the rear. It also has good feedback control due to its better rejection of unwanted sound coming in from the sides.

The hypercardioid pattern stretches the supercardioid pattern, tightening and extending front pickup and shrinking it from the sides, with a bit of increase from the rear. The hypercardioid microphone has the most side rejection of all the cardioid patterns, and can be effective for mitigating noise, room reverberation and feedback. But it's very unforgiving of off-axis vocals.

A shotgun mic is a hypercardioid mic that's often used as an on-camera mic. As mentioned earlier, we should try not to use an on-camera mic unless it's absolutely necessary. Instead, we should try to get whatever external mic we have as close as possible to our target sound source. If we're using a shotgun, we can extend it on a boom pole above the talent, being held outside the frame of the picture. Because of its narrow pickup pattern, sound picked up by a shotgun can easily get too far off-axis. So the shotgun mic must be aimed directly at our subject. In reality, if we're using a shotgun for speaking talent, we may very well need a boom pole operator wearing headphones.

Another useful mic for applications such as sporting events is the *parabolic* mic. This uses a dish to collect sound waves and then focus them onto a mic in the center of the dish. It works like cupping a hand next to our ear when we want to hear better.

Microphone Construction

Microphones are built according to their mission. Construction can be wired or wireless. *Handheld* mics can be, well, handheld. Or they can be mounted on mic stands using adaptors. *Headset* mics give a performer the use of both hands. *Lavaliere* mics can be worn on clothing. *Hanging* microphones are suspended above the source of the sound to be recorded. *Surface mount* mics can pick up sounds over a wide area, from the material to which they are mounted. *Wireless* microphones can greatly increase freedom of movement. They can have a single fixed or selectable multiple channels.

Working the Mic

As mentioned earlier, the distance at which a microphone is placed relative to its audio source is a critical consideration. In general, close and on-axis are good. When dynamic microphones are used very close to the audio source, though (within about a quarter-inch or so), the bass frequencies increase relative to the high and mid-range frequencies. This is known as the *proximity effect*. Condenser mics don't have proximity effect but tend to distort more easily than a dynamic when the sound source is too close. Because of this, condenser mics should generally be worked from a little further away than a dynamic, but not so far as to pick up too much background sound.

When working with a microphone at close range, it's generally best to use a moderate vocal attack. Depending on the sensitivity of the diaphragm and the angle of attack, some sounds such as popping a "p" can result in distortion. A sibilant sound such as "s" may also create the need for adjusting the angle of attack. *Swallowing the mic* means working it too tightly for the amount of vocal attack used. This results in diffraction from the squeezing of the sound wave, and in distortion if the diaphragm reaches its physical movement limit.

So let's summarize our microphone selection criteria.

Of the two basic types of microphone elements the dynamic mic is the one that can take the most abuse. The diaphragm in this microphone is toughly constructed. The Shure SM58 is a dynamic microphone with excellent vocal response, and it's the world's most popular stage mic.

A high-quality condenser mic is used for recording vocals and some instruments in many studios. Depending on the amount of background sound present, a condenser such as the Shure Beta 87A can also make a good on-location mic. A condenser mic requires a power source, which can be either a battery or phantom power supplied by the mixing console. A good condenser mic has a very flat frequency response curve, and captures small nuances with precision. However, the sensitivity of a condenser also makes it prone to distortion when worked poorly.

For on-location video, a lapel mic such as the Sony ECM-44B is often the best choice since it sounds good and can be easily worn on clothing.

Part Five:
Personality Performance Basics

Chapter Fourteen: Vocal Performance

For interpersonal communication, the most fundamental performance technique is the use of the voice. Vocal performance is also known in broadcasting as voice acting. Part Five of this book is designed to present that, plus some other interpersonal communication techniques.

These work much like musicianship, where having skills with scales, intervals, and harmony doesn't ensure that hit recordings will be made. However, craft in music is a prerequisite to artistry. For us speech communicators, learning tactical and strategic craft doesn't guarantee successfully meeting a communication objective. However, it does provide tools that can be used in mapping our intentions and navigating a planned path. Like musical craft, communication involves both knowledge and physical skill. So we learn some basics and apply them through practice.

We tend to think of a spokesperson as being an actor or athlete who's paid to speak on behalf of a company or its product and who thereby becomes associated with it. But just as importantly, anyone is a spokesperson if he or she has contact with any of the company's stakeholders, particularly customers or prospects, at any point in the process from product manufacture to distribution to consumption and customer service after the sale.

Tools of the Craft

A number of tools can be used to transfer ideas, images, and emotions with the voice. These include pitch, intensity, pauses and pacing plus the effective articulation of consonants, vowels, and diphthongs. Grammar and vocabulary are also important. And one of the most important things is to remember that the body and mind work together, so we'll sound more like we want to if we try to look like we want to sound. That means that we should put a smile or other appropriate expression on our face and use complementary bodily movements.

Dialects

There are three major speech dialects in the United States. They are General American (GA), Eastern American (EA), and Southern American (SA). GA is the dialect most often used in commercials. EA and SA contain some different vowel and diphthong sounds. Each of the major dialects contains sub-dialects.

Articulation

As in the last chapter, please bear with us through some of this information. It may seem to be a bit technical, particularly when we get to all of the various phonetic sounds in articulation. But hang in there. It provides an important foundation that'll come in handy later.

Articulation refers to the act or manner of producing speech sounds and joining them together. The International Phonetic Alphabet (IPA) is a special system in which each sound is represented by only one symbol. In this book, we won't use IPA symbols to represent phonetic sounds. We don't want you to have to learn a whole new alphabet, so we'll keep it easy. The word *phonetic* means "pertaining to the sounds of speech and their production." For our purposes, we'll identify 42 phonetic sounds in the GA speech dialect: 11 vowel sounds, 5 diphthongs, 21 consonant sounds, and 5 combination consonant sounds. In the EA and SA dialects, some of these sounds are modified or replaced. Let's look at each GA sound and how it's produced.

Vowel and Diphthong Formation

Vowels and diphthongs are formed at specific places inside the mouth. If you say them out loud as you read this, you can feel their placement. The highest formant vowel is the EE sound (as in meet), which is formed just behind the top front teeth. High-formant vowel sounds

212

continue with IH, AY, and EH, moving back and down, and ending with the A sound (as in bat), which is formed in the middle rear of the mouth. The lower formant vowels begin with AH (as in father) and move forward along the lower part of the mouth through AW and OU (as in boat) to OO (as in boot), which is formed just behind the lower front teeth. The final two sounds curl backward in the middle of the mouth. They are U (as in put), which is front-middle, and UH (as in mud), which is center-middle formant. A diphthong is a combination of two vowel sounds. Symbols and examples for each vowel and diphthong sound are listed below.

Vowel Sounds

1.	EE	weed, feed, need, reed
2.	IH	bit, fit, sit, knit
3.	EH	bet, fed, red, said
4.	A	fat, rat, sat
5.	AH	father, lot, rot, shot
6.	AW	fall, bought, sought, naught
7.	OO	blue, shoe, new, zoo
8.	U	foot, bull, cook, hook
9.	UH (Stressed Syllable)	butt, dumb, mud, suffocate
10.	UH (Unstressed: Schwa)	Any vowel, unstressed syllable. parachute, cinema, suffocate
11.	ER	burn, term, girl, church, teacher

Diphthong Sounds

1.	AY	late, bait, wait, fate
2.	OU	no, boat, float, vote
3.	OW	how, now, brown, cow
4.	AI	ice, white, night, light
5.	OY	boy, joy, toy, loiter

Consonant Sounds

Consonants are either voiced or voiceless. There are five manners of consonant articulation, with seven articulation places. The formation of consonants is therefore a combination of voicing, manner, and place. Consonant sounds are generally consistent with their spelling, so we'll use only a few additional phonetic spellings for them.

The *manners* of consonant articulation are:
> *Fricative*: movement of air through a constricted channel.
> *Glide*: movement toward the vowel it precedes.
> *Nasal*: formed in the nose.
> *Stop*: the oral channel is closed and then reopened in a plosive phase.
> *Semivowel*: resembles a vowel, but the mouth is not as open as with a vowel.

The *places* of consonant articulation are:
> *Dental*: tongue touches the teeth.
> *Alveolar*: tongue approaches or touches the alveolar ridge.
> *Palatal*: tongue approaches or touches the hard or soft palate.
> *Velar*: tongue approaches the velum.
> *Glottal*: sound occurs in the space between the vocal folds.
> *Labial*: sound is formed between the two lips.
> *Labiodental*: the upper lip touches the lower teeth.

Now let's look at how some consonant sounds are made. Again, if you say them out loud as you read this, you can feel their manners and places of articulation.

Stops: Stop consonants come in voiced/voiceless pairs, with the manner and place of articulation being identical. The voiced/voiceless stop pairs are B/P, (labial/stop) D/T (alveolar/stop), and G/K (velar/stop).

Fricatives: The H sound, as in "heavy", is a glottal fricative. The other eight fricative sounds are voiced/voiceless pairs. They are V/F (labiodental fricative), the voiced/voiceless TH, as in This/Thistle (dental fricative), ZH/SH, as in Mirage/Ship (palatal fricative), and S/Z as in Sue/Zoo (palatal fricative).

Nasal: M is a labial nasal consonant, and N is an alveolar nasal sound. These are the only two consonant sounds that are formed in the nose.

Semivowels: L is an alveolar semivowel, and R is a palatal semivowel.

Glides: W (as in wet) is a labial glide, and Y (as in yes) is a palatal glide.

Combination Consonant Sounds: There are five combination consonant sounds. They are NG (as in being and bank), TSH (as in church), DZH (as in jest), HW (as in what), and YU (as in union).

Articulation Errors

Articulation errors include substitution, omission, and distortion of vowel and consonant sounds. Ordinary vowel errors include "jist" for just, and "git" for get. Some of the most common consonant errors include leaving out the "h" sound in words such as "whale" and "white", which become "wail" and "wight". Another common consonant error is dropping the "g" on words ending in "ing", making them become "in" or "een" in their endings, such as "fishing" becoming "fishin" or "fisheen".

Other common errors include the transposition of syllables, such as making "hundred" become "hunderd", and the substitution of improper sounds, such as making "February" become "Feb-u-wery".

Grammar and Vocabulary Errors

Errors in grammar and vocabulary can and should be avoided by good communicators. Every professional speaker should use grammar appropriate to the target audience. We should also build a good vocabulary and continually add to it. As a general rule, slang words and phrases should be used only when they're used by our target audience or when we're employing them with an appropriate characterization.

Our target area should be researched for unusual spellings and pronunciations, and we should study all available resources for properly saying the names of people, places and events.

The PIPPs

Now that we have a few basics down in terms of articulation, grammar and vocabulary, let's add some other skills to use in building an effective speech system for good vocal techniques. For this part of our study, we'll list the headings of Pitch, Intensity, Pauses and Pacing, with various techniques under each. Speech should have variability in all these four areas. So our acronym "PIPPs" (with apologies to Gladys Knight) means variability in pitch, intensity, pauses, and pacing.

We must properly select and vary *pitch* according to our meaning. Intonation is long-term pitch variation, while inflections and shifts are short-term pitch variations. We need dynamic vocal *intensity*, changing our volume according to the situation. *Pauses* create timing and convey the proper punctuation of speech. *Pacing* is the combined effect of rhythm and rate. Speech rhythm should fit the character and the scene, with variability when needed. A good average rate of speech is around 165 words per minute.

The ways that we combine and vary our pitch, intensity, pauses and pacing can create interesting, effective phrasing in our speech. Let's look more closely at each component of the PIPPs.

Pitch

In speaking, pitch involves four major areas: register, range, melody, and modulation. Let's review each.

Register: Singers sometimes refer to the vocal registers as being the chest voice and the head voice. For our purposes, we'll use the term register to describe which one-third of the pitch range of our voice is being used: lower, middle, or upper. For example, the lower register is often used to help the communicator achieve an air of authority and believability.

Where the voice is "based" is determined by the use of the *habitual pitch* (HP). The habitual pitch is the one that we use most often when speaking. It's the note that we move toward and away from when we're going up or down on the musical scale. The HP that we use will depend on the perception of our character that we want to convey at a given time.

Range: While a professional singer or actor will sometimes utilize a pitch range of three octaves or more, a good speaker should generally use at least a two-octave range. That means we should develop the ability to produce good tone throughout all of the notes twice through the major scale (doe, ray, me, fah, so, lah, tee, doe, ray, me, fah, so, lah, tee, doe). We can practice this daily to build strength and as a vocal warm-up exercise. And when we speak in applications like commercials, we should generally try to use most or all of the notes in our range.

Melody: In our melody, we're concerned with the intervals, note selection, and pattern. Let's look at each.

Intervals: The distance between notes is called the interval. For example, each note of the major scale (doe, ray, me, fah, so, lah, tee, doe) is given a number of one through eight, with the interval being the note's number in the scale. The *tonic* or beginning note of the scale (*doe*) is both the first note and the first interval. *Ray* is the second interval from the lower doe, *me* is the third interval, *fah* is the fourth, *so* is the fifth, *lah* is the sixth, *tee* is the seventh, and the upper *doe* is the eight interval (or octave) away from the tonic note. If there's a note between the two "perfect" notes of the scale's interval, we call that a sharp or a flat depending on whether it's higher or lower than the normal interval in the key we've chosen. For example, in the key of C major the 5th interval is G, which we would call a G flat (Gb) if we take it down ½ step on the chromatic scale. It would be called F sharp (F#) if we are sharping the 4th note of the scale, F, rather than flatting the 5th note of G. Same note, different name.

Again, in speaking we should try to use a wide variety of notes and our full range. Although actually using a different note on every syllable is impractical, this can be a good perceptual goal. If we try for the *feeling* of using a different note on every syllable, we can avoid monotonous speech. The root word of monotonous is, of course, monotone. It means a series of pitches that are the same or too similar.

Note Selection: Much of the time, communicators work from a script rather than speaking on an extemporaneous basis. Poor note selection can help "tip off" the listener that the words are scripted. We need to be aware of our range. How many notes of the scale are we using, and how are they flowing? Are they going up and down smoothly? Are they flowing in a consistent pattern, or is it too erratic? Most importantly, does our note selection make sense with what we're saying? Note selection can complement the literal meaning of the words. Notes can also contrast with the literal meaning of words, creating contrary meanings such as sarcasm. We can imagine our speech segment written in musical notation, called tablature. Here's a sample showing a radio broadcaster with a simple message.

K B B   B . . . . .   It's 3: Six-Teen.   Hi!

Patterns: Care must be taken that the series of notes in nearby phrases are not too similar-sounding. Successively similar note selection is referred to as "patterned speech". Obvious patterns in note selection can make us sound phony (intentionally or unintentionally), can lead to a loss of credibility, and it's boring. A common error causing perceived patterned speech is to habitually begin or end successive phrases with the same top or bottom note.

Modulation: In music, the term modulation refers to a change in key. In speaking it means a pitch variation, which can occur in either the short term or the long term. The production of vocal tone is called *phonation*. Modulation can occur either during or between phonations.

Inflection: Inflection is short-term pitch modulation. It occurs *during* phonation. For illustration, let's say the word "go" for about two seconds, using two different notes and making the one word a declarative statement. Declarative statements typically end with a down

218

inflection, which means that the last note spoken is lower than the next-to-last note. Now we'll say the word "go" again for about two seconds with two notes, this time making the one word a question. Questions requiring a response generally end with an up inflection. This means that the last note is higher than the next-to-last note. Up inflections are also used when listing things, with the final item requiring a down inflection to infer that the list has been completed. To illustrate, let's use this line: *The cat, the dog, the bird, and the owner all played in the yard.* To make a statement, the words cat, dog, and bird will receive an up inflection, while the words owner and yard get a down inflection. To make a question, we'll give these two words an upward inflection. Inflection marks may be placed in copy by placing a small arrow at the appropriate place, pointing either up or down.

Shift: A shift is a modulation of pitch *between* phonations. That is, the beginning of the succeeding word is significantly higher or lower in pitch than the ending of the preceding word. For practice, let's use the two-word phrase *Get out*, as if we're an impatient parent informing a child to leave the hot tub. For our declarative statement, we'll make the shift downward. That is, the word "out" begins lower on the musical scale than the note ending the word "get". Now we'll play the role of the child, responding with the same phrase asking a question. We'll use a wide upward shift first, to denote disbelief. Next, we'll use a smaller shift, simply asking for confirmation.

Intonation: Intonation refers to modulation of pitch over a longer term. It's the general pattern of note selection throughout the entire sentence being spoken. For illustration, let's take a downward intonation beginning with a note near the top of our two-octave range and ending with a note near the bottom, generally moving smoothly downward throughout this sentence: *I told you not to spend more than a half hour in that tub.* There should be some upward movements in note selection throughout the sentence, but the general pattern is downward. To alter the meaning, and add a feeling of irritation and frustration, let's take an upward intonation for the same sentence. We'll start near the bottom of our two-octave range, and end near the highest note that we can produce. Intonation may be marked in copy by placing a long arrow over the entire sentence indicating the intended direction.

Intensity

Vocal intensity means controlling volume, which is often done through changes in our tension. For our purposes here, we'll practice four levels of vocal intensity on a line of copy, moving from a quiet whisper through normal conversation to shouting and then screaming. Rehearsing these different intensity levels can give us a virtual volume control for our voice. Here's the practice line: *Let's get out of here.*

Voice coaches tend to yell that our vocal support should come from the diaphragm, which is muscle located at about the level of our belt. So to avoid irritating them, we'll think of air as getting depleted and then replenished from the bottom, rather than the top, of our lungs.

Relaxation/Tension: Since the voice is essentially a stringed wind instrument, we need good breath control plus controlled relaxation and tightening. Tension levels should be considered when planning vocal effects. A good practice exercise is a 7-step model of muscular tension throughout the body. A level of 0 means we're unconscious, and a level of 4 is the middle with a level of contentment. We'll begin with total relaxation of the entire body at level 1. We'll then move in steps toward total tension at level 7, where we'll tighten up as if we're in a rage or in a fight for our life.

Shape: Maintaining the shape of an instrument is also essential to tone generation. To illustrate, let's look at a grand piano. The shape of its resonating cavity is largely responsible for its tone. In the same way, the resonating cavities for our voice must maintain their proper shape. If we slump while sitting in a chair, the shape of our chest will change. Both our vocal support and lower resonance can suffer. We can think of our lungs as building two round cylinders. We try to maintain that roundness, as opposed to flattening the chest cavity as air goes in and out, although in reality the lungs do flatten somewhat. If we fail to open our mouth and nose properly, our upper notes will lose space in which to resonate. Constricting the shape of our body's cavities can have roughly the same effect as stuffing our grand piano full of dirty laundry. Let's analyze the cavities of our body and our resonance by separating our notes into what singers call the chest voice and the head voice.

Chest Voice: We can call our lower notes the chest voice because we tend to feel them resonate and produce harmonics in the lower throat and chest cavities. This is due in part to the physical length of low-pitched sound waves. We should sit or stand up straight to get the best tone production in our lower register. We get the feeling of moving our resonance back and down on lower notes.

Head Voice: We can refer to the pitches in our middle and upper registers as the head voice. They have shorter wavelengths, and we tend to feel them up higher in our body. We may notice that our middle register notes seem to resonate and produce harmonics in the upper throat and the rear of our mouth in the area of the soft palate, while our upper register notes feel like they produce resonance more forward in the head, including the area of the hard palate and nasal cavities. So it's important to keep all of these passages open and properly shaped.

Projection and the Phonation-to-Air Ratio: A dictionary definition of projection is to "shoot out or forth". Essentially, when we project the voice we give it sufficient intensity to be heard over distances. Projection is a function of the muscles of the vocal production instrument, and of the placement of our vocal tones for resonance. Like other physical skills, the voice can be improved through exercise and practice. The phonation-to-air ratio refers to the amount of tone production generated by the volume of air passing the vocal folds. We can make the voice more full by generating maximum phonation, or more "breathy" by generating little phonation so that mostly air passage is actually heard by the listener. Generally, our goal is maximum phonation for minimum air passage. A good exercise is to hold a lit candle approximately six inches from the mouth, and practice reading copy without blowing out the candle. Our caring lawyers remind you to exercise caution when doing this exercise so as not to set yourself aflame.

Intensity Dynamics: Intensity changes may be broken down into long-term and short-term. The long-term illustrations below show a disc

221

jockey doing a brief introduction of a song. The first long-term intensity change is the *crescendo*, which begins with low and ends with high intensity.

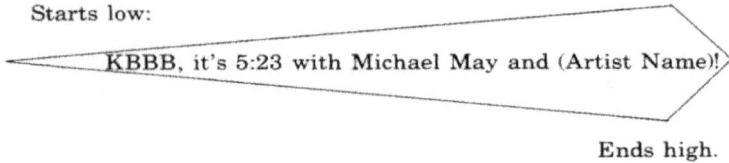

Starts low:

KBBB, it's 5:23 with Michael May and (Artist Name)!

Ends high.

The other long-term intensity change is the *decrescendo*, which starts with high and ends with low intensity.

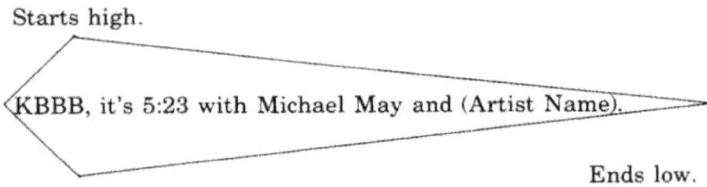

Starts high.

KBBB, it's 5:23 with Michael May and (Artist Name).

Ends low.

Short-term intensity changes are called *stress*, which is relative vocal prominence of a syllable within a word, a word within a phrase, or a phrase within a sentence. The term *emphasis* is used to refer to the effect created by stressed words and phrases. While stress is a vocal tactic, emphasis is an intention.

The three degrees of stress are *primary*, *moderate*, and *unstressed*. Connecting words such as articles and prepositions are typically unstressed, except for unusual meaning. Emphasis can be indicated in a script by placing a double line underneath words of primary stress, and a single line under words of moderate stress. Unstressed words receive no marking underneath.

Pauses

One of the most important skills of the professional speaker is the placement and lengths of pauses. These are the speaking equivalent of punctuation marks, and are generally taken in four lengths.

Quarter Beat. These may be taken at non-punctuated phrase breaks. Vertical slashes can be placed in copy to remind the speaker where he or she intends to take such pauses.

Half Beat. These are taken at commas. Commas and periods need not be slashed, but punctuation marks may need to be added to copy in places where we want them to be but they perhaps aren't.

Full Beat. These are taken at periods, question marks, and exclamation marks.

Longer than Full Beat. These are taken for dramatic purposes, and are often indicated by three periods (...).

Pauses are normally taken only at phrase breaks, including punctuation marks. In cases such as an intention to create the sound of a confused or uneducated character, or where we intend to express sorrow or other emotions, we may take pauses within phrases. A common mistake is to hurry through what we say, taking too few pauses.

Long sentences should be broken down into shorter ones, using pauses to break them into little bites that are easy to digest. A good rule-of-thumb is to keep spoken sentences to seven seconds or less, with plenty of verbally punctuated phrase breaks. Pauses and inflections work together. Extemporaneous declarative thoughts can be segmented through the use of plenty of *down-inflection/pause* sequences. These help us avoid verbal run-on sentences. In addition to sentence ends, they may be used at non-punctuated phrase breaks and commas. An *up-inflection/pause* sequence may also be used at non-punctuated phrase breaks and commas, but these are less common and alter meaning. Up-inflection/pause sequences are commonly used in lists of items.

Like our earlier practice, let's say the following list using an up-inflection at the end of the first three items, with a down-inflection at the end of the last item: *a shirt, pants, a belt, and a shoe.* The final down-inflection says that the list is complete. Now let's practice it by ending *all* of the items in an up-inflection. This sends one of the following messages: either our list is not yet complete, we're unsure of ourselves, or we're asking a question.

Pacing

Pacing is the combined effect of the rate and rhythm of speech. *Rate* refers to the number of words per minute (WPM), also called the rate of speech (ROS). *Rhythm* refers to the regularity of speech. Rhythms include steady, irregular, stammering, and jerky speech. A major enemy of the communicator is the stumble. This is a mistake that requires restarting a phrase or correction of a word. The main culprit causing stumbling is too fast a rate of speech. Speaking is like running down a hill. When we go too fast, we can lose control. The best thing to do when stumbles occur is to slow the ROS.

An easy beat to pace is a 4/4 beat, because it's the one we hear most often. This meter is referred to as *common time*. Let's look at some musical note values.

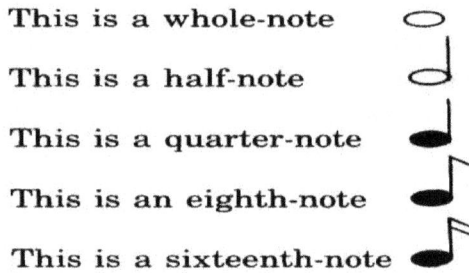

This is a whole-note

This is a half-note

This is a quarter-note

This is an eighth-note

This is a sixteenth-note

Each split of a note divides its metric value in half. A half note is worth half as many beats as a whole note, and a quarter note is worth half as many beats as a half note. The *time signature* 4/4 means that there are four beats in a measure, and the quarter note gets one beat. So a half note appearing in any measure would get two beats, and a whole note would last for four beats. It would take two eighth notes, or four sixteenth notes, to occupy one full beat.

In learning to count eighth notes, we can say *one-and-two-and-three-and-four-and.* We can learn to count sixteenth notes by saying *one-E-and-E, two-E-and-E, three-E-and-E, four-E-and-E.* When the melody stops momentarily, the pause is denoted by a *rest*. A quarter rest is a one beat pause in 4/4 time. It looks like this:

Let's tap out some meter, using the above notes. First, let's count in common time.

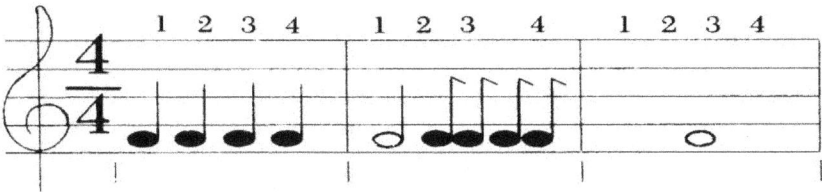

Now let's count out some notes using 3/4 meter, or *waltz time*. The 3/4 time signature means that there are three beats in a measure, and the quarter note gets one beat.

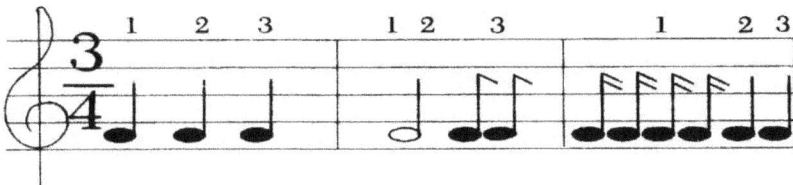

Outline of the PIPPs

Here are the PIPPs presented in the form of a brief outline, with related items listed below each PIPP. This can be an aid in learning and remembering them.

Pitch
        a. Register (placement of habitual pitch)
        b. Range (2 octaves)
        c. Intonations (long-term up or down trend in pitch)

225

d. Inflections (variation of pitch *within* a phonation)

e. Shifts (variation of pitch *between* phonations)

Intensity

a. Volume (the amount of amplitude)

Crescendo (up-building, long-term variation)

Decrescendo (downward, long-term variation)

Stress/Emphasis (relative vocal prominence)

b. Support (shape of instrument/resonance)

c. Air/Phonation Ratio (amount of audible air passage)

d. Tension (muscles according to intended effect)

Pauses

a. ¼ Beat (used at unpunctuated phrase break)

b. ½ Beat (used at comma)

c. Full Beat (used at period)

d. Longer than Full Beat (used for dramatic purposes)

Pacing

a. Rhythm (consistency of meter)

b. Rate (speed measured in WPM)

Copy Notations

Crescendo: <

Decrescendo: >

Inflections and Shifts: Short up or down arrow above the syllable.

Intonation: Long up or down arrow above the phrase or sentence.

Pauses:

Unpunctuated phrase break: vertical slash

Commas, periods, and other punctuation marks: for ½ and full beats.

Dramatic Pause: Three dots (…) on either side of the word/phrase.

Rate: When needed, we write slow, medium, or fast.

Rhythm: Where relevant, we write out that we'll be smooth, broken, stammering, or jerky.

Stress/Emphasis: Stress is a vocal tactic that can be used to achieve the intention of emphasis. Emphasis is denoted by one underline beneath words receiving moderate stress, and two underlines beneath words receiving primary stress.

Long-Term and Short-Term Impressions

Long-term impressions are those which become evident to the listener over an extended period such as a sentence or paragraph.

The following are long-term impressions:
1. Habitual Pitch (most-often-repeated pitch)
2. Crescendo (up-building intensity)
3. Decrescendo (down-building intensity)
4. Intonation (pitch variation over a long period of time)
5. Rhythm (consistency of meter)
6. Rate (speed, measured in WPM)
7. Grammar (proper relative use of classes of words)
8. Vocabulary (proper understanding and use of word meanings)

Short-term impressions are those which become evident to the listener over a quick period such as within a single word or phrase.

The following are short-term impressions:
1. Tonal Phrasing (think "use a different note each syllable")
2. Stress/Emphasis (relative vocal prominence)
3. Inflections (short-term pitch modulation during phonation)
4. Shifts (modulation of pitch between phonations)
5. Pauses (the speaker's "punctuation marks")
6. Articulation (use of proper vowel and consonant sounds)
7. Avoidance of Slang (language not appropriate for the target)
8. Pronunciation (use of proper sounds of words)

Character Voices

Character voices fall into two fundamental categories, which are general and specific. A *general* characterization is of a type. It could include those with foreign accents, as well as stereotypical characters such as cab drivers, hillbillies, or football coaches. It might also include vocal characterizations of non-humans, such as Martians or Leprechauns. We simply map out the vocal tactics to be used, building the characterization from scratch. A *specific* characterization is of an actual person. This is also known as an impression or impersonation, and requires a high degree of believability in order to be effective. These require studying recordings of the subject, with accompanying practice in imitating the characteristics of the individual's voice one phrase at a time. Listed below are some methods that can be useful in planning and constructing vocal characterizations. They can be used separately or combined.

Change Pitch, Intensity, Pauses, and/or Pacing: One of the simplest ways to quickly create a character voice is to alter one or more of the PIPPs.

Change Voice Quality. Four voice quality modifications are:
> *Nasality:* (Sounds other than M and N are formed in our nose.)
> *Breathiness:* (We use a high air/phonation ratio.)
> *Harshness:* (We use high intensity at our lowest pitch levels.)
> *Hoarseness:* (We combine breathiness and harshness.)

Use a Dialect or Accent. For example, we might be able to do English accents for Southern American, Eastern American, British, Irish, Scotch, and Australian. We might also be able to do accents for other languages or ethnicities such as Russian, Japanese, Mexican and Italian.

Cradle Phrases can be used to support character voices. These are words and sayings that such a character is known to use. For example, a cowboy might say "Howdy, ma'am", and a Frenchman could say "Oui, oui, monsieur."

Vocal Skills Exercises

Just for the moment, let's accept the proposition that 93% of the meaning we transfer when speaking to another person comes from how we look and sound when we say the words. (Hey, even if it's less than that, say 50%, it's still critical). It's been said that the great acting coach, Stanislavski, used to ask something extraordinary from his actors. After learning their scripts, he required them to perform the entire play while saying no actual words. They were only allowed to use nonsense sounds, such as tra-la-la. Stanislavski wanted them to try to put across the entire meaning through their stage movements and the sounds of their speech. Following are some exercises designed to help develop communication skills while reading text.

   1.   Eyes Right.   One problem to overcome can be the tendency to read one word at a time, rather than in phrases. For this exercise we mark a piece of copy with vertical slash marks at all unpunctuated phrase breaks. We hold the right index finger in the center of each line for visual reference, moving the finger down as each line is read. We keep the eyes reading a full phrase ahead of the one being spoken. We read for only 1 second and look away for 4, speaking the memorized phrase(s). Then, 1 second before finishing the memorized phrase(s), we look back at the copy for 1 more second and read ahead again. The goal is to look at the script only about 1 second in 5, which forces us to speak the copy in phrases.

   2.   Chat and Read.   Sometimes, such as in a radio or TV broadcast or a telemarketing conversation, the communicator must mix purely adlib live talk with vocal interpretation of a written script. The listener should not be able to tell when one ends and the other begins. This exercise lasts approximately thirty seconds. For the first ten seconds, we speak adlib. For example, we talk about something seen on television the previous evening. Then we read ten seconds of copy. Finally, we adlib for ten seconds more. The goal is to make the vocal delivery sound exactly the same for both our adlib conversation and our vocal interpretation of the written copy.

CRITIQUE SHEET: VOCAL PERFORMANCE TECHNIQUES

NAME: _____ DATE: _____ SCORE: _____

I. PITCH
_____ A. Use All Three Registers (Thirds of Voice): Lower, Middle, Upper
_____ B. Habitual Pitch (Normal = 1/3 Up in Lower Register; doe, ray, me)
_____ C. Use HP More Often (Note should "run through" voice)
_____ D. Use More Notes Overall (Feeling of different note every syllable)
_____ E. Use Wider Melodic Intervals (Distance between notes)
_____ F. Melody Must Make Sense with Message
_____ G. Avoid "Patterned" Speech (Same note sequence repeated often)
_____ H. Vary Dynamics in Pitch (Long = Intonation, Short = Inflection)

II. INTENSITY
_____ A. Relax! Undue Tension Tightens Your Vocal Instrument
_____ B. Sit or Stand Straight to Maintain Proper Shape of Instrument
_____ C. Lower Notes Resonate in Throat and Chest Cavities (Chest Voice)
_____ D. Higher Notes Should Resonate in Cavities of Head (Head Voice)
_____ E. Support Voice from Diaphragm, NOT Throat
_____ F. "Project" More (Maximum phonation for minimum air passage)
_____ G. Vary Dynamics in Intensity (Crescendo, Decrescendo, Stress)
_____ H. Connecting Words Normally Unstressed (a, and, the, of, to, etc.)

III. PAUSES
_____ A. Errors in Lengths of Pauses
        1. Quarter-Beat: Non-punctuated Phrase Break
        2. Half-Beat: Comma
        3. Full-Beat: Period or Other Punctuation Mark
        4. Longer Than Full-Beat: Dramatic Purposes
_____ B. Too Many Pauses. Normally Taken Only at Phrase Breaks
_____ C. Too Few Pauses. Take More Pauses for Better Timing
_____ D. Use Shorter Sentences
_____ E. Use More Down Inflection/Pause Sequences for Easier Understanding.

IV. PACING
_____ A. Stumbles! Slow Down Rate of Speech, and Pace Deliberately
_____ B. Rate of Speech Too (Circle)   Fast   Slow
_____ C. Attack (Of Beginning Sound): Too (Circle) Harsh, Gentle, Slow, Fast
_____ D. Release: Holding Too Long (Ending Sound) of Word: _____
_____ E. Pacing Too Steady
_____ F. Pacing Too Irregular

V. ARTICULATION
_____ A. Vowel Error(s): Substitutn, Omiss, Distortn (Git, Jist, Fer, Etc.) _____
_____ B. Consonant Error(s): Sub, Om, Dist (Hunderd, Drop G, Etc.) _____

VI. GRAMMAR/VOCABULARY
_____ A. Inappropriate Use of Slang Words/Phrases _____
_____ B. Mispronunciation(s) _____

Chapter Fifteen: The Subtext - More than Words

The term *subtext* refers to perceptual superimposition. For our purposes, we'll divide the subtext into the tactical and the strategic. We use performing arts terms in this chapter that work well for our goal, which is to clearly and concisely explain some fundamental concepts of constructing and performing characters. Other names for similar ideas may be used elsewhere but ultimately they've probably all been adapted from what Stanislavski taught more than a century ago.

Subtext adds layers to the literal meaning of words much like computer programs are used to superimpose layers of varying transparency above or below primary graphic and video files.

If we're not aware of our subtext, we can sometimes unintentionally communicate the wrong things. For instance, in performing during a commercial, meeting someone in the business office, holding a staff meeting, or talking on a sales call, we might wish to be perceived as friendly, concerned, and helpful. However, some unintended communication signal could cause the other person to perceive us differently. We might accidentally come across as aloof, opinionated, pushy, nervous, uncertain, or uncommitted.

We've said it before and it bears repeating. In spoken communication, words are not meaning. Words *carry* meaning. To illustrate, an elementary stress exercise in a three-word sentence reveals three entirely different meanings. (DRIVE home now. Drive HOME now. Drive home NOW.)

Objectives, Strategies, and Tactics

Communication objectives are our overall goals such as entertaining, informing, gaining information, influencing thought, changing behavior, negotiating, or closing a sale. Our strategic elements may be expressed in terms of the underlying thoughts, observations, feelings, and needs that we want to transfer. Tactical communication involves the specific physical techniques that we'll use.

Tactical Subtext

The tactical subtext is superimposed within how we look, what we do, and the short-term sounds of what we say. It involves the vocal skills detailed in Chapter Fourteen, plus sensory and emotional transfer through our facial expressions, bodily positions, and movements. In this book, we'll refer to each tactical component that we use as a *pulse*. We'll write pulses of tactical subtext on the copy above the text, using symbols like punctuation marks, pause slashes, stress underlines, and intonation arrows. We may also want to jot down some reminder notes regarding facial expressions, bodily positions, and movements.

Strategic Subtext

The strategic subtext is superimposed within our physical activities, plus in the longer-term sound of our text by employing enhanced or substituted meaning. This additional meaning could be a complementary message that reinforces the literal meaning of the words being spoken, or a contra-textual message such as sarcasm that replaces the literal textual meaning. For illustration, let's use the phrase *"You did that just perfectly."* A complementary example might be *"I really appreciate your skill."* Contra-textual subtext could be *"You really screwed that up"*. In our practice here, strategic subtext is written in the margin beside the copy.

Spine of a Character

The *spine* is the backbone of a character's role. We'll refer to it as the combination of two things: the superobjective and the through-action. The *superobjective* is the driving motivation that influences the character's thoughts and intentions. The *through-action* is an overriding pattern of behavior that impacts the character's activities. The through-action helps the character accomplish the superobjective.

Circumstances of a Character

The *circumstances* of a character are the conditions under which he or she exists at a given time. These include the following:

Setting
>Atmosphere
>Place
>Time
>Event

Physical traits and conditions
Mental traits and conditions
Relationships to others
Objectives
>Physical/Material
>Mental/Emotional

Obstacles

For some types of marketing scripts, we build a plot. The fundamental elements of it, or of any other plot for that matter, include our *characters*, their *objectives*, the *obstacles* that are in the way, and the *resolution*. As a performer, we want to play our role convincingly, so we need to particularize the circumstances and personalize the character.

The dictionary defines *particularize* as meaning "to give particular details and to be specific." We begin by defining, visualizing, and feeling the setting. It begins with the atmosphere, which refers to both the weather and the mood. We might have a sunny day, a stormy night, fog, euphoria, depression, enthusiasm, or a feeling of electricity. What is the place and time? Where are the character(s)? Are they in the city? Are they in the country? Are they at work? Are they at home? Are they in a supermarket checkout line? Are they stuck in traffic on the freeway? What event is going on? Are they at a grand opening of a new store? Are they waiting for a concert to begin? Are they watching a sporting event? Are they driving home from work?

To *personalize* characters is to personify the fictitious. We need to know them and understand how they'd react in a given situation. As in real life, we initially mentally assign characteristics to them. Later, we might modify these as we get to know the character better.

Now let's consider conditions. In addition to traits, it's important to know our characters' physical and mental states. *Physical conditions* include things like being tired, hungry, hot, cold, and any other helpful or handicapping qualities. *Mental conditions* can include being irritated, angry, excited, sad, drunk, or any other state of mind.

What is the character's *relationship* to the other people in the scene? If we're in a commercial or marketing presentation with another person, our relationship to that person will color how we say what we say. For example, our approach may be very different with our employer than with our honey.

We also need to know each character's objectives. *Physical* objectives can include things like eating, sleeping, romance, or better health. *Material* goals include anything in terms of possessions. *Mental* goals can include looking for self-esteem or status. *Emotional* objectives include joy, satisfaction, revenge, or any other emotions.

Obstacles are things impeding a character's ability to accomplish objectives. Characters become more interesting when we not only construct goals for them to achieve, but stick obstacles in their way. The audience becomes interested in seeing how they overcome these challenges to achieve *resolution*.

Unit Objectives, Intentions, Actions and Activities

In this book we use the term *psychophysical communication*, which just means that the sum total of what we communicate comes from the interaction of the mind/body system. So let's break this into two components which are, um, mental and physical. Mentally, our objectives are met by systematically accomplishing each planned intention. Physically, our actions are comprised of activities whose smaller parts are pulses.

We'll break down the time blocks of each scene into *units*. Each unit has an objective. One marketing example of a unit could be the product demonstration in a two-minute content video that we'll upload to our website. Another example might be the body copy section of a 60-second radio spot.

Unit objectives are accomplished in strategic segments, using what we'll call *intentions of the moment*. One example of a *moment* could be the assembly during the product demonstration unit in the previous paragraph. Another might be the differentiation phase of the body copy unit in the above paragraph's 60-second radio spot.

A character acts in pulses of activity according to each intention of the moment. Intentions can be stated in internal or external terms. To state it internally we focus on ourselves, using the first person narrative. To state it externally we use the second or third person narrative in terms of you, he, she, they or it.

Here's an example of an externally stated intention: *"He's bragging like a jerk."* As an internally stated intention, it could be *"I can do that better than he can."* Another externally stated intention is *"This will be tremendous!"* To state that internally, we might say *"I'll feel great!"* Here's a final example of an external intention: *"He'll finally make it happen!"* Stated internally, this could be *"I'll make him so embarrassed!"*

Here's how activities, actions, intentions and objectives work together. A character goes into action as the result of an objective. Each moment of a unit involves a single thought, so every thought change brings a different moment. Intentions are the thoughts and feelings that cause our activities to change from moment to moment. The combined intentions of the moments define our strategic path. Activities accomplish intentions, adding up to the action to meet the unit objective.

Bringing Scripts to Life

Sometimes we write our own script. Other times we're required to interpret a script written by someone else. In either case it's our portrayal of the intentions, along with our approach to the tactics of accomplishing them, that makes our performance unique. No other person can duplicate the individual shading that we bring to the role. The copy lives through our personality.

Superobjectives and Through-Actions

Personality scripting involves considering our characters' superobjectives and through-actions as we're defining our units and constructing objectives. We break each unit down into individual intentions and activities that fit a character's superobjective.

For example, if the character's superobjective is to get the girl, then most every action is designed to put him in a position to impress her. He's always doing things for her and buying her gifts. If our character is a boxer whose superobjective is to be the best prizefighter in the world, then he's constantly trying to get into peak physical condition, and to meet promoters who can get him the better fights.

Here are a few more examples of superobjectives and through-actions. Let's say a person wants to be a U.S. Senator. He's always trying to meet influential people and build a political base. Or, if our character's father had been murdered in front of her eyes when she was a child, then she could be obsessed with finding the person who did it. She's continually digging for more details of the case and tracking down leads that no one else ever followed.

Meter: The Flow of Our Performance

We'll use the term *meter* to refer to the flow of activities in achieving action. A good metric aid is to tap our foot, or to keep a finger acting as a metronome. Meter happens from moment to moment.

When we stumble we should try to recover on beat. If this is happening when we speak, we probably need to slow our rate of speech. Then we can practice both our adlib lines and scripted copy until we can perform each at the required speed without stumbling.

At any given time, a character has a *tempo*. This varies with the *rhythm* of the setting, which is substantially different in various situations. For example, the rhythm of a funeral could be slow, tentative, and remorseful. It's a world away from a Super Bowl party where things are fast-paced, spontaneous, and the beer is flowing freely.

Being In Character

A good personality doesn't just mimic a character. He or she *becomes* the character. Appropriately, this is called *being in character*. Once we mentally become a character, we shouldn't *break character* by going back and forth between our real self and the character, popping in and out of the role. For example, if we use a name other than our given name in a marketing performance such as a demonstration video, we should have others refer to us only by that character's name throughout the entire production, even between takes.

It's sometimes helpful to try to keep our character physically *centered*. This centering is a psychophysical concept assigning a part of the body as a thought-focus. This might be referred to as an imaginary, emotional, or motive center. To better understand and feel the center, we consider the character's outlook, feelings, perceptions, and motivations.

For example, a character with an abnormality may become very self-conscious about, and therefore focused on, the affected area of the body. If she has a scarred lip, she may feel that people tend to look at her mouth rather than into her eyes. A person who has rotten teeth may try to keep his upper lip low, covering his teeth when he talks. When he smiles, it's with his lips closed. A well-endowed woman may wish people looked at her face all the time, but gets irritated when she knows where they're actually looking when her eyes are turned away.

An exceptionally tall person may habitually stoop in order to try to become closer to the height of others nearby. What we all want most is what we don't have.

Clichés often grow from truth. So a cynical character might literally speak out of the side of his or her mouth. If our character becomes sentimental and wants to smooch, the center of that character might move to the lips. A weight lifter could be centered in the pectorals, with a booming, chesty voice. If our character is a frequent beer drinker, (s)he could be centered around a big stomach, saying "Hey, I've got a lot of money invested in this belly." A busybody could be centered in the ears, always leaning the side of the head toward a conversation between others, hoping to pick up a little gossip. A socialite could be centered with the nose upturned in a better-than-thou attitude.

Sample Ad Copy Marked for Subtext

Following is some sample ad copy from the Radio Advertising Bureau. Their base copy has been modified for our client and subtext has been added. In the copy, underlines represent words receiving stress, and forward slash marks (/) represent unpunctuated phrase breaks that receive ¼ beat pauses. This particular piece of copy is primarily based in emotion, rather than logic or intellect. In other words, it's institutional copy that talks about some feelings of a customer and associates them with the bank. It doesn't focus on specific products and services of the bank.

The final page of this chapter contains a Subtext Prep Sheet.

Subtext	Fourteenth National Bank
Relatives are silly.	Everyone who mattered /was there. And everyone there/ was a clown….making faces, funny noises, and doing whatever else people do/ whenever there's a baby around.
Mom and Dad are pretty cool.	A baby…with the tender, soft eyes of its Mother, the proud set jaw of its Father,
Everybody's bonding.	And, according to every relative in the room, something of theirs. Grandma's nose, Grandpa's mouth, Uncle So-and-So's ears, and on and on.
This could get confusing.	Until you might wonder…Does the poor child/ have anything of its own?
I'm so proud.	It does. It has a future. For this baby, born somewhere in the United States today, or maybe tomorrow, is destined to be/ our future President.
Wait 'til you hear this!	And the baby…is a GIRL!
The future is in good hands.	Youth…part of the tradition/ that this country was built on. And will continue to build on…the tradition of strength.
We're proud to be part of your future.	Today, Fourteenth National Bank/ upholds that tradition…because if you can build a nation on it, you can build a bank on it. Fourteenth National Bank…a tradition of strength, when money matters. Member FDIC.

SUBTEXT PREP SHEET
Character Construction

Physical
- Age _____
- Height _____
- Weight _____
- Hair _____
- Clothing _____
- Physical Condition _____

Mental
- Outlook _____
- Mood _____
- Perceptions _____

Relationship to Others _____

Emotions _____

Affective Memories
- Emotional Recall(s) _____
- Sense Memories
  - See _____
  - Hear _____
  - Feel _____
  - Smell _____
  - Taste _____

Spine
- Super-objective _____
- Through-action _____

Setting
- Atmosphere _____
- Place _____
- Time _____
- Event _____

Mark Copy for Stress and for Phrase Breaks

Vocal Approach
- Physical Tension (1 – 7) _____   Habitual Pitch _____
- Range _____   Intensity/Quality _____
- Rate of Speech _____   Tempo _____

Psychophysical Elements
- Movements _____
- Facial Expressions _____

Unit Objective _____

Required Action _____

Obstacles(s) _____

Intentions of the Moments (Write in Copy Margin, Left of Text.)

Chapter Sixteen: Becoming the Part with Characterization

It's been said that character is what we do when no one is watching. Well, *characterization* is what we do when someone *is* watching. Our very believability begins with our characterization, because other people perceive us through the traits we convey. Sometimes it's okay to act out our part based mostly on physical planning. Maybe we're doing a video voiceover where we aren't seen. Perhaps we're on the radio, doing an audio podcast, or someplace else where the audience can't see us at all. Or maybe we're visible, but the audience can't see us up close. So they really can't tell if we're overplaying or underplaying a bit.

But that's not the case in personal selling. There, our prospect is an arm's length away. And if we're on-camera in a video, our viewer can see us that close or even closer. In short, in some situations we can't just *act* the part. We have to *be* the part. Sure, we still need to do all of our physical planning. But even more importantly, we should define exactly what we want others to perceive and then be absolutely true in our performance. We can't *pretend* to feel the subtext. We have to actually feel it.

What we perceive to be real becomes so, according to our point of view. Someone once said that whether the glass is half empty or half full depends on whether we're drinking or pouring. In performance, as in real life, reality exists from a point of perception.

Videographers and cinematographers use the principle that if something is in the picture, it exists. If it's not in the picture, it doesn't. We've said it before and it bears repeating. In any of the various media channels, human reception comes through some or all of the following: sight, sound, and emotional feelings. For those of us who are physically present with our receiver, we may also transmit in terms of physical touch, smell, and taste.

In order to begin to influence the perception that other people have of us, we first have to define what we *want* it to be. We reveal it to others through what we say and what we do. Our actions and our dialogue transmit it, with or without our consent. So, characterization is simply the process of identifying and transmitting traits. Trait analysis is the first step. We look at ourselves, other people, things, or animals and decide on some traits that we want to reveal. Characterization involves two fundamental steps: character construction and character portrayal.

The first, *character construction*, means that we look for qualities that could exist for a character of the type to be portrayed. A trait list is drawn up, often using human models. Animals and inanimate objects may also be used. For instance, a character might be modeled after analysis of an athlete, a cougar, a river, or all of the above.

The second step is *character portrayal*. This means we have to effectively reveal our character and message to others through the five human channels. First, we make sure that what we say is consistent with those traits. Then we decide how we'll use our voice. Next, we plan our non-verbal communication. This involves our facial expressions, our bodily movements, and sometimes even the way we touch others such as our handshake or a hug. And if we're seeing someone up close and personal, as in a business office or in personal selling, we must also be conscious of how we smell. One fast way to leave a bad impression is to forget to use antiperspirant on a hot, humid day. Another is to have bad breath, which communicates not only through the "smell" channel but can actually leave a bad taste in the other person's mouth.

In the psychophysical mind/body system, actions create feelings and feelings lead to actions. If we plan and perform well, others will be more likely to perceive what we intend to communicate.

Building a Mental Image

Building a characterization first involves forming our own crystal clear visualization of the character. Once we've identified the key traits, we get in character by thinking and acting as if we had them. As a small-town teenager suddenly finding himself working with Dick Clark, who was the biggest promoter in rock and roll at the time, I was intimidated. So I said "Mr. Clark, I'm just a kid from Springhill, Louisiana. I don't know what to do around all these rock stars." He said "Michael, wherever you are just act like you're supposed to be there." That was one of the best lessons I've ever learned. It means that whenever we play any role, we leave our own traits and insecurities behind. We just act and think like the character that we want to portray in order to have believability.

We can apply that philosophy to our lives in general. Our thoughts literally create us, and our life becomes what we *think* it to become. Circumstances may create some of our thoughts, but mostly it's the other way around. Religious leaders and philosophers have been telling us for centuries that we're simply the physical manifestation of what we allow our minds to think about.

Let's peek back into our Psychology 101 textbook. Our self-image was formed initially in the first few years of our lives. As children, we believed what others told us about ourselves. If our parents and other significant people in our lives said that we were good looking or smart, we believed it. On the other hand, if they claimed that we were ugly or stupid we believed that, too. So we began our lives with an initial image of our worth and potential based on what others told us throughout our early childhood years. Later, though the inner child remains, we learned to adjust our self-image based on our own experiences in life.

And just like us, our characters are the products of their minds. When we're building a character, one of the first things we need to do is to define the character's life experiences and the resulting traits. Then we can create a visualization based on those plus the character's present circumstances. One helpful tool is to write a *backstory* that describes a brief history of and a typical day in the life of our character. This can be done for both the character that we're portraying and for the one with whom we're trying to communicate, such as a marketing prospect.

Defining, Scripting, and Portraying Characters

Repetition establishes traits. The fact that a character has said or done something once doesn't make it a trait. It becomes a trait when it's said or done repeatedly.

Character Construction

In building our character, we'll look at five major trait categories: Physical, Mental, Emotional, Speech, and Social. Each of these categories is listed below, with some examples of traits that could be used in character definition. The list given is just a foundation that can be added to over time. A great resource for this is the book *Building Believable Characters* (Marc McCutcheon, Writer's Digest Books, Cincinnati, 1996).

Physical

    Age
    Height
    Weight
    Body Type
    Physical Condition (Thin, overweight, fit, athletic, etc.)
    Posture
    Ethnicity
    Clothing Worn
    Grooming
    Hair
    Facial Expressions
    Bodily Movements
    Mannerisms
    Gestures
    Physical Abilities

Mental

General Personality Type
Temperament
Wit & Charm
Habits
Quirks
Strengths
Weaknesses
Areas of Expertise

Emotional

Attitudes
Psychological Issues
Outlook
Feelings
Perceptions
Prejudices
Phobias

Speech

Sound
> Pitch
> Intensity
> Pauses
> Pacing

Topics
> Work
> Politics
> Kids
> Religion
> Neighbors
> Politics

Social

Vocational
Avocations (Sports, Hobbies, Interests, etc.)
Favorite Pastimes

Lifestyle
Relationships
Goals
Motivating Forces
Obstacles
Professional Achievements
Virtues
Bad Habits
Vices

The choice of a name is important in making the character relatable and memorable, particularly if we're constructing a character that we'll use regularly. It's hard to imagine Progressive Insurance's *Flo* by any other name. Our characters may exhibit some weaknesses, flaws, and vulnerabilities in order to make them seem more human.

Character Modeling

We can model our characters internally or externally. *Internal* character modeling means taking a look at our own attributes, perceptions and memories.

External character modeling could utilize the traits of other persons. In using human models, we might remember or read about other people, or we could go out and watch them. A good observation exercise is to go to a busy place such as an airport terminal. As we look at people passing by, we can assign characteristics to them from a traits list or write down other things that we might observe or imagine in them.

Other good external character-modeling sources are inanimate objects and animals. We can start by naming some associated characteristics. Perhaps we'd study a couch, a highway, a truck, a lion or a squirrel. We could say that someone is as sharp as a razor. We might use an analogy saying *"He's like a snake. He slithers around, hissing, and spreading his venomous lies."* We could base a character on a horse. Its torso is sleek with well-defined muscles, so we could have our character wear something to showcase that. The horse has strong but thin legs plus a hairy mane on top of its long neck. Perhaps it's a Tennessee Walker with a peculiar gait. It makes a deep-throated whinny. All of these traits could easily be assigned to a human character. Here are a few examples of other animals that could be used as models for human characterizations: a turtle, gorilla, eagle, vulture, bulldog, frog, and alligator. A good exercise is to think about each of these and write down traits that could be assigned to a human.

Portraying Characters

Okay, *constructing* the character was the easy part. Now we have to play the role. In portraying our character, some major tools are:

> Tension and Muscle Memory
> Concentration
> Affective Memory
> Circle of Attention
> Public Solitude
> Truth (Naiveté)
> Imagination
> Visualization
> Vocal Techniques
> Body Position and Bodily Movements
> Facial Expressions

Some items in the above list are detailed elsewhere in this book. Of those remaining, perhaps truth is the most important concept. This refers to naiveté like that with which a child plays a role. No one has to teach a child how to play. We were born with acting ability. One of the most convincing performances we'll ever see could involve a four-year-old pretending to talk to Dad on the telephone. She exhibits total belief in the reality of the toy phone, and complete concentration on what she "hears" her father saying through the earpiece. She answers imaginary questions with conviction.

As adults, we can also practice improvisational exercises. They can help us remember how to perform with the truth of a child, and can also assist us in developing our adlib abilities.

247

Another tool is tension…good old tightness in our muscles or the lack thereof. As discussed in Chapter Fourteen, our tension levels range from total relaxation as when we're about to faint to maximum tightening of the body as in a state of terror or rage. Let's try an exercise, beginning with complete relaxation at level 1. We then totally tense the body to its maximum at level 7, over a time period of about 35 seconds. Every 5 seconds or so, we note the difference in our muscular tension level. We try to commit each position to muscle memory.

Athletes in every sport depend on muscle memory as an integral part of what they do. The golfer calls on it for his or her swing. The quarterback needs muscle memory to know how much exertion will make the ball fly the precise distance to the pass receiver. Dancers and musicians rely on it for the movements of their legs and fingers. And in our communication performances each of our movements should have a purpose, being gauged and timed appropriately.

As we begin doing characterization exercises, we should practice *concentration*. This is total belief in the reality of our props and the imaginary things that are happening around us. We should also practice a concept called the circle of attention and another called public solitude. In utilizing the *circle of attention*, we mentally construct a protective shield around ourselves and create a reality inside the resulting bubble. Inside it, we're not distracted by reality. All imaginary objects inside our bubble become real, and all reality outside becomes non-existent. The concept is similar with *public solitude*. Here, we develop the ability to do very private things in public. For example, if we're called upon as a performer to do a love scene, we must be able to do it in front of others as if no one else is there except our partner. We have to sound and look truthfully loving and passionate.

Affective Memory and Imagination

When we perform, *affective memory* is sense memory combined with emotional recall. *Imagination* is affective memory plus truth. Our work with imagination will begin with sense memory.

248

Sense Memory

Sense memory refers to the ability to recall sensations experienced by the five senses. If we're going to stimulate the senses of others, we first have to learn to stimulate our own using just our minds, because it's hard to transfer feelings that we don't have. We learn to actually feel what we think, and this starts with simple physical sensations.

An easy place to begin is with a coffee cup. We pick up an empty one and try to experience the sensation of heat on our fingers as we hold it. Next, we might put a small pillow on our lap and treat it as if it's a puppy. At the dinner table, we could eat some mashed potatoes and use our sense memory to experience the taste of ice cream. We could take a mop and turn it into a dance partner. Once we've practiced some simple feelings like those above, we can try thinking in terms of the more complex sensations of atmospheres. First, let's imagine that we're sitting in the warm sunshine and remember how the heat feels. Then we'll mentally move into the rain, recalling the experience of having our clothes and hair wet with water running down our face.

Performance Triads

Musicians work with chords. These are built on triads, which are a combination of three notes. Let's work with some performance triads using our own three-note chords. We'll practice this simple building block for an elementary performance: atmosphere, object, and activity.

To begin, let's place ourselves in a steamy bathroom. We'll use our index finger as a toothbrush and brush our teeth. Next, let's put ourselves in a graveyard on a misty, overcast day. Our ink pen will become a flower that we'll place on the headstone of our friend's grave.

A list of some simple performance triads is provided on the next page. After that is a sheet on which we can build triad elements and then perform these very basic scenes. Following the sense memory triad exercises we'll discuss the other element of affective memory, which is emotional recall.

Atmospheres
1. In a long checkout line, irritated
2. In front of a computer screen, engrossed
3. On a barstool in a pub, drunk
4. In a hot kitchen
5. At home, in a hurry to watch football game
6. In an artist's studio, in front of easel
7. In a doctor's office, waiting for intravenous blood sample
8. In front of flaming residence, possible children inside
9. Football player on sidelines, behind in fourth quarter
10. In photography studio with beautiful model
11. In a basement beneath a burst pipe spraying water
12. In driver's seat of large truck (semi)

Objects
1. Carton of milk
2. Keyboard
3. Glass of beer
4. Skillet and spatula
5. Remote control
6. Paint brush/pallet
7. Shirtsleeve (rolling up)
8. Fire hose
9. Helmet
10. Camera
11. Pipe wrench
12. Gearshift lever

Activities
1. Lay the carton on checkout counter, write check
2. Type in copy, make corrections
3. Take drink, spill on bar
4. Make omelet
5. Changing channels to try to find game
6. Painting on canvas on easel
7. Having needle inserted in vein
8. Pulls off truck, attaches to hydrant
9. Puts on helmet, snaps chin strap.
10. Sets camera down, frames photos with hands.
11. Tighten the leaky connection
12. Look in rearview mirror, and back truck into tight spot.

Performance Triad Exercises

Atmosphere:

Object:

Activity:

Atmosphere:

Object:

Activity:

Atmosphere:

Object:

Activity:

Emotional Recall

The next element in affective memory is *emotional recall*. In our practice chart for psychophysical communication, 4 conditions and 30 emotions are listed. In the exercises below we'll utilize emotions that are not listed there, in order to avoid duplication.

An internal approach to feeling and transferring emotions depends on emotional recall. This is simply reaching back in our past and recalling a situation that made us feel the particular emotion. The exercise below is designed to help develop this technique. We write, using sensory language, a short essay of one page or less describing the experience. Then we name the story and remember it sufficiently so that just thinking the name of the story will give us a clear enough mental picture of the memory to lead us to feel the recall of the emotion. Here are ten emotions for this exercise, with definitions from Funk and Wagnall's Standard Desk Dictionary.

Passion: an intense, extreme, or overpowering feeling; hardened affection or love, with intense sexual desire or lust; an outburst of strong feeling, such as overwhelming anger or rage.

Ecstasy: the state of being beside oneself through overpowering emotion; intense delight or rapture.

Inspiration: the infusion or arousal within the mind of some idea, feeling, or impulse, especially one that leads to creative action.

Empathy: the intellectual or imaginative apprehension of another's condition or state of mind.

Despair: utter hopelessness and discouragement that leaves the mind apathetic or numb.

Jealousy: fearfulness or suspiciousness of being displaced by a rival in affections or favors; vindictiveness toward another because of supposed or actual rivalry.

Greed: selfishness in grasping for possession.

Sympathy: the quality of being affected by the state of another's feelings, correspondent in kind; grief or pain awakened by the misfortunes of others.

Anguish: excruciating mental or bodily pain; agony, torture.

Pride: a proper sense of personal dignity and worth.

Body Language

Body language can transmit meaning through our planned or involuntary movements, poses, and gestures. In terms of *bodily movements*, one important consideration is that every individual occupies *personal space*. The amount required depends on the relationship between the individuals involved. We can create an irritating, aggressive, or threatening situation with someone simply by invading this space. And rapid or aggressive movements can cause a defensive reaction. Or on the flipside, we could communicate rejection or apprehension by remaining too far away. Examples of *bodily positions* or *poses* that communicate feeling are slumping, relaxing, arms open and welcoming, or arms crossed. *Gestures* are also tremendous communication tools. One example is to raise our hands in a protective, aggressive, invasive, or threatening way. Or if we shake our fist, scratch our head, or put our hands on our hips our message can be very clear.

Facial Expressions

Charles Darwin believed that facial expression is a form of communication that's innate. He said that humans are born with the ability to understand some basic facial expressions, and that these make up a universal language.

Facial expressions can be planned in order to assist communication. We sometimes communicate unintentionally through spontaneous facial expressions. Even though we've learned to use sophisticated social masks, facial expressions quite often reveal what we're actually thinking and how we really feel. These can come from emotions or they can involve our present state of being, such as pain or exhaustion.

One fine book on this topic is *The Artist's Complete Guide to Facial Expressions* (Gary Faigin, Watson-Guptill Publications, New York, 2008), which explores them for the artist who draws. This book grew from his studies with actors, painters, sculptors, and others. It also leans heavily on the work of a leading authority on facial expressions, Paul Ekman, Ph.D., who's a professor of psychology at the University of California Medical School. Ekman's book *Emotions Revealed, 2nd*

Edition (Times Books, Henry Holt and Company, New York, 2007) provides an in-depth study of how emotions are conveyed through facial expressions. Ekman identifies six basic emotions as the only ones that are universally recognized purely from facial expressions. They are:

Sadness
Anger
Disgust
Surprise
Fear
Joy

Faigin says that these six basic expressions can be varied in their intensity and combined in different ways to create the expression of any emotion. For example fear might be combined with surprise, or anger might be combined with disgust. Mixing the fundamental facial expressions works in the same way that combining the red, green and blue in our RGB video model can create any color on a screen.

Our face continually changes according to what we're feeling and thinking, communicating our feelings and thoughts to others. Faigin points out that there are over twenty muscles in the face, and about half of them serve no other purpose than facial expression. Meaning is imparted facially by the positions of the brows, the eyelids, the nostrils, and the lips. While most muscles in our body pull on bones, the facial expression muscles pull on the skin. Very small movements of these muscles can create large changes in facial expression. As we age, we develop permanent wrinkles created by our repeated facial expressions.

All parts of the face are involved to some degree in facial expressions, but the two biggest areas of expression are the eyes and the mouth. The nose is sometimes involved as a major contributor, in expressions such as fear or rage that involve flaring the nostrils.

When we speak of the eyes in facial expressions, we include the brows and the eyelids. In fact, the eye itself doesn't change much during expression. It's the interaction of the eyelids and the brows that reveal emotion. For instance, let's take the thought *What do you mean?* To help communicate it, we could raise the outside of only one of our two brows. To convey a feeling of distress, we might raise the innermost part of one brow. Brow lifting can be used to communicate lots of things. For illustration try fear, surprise, and sadness.

Psychophysical Communication Planning

As mentioned earlier in this chapter, the term *psychophysical* refers to the interaction of the mind and body, with each influencing the other. Physically generated techniques can be used as learning tools, activating the mind/body system in order to more effectively feel and communicate the emotions and conditions that we intend to show.

The exercises on the next page detail a psychophysical plan of action for giving 34 different meanings to the sentence *"I have never met anyone like you in my life"* using different emotions and conditions. Of course, different performers will use other psychophysical strategies in communicating these. And we ourselves might portray the same emotions and conditions in varying ways at different times depending on the context. Therefore, this exercise is not to be considered a definitive way of portraying any of the emotions and conditions presented. Rather, this should be considered just a starting place for practice in building psychophysical plans of action for learning to intensely feel various emotions and conditions. Experimentation in both physical planning and emotional recall helps us perform more effectively.

255

Psychophysical Communication Exercise

SCRIPT: "I have never met anyone like you in my life."

EMOTION	A strong feeling impulsed to express	Tnsn	HP	RANGE	INTENSITY	RATE	PACE	POSITION/MOVEMENT	EXPRESSION
1. Sadness	**Sorrowfullness or depression in spirits.**	**2**	**Low**	**Mod**	**Sobbing**	**Med**	**Jerky**	**Look up, shake head**	**Face dark with pain**
Depression	Low spirits, deep dejection, withdrawal.	1	Low	Narrow	Whimpering	Slow	Irregular	Look down, shake head	Long-faced
Despondenc	Paralyzing despair, coupled w/deep sorrow	2	Upr	Wide	Strained	Med	Sing-Songy	Raise hands helplessly	Stare catatonically
Shame	Painful sense of guilt and degradation.	2	Upr	Wide	Breathy	Slow	Deliberate	Look away from eye contct	Smile self-consciously
Sorrow	Pain/distress because of loss or misfortune.	2	Low	Mod	Crying	Med	Jerky	Put hands behind neck	Downtrodden
Grief	Deep sorrow caused by loss/remorse/affliction	3	Mid	Wide	Cracking	Slow	Deliberate	Shake head in disbelief	Eyelids half-closed/frwng
2. Anger	**Sudden and strong displeasure and antagonism.**	**14**	**Low**	**Narrow**	**Harsh**	**Fast**	**Deliberate**	**Aggressive movements**	**Mouth scowling**
Rage	Extreme violence, wrath, anger and fury.	15	Upr	Wide	Shreiking	Fast	Deliberate	Sahke fist violently	Wide-eyed, flaring nstrls
Trepidation	A state of agitation, alarm, or perterbation.	10	Low	Wide	Fuming	Fast	Deliberate	Run hands through hair	Eyes darting
3. Disgust	**Feelings of repulsion, loathing, or nausea.**	**8**	**Low**	**Wide**	**Hissing**	**Med**	**Deliberate**	**Put hands on hips**	**Scorching**
Agitation	A feeling of trepidation, alarm, or perterbation	6	Low	Wide	Fuming	Fast	Deliberate	Run hands through hair	Glaring
Hate	An extreme feeling of dislike or animosity.	3	Upr	Wide	Hysterical	Fast	Deliberate	Point threateningly	Teeth clenched, lips tight
Indifference	Unconcerned, with no feeling or interest.	5	Low	Wide	Soft	Slow	Deliberate	Nod derisively, eyes up	Smirking
Conceit	Undue self-esteem; arrogance: overbearingness	12	Low	Wide	Snickering	Med	Deliberate	Cringe at the thought	Sneer
Resentment	Anger and ill will in view of wrong or injury	11	Mid	Wide	Taunting	Med	Deliberate	Slowly move head side-to-side	Mocking
Loathing	Great hatred, revulsion, or disgust.	8	Low	Wide	Hising	Slow	Deliberate	Purse lips	Scouring
4. Surprise	**A sudden state of astonishment.**	**12**	**Upr**	**Wide**	**Loud**	**Fast**	**Smooth**	**Recoil head**	**Widen eyes**
Disappointmt	Feeling of failure to fulfill desires/hopes	4	Low	Mod	Soft	Med	Irregular	Nod head side-to-side	Dejected
Shock	Sudden and severe agitation of the mind.	14	Upr	Narrow	Strangled	Fast	Stammering	Throw hands up	Mouth open widely
5. Fear	**Deep awe and dread of danger, trouble/terror**	**14**	**Upr**	**Narrow**	**Wailing**	**Fast**	**Jerky**	**Raise hands defensively**	**Eyebrows raised, mouth open**
Uneasiness	Unsettled/disturbing condition. Syn: disquiet	9	Low	Mod	Constricted	Fast	Stammering	Scratch neck nervously	Licking lips
Worry	Uneasiness of the mind; fretfullness.	9	Low	Mod	Moderate	Fast	Jerky	Bite nails	Eyes scan left to right
Horror	Extreme fear, repugnance, or dread.	15	Upr	Narrow	Screaming	Fast	Stammering	Hands raised straight up	Head shaking wildly
Concern	Troubled; affected with anxiety or interest.	6	Low	Mod	Moderate	Slow	Rhythmic	Chew lip nervously	Eyes searching
Compassion	Pity for another w/mercy and desire to help.	6	Low	Mod	Sobbing	Med	Jerky	Nod knowingly	Smile graciously
Desperation	Energized despair, reckless of consequences.	15	Upr	Mod	Maniacal	Fast	Irregular	Wave arms erratically	Wild-eyed
6. Joy	**Strong feeling of happiness/gladness/delight**	**12**	**Upr**	**Wide**	**Roaring**	**Fast**	**Rhythmic**	**Arms up and wide**	**Smiling broadly**
Love	Deep devotion or affection for another	3	Low	Nar	Breathy	Med	Rhythmic	Blink eyes suggestively	Stare adoringly
Affection	A fond attachment or kind feeling.	8	Low	Mod	Moderate	Fast	Rhythmic	Cross hands over chest	Eyes inviting
Desire	To wish or to long for. To ask for or crave.	8	Low	Mod	Moderate	Fast	Deliberate	Blink eyes, look up	Dreamy
CONDITION	**The state or mode of existence**	**Tnsn**	**HP**	**RANGE**	**INTENSITY**	**RATE**	**PACE**	**POSITION/MOVEMENT**	**EXPRESSION**
Drunk	Feeling faint, dizzy, weak, or swooning.	3	Low	Nar	Breathy	Slow	Sputtering	Rotating upper body slowly	Eyes unfocused, lids half closed
Fatigue	Weary as a result of physical/mental exertion	1	Low	Nar	Panting	Slow	Stammering	Slouch in seat, arms limp	Tongue out, eyes drooping
Composure	Calmness, serenity, and tranquility of mind.	7	Low	Mod	Moderate	Med	Regular	Posture confidently	Serenity
Pain	Physical suffering from sickness or injury	6	Low	Wide	Wheezing	Slow	Irregular	Look aside, shake head	Abandonment

About the Author

Michael has been a broadcaster since Marconi was a kid, with experience ranging from news reporter to disc jockey, account executive, program director, manager, and station owner. He has also done several thousand live onstage performances in bands, as an emcee, a mobile disc jockey and a karaoke host. As a teenager, he worked as a performer for Dick Clark on ABC-TV and on his touring show *The Dick Clark Caravan of Stars*. Michael has also acted in plays in college and community theatre, and worked for a time as a touring actor. His background in music and acting led him to write two books in the 1980's on training radio broadcasters. The industry's number one trade magazine, *Radio and Records*, called his first book "a cut above the rest." These texts were used in training programs at broadcast stations, schools and colleges in all 50 states and several foreign countries. For 19 years, Michael taught classes at the postsecondary level in broadcast performance, production, and marketing.

He has owned a variety of small businesses including, since 2004, Michael May Marketing, Inc. This is an advertising agency located in Billings, Montana that does media planning and buying plus radio and TV production and other marketing services for its clients.

Michael is a karaoke addict who points out that it's a good performance outlet for businesspeople that doesn't take much time, requires no preparation, and can be both fun and rewarding. And hey…if you need an excuse for a good cold beer, there it is.

He does a weekly radio show and is an instrument-rated private pilot whose favorite expression is *Go Broncos!*

His Facebook name is Michael Wayne May. Join him there at www.facebook.com/michaelwaynemay.

Email him at: michael@michaelwaynemay.com.

Resources and Recommended Reading

Philip Kotler and Gary Armstrong, *Principles of Marketing*, 15th Edition, Prentice Hall, Upper Saddle River, NJ, 2013.

Richard L. Sandhusen, *Marketing*, 4th Edition, Barron's, Hauppage, NY, 2008.

James E. Finch & James R. Ogden, *Principles of Marketing*, 6th Edition (Revised), Research & Education Association, Piscataway, NJ, 2013

Al Ries and Jack Trout, *Positioning: The Battle for Your Mind*, McGraw-Hill, New York, 2002

Rosser Reeves, *Reality in Advertising* , Knopf, New York, 1961

Alexander Hiam and Charles D. Schewe, *The Portable MBA in Marketing*, 2nd Edition, John Wiley & Sons, Inc., New York, 1998

Ronald D. Gesky, Sr., *Media Planning & Buying in the 21st Century*, 2nd Edition, 2020: Marketing Communications, LLC, Auburn Hills, MI 2013

Charles Futrell, *ABC's of Relationship Selling through Service*, 12th Edition, Irwin, Chicago, 2012

Stephen Castleberry & John Tanner, *Selling: Building Partnerships*, McGraw-Hill, New York, 2013

Walter J. Wessels, *Economics*, 5th Edition, Barron's, Hauppage, NY, 2012.

Lorrie Thomas, *The McGraw-Hill 36-Hour Course: Online Marketing*, McGraw-Hill, New York, 2011

Liana Evans, *Social Media Marketing*, Que Publishing, Indianapolis, 2010

B. J. Mendelson, *Social Media is Bullshit*, St. Martin's Press, New York, 2012

Robert Liljenwall, *The Power of Point-of-Purchase Advertising: Marketing at Retail*, Point-of-Purchase Advertising International, Washington, DC, 2004

Bob Stone and Ron Jacobs, *Successful Direct Marketing Methods*, 8th Edition, McGraw-Hill, New York, 2008

Robert W. Bly, *The Copywriter's Handbook*, 3rd Edition, St. Martin's Press, New York, 2005

Joseph Sugarman, *The Adweek Copywriter's Handbook*, (Wiley, 2006)

Richard Bayan, *Words That Sell*, Contemporary Books, Lincolnwood, IL, 2006

Joe Toplyn, *Comedy Writing for Late-Night TV* (Twenty Lane Media, Westchester, NY, 2014)

Gene & Linda Perret, *Comedy Writing Self-Taught Workbook* (Quill Driver Books, Sanger, CA, 2015)

Garrison Keillor, *Pretty Good Joke Book* (HighBridge Company, Prince Frederick, MD, 2009)

Pat Williams, *Winning with One-Liners* (HCI Books, Deerfield Beach, FL, 2002)

Louis Safian, *The Gargantuan Book of Insult, Offense, and Effrontery* (Skyhorse Publishing, New York, 2014)

Grant Tucker, *5,000 Sidesplitting Jokes and One-Liners* (Skyhorse Publishing, New York, 2013)

Geoff Tibbals, *The Mammoth Book of Jokes* (Running Press, Philadelphia, 2006)

Milton Berle, *Milton Berle's Private Joke File: Over 10,000 of His Best Gags, Anecdotes, and One-Liners* (Three Rivers Press, New York, 1992).

Milton Berle, *More of the Best of Milton Berle's Private Joke File: 10,000 of His Best Gags, Anecdotes, and One-Liners* (Three Rivers Press, New York, 1992).

Jane Imber and Betsy-Ann Toffler, *Dictionary of Marketing Terms*, 4th Edition, Barron's, Hauppage, NY, 2008.

Charles Doyle, *Dictionary of Marketing*, Oxford University Press, New York, 2011.

Dr. Abraham H. Maslow, *Motivation and Personality*, 3rd Edition, Longman, New York, 1987

Earl Nightingale, *The Strangest Secret*, Merchant Books, New York, 2013

Napoleon Hill, *Think and Grow Rich*, Tarcher/Penguin, New York, 2005

Sigmund Freud and A. A. Brill, *Wit and Its Relation to the Unconscious*, Dover, New York, 2011

Paul Ekman, Ph.D., *Emotions Revealed*, 2nd Edition, Holt Paperbacks, New York, 2007

Henry H. Calero, *The Power of Nonverbal Communication*, Silver Lake, Los Angeles, 2005

Gerald I. Nierenberg and Henry H. Calero, *How to Read a Person Like a Book*, Pocket Books, New York, 1990

Gary Faigin, *The Artist's Complete Guide to Facial Expressions,* 2nd Edition, Watson-Guptill Publications, New York, 2008

Julius Fast, *Body Language*, 2nd Edition, M. Evans and Company, New York, 2002

Constantin Stanislavski, *An Actor's Handbook*, Theatre Arts Books, New York, 2004

Constantin Stanislavski and Elizabeth Hapgood, *An Actor Prepares, 41st Printing*, Routledge/Theatre Arts Books, New York, 1988

Constantin Stanislavski and Elizabeth Hapgood, *Building a Character, 23st Printing*, Routledge/Theatre Arts Books, New York, 1994

Constantin Stanislavski, *Creating a Role*, Routledge/Theatre Arts Books, New York, 2014

Marc McCutcheon, *Building Believable Characters*, Writers Digest Books, Cincinnati, 1996

Anne Utterback, Ph.D., *Broadcast Voice Handbook*, 4th Edition, Taylor Trade Publishing, Lanham, MD, 2005

Grant Fairbanks, *Voice and Articulation Drillbook*, Joanna Cotler Books, New York, 1960

David Meerman Scott, *The New Rules of Marketing & PR*, 4th Edition, John Wiley & Sons, Hoboken, NJ, 2013

Andrew Macarthy, *500 Social Media Marketing Tips*, CreateSpace, 2013

Dave Kerpen, *Likeable Social Media*, McGraw-Hill, New York, 2011

Bob Lotich, *How to Make Money Blogging*, CreateSpace, 2013

Raymond E. Webster, Ph.D., *Introduction to Educational Psychology*, Research & Education Association (REA), Piscataway, NJ, 2006

Christine McCormick and Michael Pressley, *Educational Psychology*, Longman, New York, 1997

Sharan Merriam and Laura Bierema, *Adult Learning: Linking Theory and Practice,* Jossey-Bass, San Francisco, 2013.

Federal Aviation Administration, *Aviation Instructor's Handbook,* Aviation Supplies & Academics, Newcastle, WA, 2008

Steve Stockman, *How to Shoot Video That Doesn't Suck* , Workman Publishing, New York, 2011

D. Eric Franks, *Videopia,* Lulu Publishing, Raleigh, NC, 2009

Jim Owens and Gerald Millerson, *Video Production Handbook,* 5th Edition, Focal Press, New York, 2013

Barry Braverman, *Video Shooter,* 2nd Edition, Focal Press, New York, 2010

Douglas Spotted Eagle, *Vegas Pro 11 Editing Workshop,* Focal Press, New York, 2012

Steve Grisetti, *The Muvipix.com Guide to Photoshop Elements & Premiere Elements 12* (Muvipix.com, Amazon, 2013)

Index

3/4 Time Signature, 225
4/4 Time Signature, 224
4-P's of Marketing, 15
5-P's Personal Selling Model, 66
Ability, 26, 28, 29, 32, 41, 65, 71, 82, 109, 120, 169, 201, 217, 234, 247, 248, 249, 253
Acoustics, 193, 199
ADI, 102
Adobe After Effects, 191
Adobe Flash, 191
Advertisement Life Cycle, 59
Advertising, 53, 59, 150
Advertising Agency, 97
Advertorial, 104, 154
Affective Domain, 33
Affective Memory, 247, 248
AIDA, 26, 73, 152, 165
Allusion, 123, 173
Ambush Marketing, 155
Amplitude, 194, 197, 199, 202, 226
Analog, 181
Analogy, 155
Analogy, Metaphor and Simile Advertising, 155
Angle of Incidence, 194, 205, 206
Announcement Advertising, 156
Aperture, 185
Area of Dominant Influence, 102
A-Roll, 193
Articulation, 212

Articulation Errors, 215
Aspect Ratio, 184
Association, 36, 119, 120, 121, 124, 137, 139, 155, 168, 169, 171, 173, 174, 177
Attention, 27
Audience Estimates, 95, 101, 102
Audio, 112, 115, 181, 183, 187, 189, 190, 192, 193, 197, 199, 203, 207, 231
Audio File, 190, 191
Average Ratings, 98
B2B, 59, 72, 77
B2C, 59, 72, 77
Back Light, 186
Backdrop, 187
Backstory, 243
Balance, 188
Banner Ads, 60, 108, 160
Banner Blindness, 92, 108
BAT Formula, 31
Beauty Shot, 187
Before and After Advertising, 156
Being In Character, 237
Berners-Lee, Tim, 107
Billboard, 27, 61, 69, 105, 161
Bit Depth, 197
Blend Line, 134, 135
Blog, 61, 110, 162
Blog Backlink Strategy, 110
Blogosphere, 110
Body Language, 253
Bookends, 101
Boston Consulting Group, 39

Bounce Rate, 109
Brainstorming, 40, 168
Branding, 89, 91, 109, 158, 159, 164, 167, 182
Breakdown of Authority, 127
Break-Even Point, 45
BRM, 104
Broadcast Time Slot, 100
Brochure, 160
B-Roll, 193
Business Reply Mail, 152, 160
Business Video
    External, 179
    Internal, 179
Buyer Stages
    (a) Target, 81
    (b) Lead, 81
    (c) Prospect, 81
    (d) Customer, 81
    (e) Repeat Customer, 81
    (f) Promoter, 81
Buying Cycle, 26
Buying Motivations, 23, 26
    Emotional, 75
    Logical, 75
Buying Signal, 76
Bypass Attack, 58
Call-to-Action, 164, 170
Camera Moves
    Dolly In, 185
    Dolly Out, 185
    Pan, 185
    Tilt, 185
Camera Shots
    Angle, 186
    Beauty Shot, 187
    Close-Up (CU), 187
    Establishing Shot, 187

Extra or Extreme Close-Up (XCU), 187
    Medium Shot (MS), 187
    Over-the-Shoulder Shot, 187
    Reaction Shot, 187
    Wide Shot (WS), 187
Camera Track Slider, 186
Cannibalization, 43
Captioning, 119
Category Killer, 49
Cells, Demographic, 19
Center for Economic and Policy Research, 3
Center of a Character, 237
Channel Management, 48
Channels of Distribution, 48, 86
Character Construction, 242, 244
Character Modeling
    External, 246
    Internal, 246
Character Portrayal, 242
Character Voices
    General, 228
    Specific, 228
Chest Voice, 221
Chroma Key, 187
Chromatic Scale, 198
Chunks, 134, 135
Circle of Attention, 248
Circulation, 60
Circumstances, 127, 142, 170, 233, 243
Circumstances of a Character
    Mental Traits and Conditions, 233
    Objectives, 233
    Obstacles, 233

Physical Traits and
   Conditions, 233
Relationships to Others, 233
Setting, 233
Claritas, Inc., 20
Classified Advertising, 104, 160
Clayton Act, 49
Clichés, 172, 173, 174, 238
Click-Through Rate, 99
Client Personality Advertising,
   156
Close-Up, 187
Cognitive Consistency, 27
Cognitive Consonance, 32
Cognitive Dissonance, 27, 32
Cognitive Domain, 33
Collateral Materials, 56, 103
Comb Filtering, 199
Combination Consonant
   Sounds, 212
Comedy, 123, 124, 125, 126,
   128, 129, 131, 134, 170
Comic Character, 135
Comic of Expectation, 127
Comic of Ideation, 125
Comic of Imitation, 125
Comic of Motion, 125
Comic of Situation, 124
Commitments, 170
Common Time, 224
Communication Channel, 13,
   159
Communication Models, 13
Communication Objectives,
   231
Company-Centric Marketing, 7
Comparative Advertising, 156
Competitive Analysis, 89
Competitive Strategies

Differentiation, 85
Imaging, 85
Niche Marketing, 85
Pricing, 85
Compositing, 191
Composition, 188
Concentration, 247, 248
Concentric Diversification, 42
Condenser Microphone, 204,
   208
Conglomerate Expansion, 43
Consonant Articulation
   Manners, 214
   Places, 214
Consonant Sounds, 212, 213
Consumer Behavior, 19, 23, 26,
   149, 150, 152, 165, 170
Consumer Credit Protection
   Act, 44
Consumer Goods Pricing Act
   of 1975, 44
Consumer Market, 17
Content Marketing, 111, 161
Content Video, 31, 33, 35, 134
Continuity, 189
Contraction Defense, 58
Controls and Tracking, 90
Cookies, 109
Co-op Advertising, 49, 155
Copy Notations, 226
Copywriting, 149, 151, 159
Core Based Statistical Area, 18
Cost - Overall Expenses
   Method, 42
Cost of Ownership, 45
Cost per Average Order, 59
Cost per Click, 99, 108
Cost per Inquiry, 59
Cost per Lead, 59

Cost per Point, 95, 98
Cost per Thousand, 98
Cost per Unit Sold, 42, 59
Cost-Plus Pricing, 45
Counter-Offensive Defense, 58
Coupon Redemption Rates, 62
Coupons, 62
CPC, 98
CPM, 98, 99, 112, 113
CPP, 98, 99
Cradle Phrases, 228
Crane, 186
Creative, 123, 180, 197
Creative Brief, 87
Creativity, 9, 14, 23, 119, 128,
    136, 158, 169, 171, 173
Credit Policies, 43
Credit Rolls, 192
Crescendo, 222
Crisis Communication, 61
Crossfade, 191
Crossing, 139, 140
Cross-Promotion, 63
Cross-Selling, 63
CU, 187
Cume, 60
Current Circumstances, 89
Customer, 81
Customer Benefits, 150, 165
Customer Era, 8
Customer Loyalty, 72, 87
Customer-Centric Marketing, 7
Cut, 191
Cutaways, 193
Darkside, 125, 143, 144
Data Mining, 63
Database Marketing, 63, 107
Daydreaming, 25, 120
Daypart, 101

Deceptive Advertising, 163
Decision Influencer, 30
Decision Maker, 30
Decrescendo, 222
Defense Mechanism, 25, 126,
    127, 142
Defense or Escape Mechanism,
    127, 142
Definition, 10, 139
Demand, 56
Demand Bursts, 41
Demand States, 57, 84
    Declining, 163
    Full, 163
    Irregular, 163
    Latent, 163
    Negative, 162
    Nonexistent, 162
    Overfull, 163
    Unwholesome, 163
Demand, Individual, 28
Demand-Based Pricing, 45
Demographic Cells, 102
Demographic Segmentation, 19
Demographics, 17, 19, 52, 92,
    93, 99, 113, 151
Depth of Field, 184
Derived Demand, 43
Descriptive Advertising, 156
Designated Market Area, 102
Desire, 24, 29
Dialects
    Eastern American, 212
    General American, 212
    Southern American, 212
Diaphragm, 204, 205, 208, 220
Differentiation, 27, 29, 57, 74,
    158
Diffraction, 195

Diffusion, 30
Diffusion of Innovation, 30
Digital, 41, 91, 93, 100, 107,
    181, 187, 189, 195, 197, 199,
    200
Digital Advertising, 112
Digital Marketing, 107
Diphthongs, 212, 213
Direct Channels, 48
Direct Mail, 48, 50, 59, 60, 93,
    103, 104, 160
Direct Marketing, 50, 59
Direct Response Advertising,
    104, 152
Direct Response Marketing, 50
Direct Selling, 51
Display Advertising, 104
Dissonance of Musical Tones,
    201
Distribution Center, 49
DMA, 50, 102
Docking Windows, 190
Dolly, 185
Doppler Effect, 194
Double Entendre, 142
Downline, 52
Dr. Albert Mehrabian, 8
Drop-Shipping, 41, 51
Dutch Angle, 188
Dynamic Microphone, 204, 208
eBay, 48, 50, 115, 138, 186
Ecommerce, 50, 86
Economic Position
    Macroeconomics, 84
    Microeconomics, 84
Economies of Scale, 41
Economy in Inhibition, 124
Economy of Expenditure in
    Feeling, 124

Economy of Expenditure in
    Thought, 124
Economy of Sympathy, 125
Effective Reach, 96
Effects, 190, 191, 195
Effects Plug-Ins, 191
Elasticity of Demand, 46
Election Advertising, 153
Electronic Magazine, 115
Electronic Noise, 203
Electronic Promotion, 115
Email Marketing, 115, 161
Emotional Motivating Factors,
    170
Emotional Recall, 248, 252
Emotional Situation
    Advertising, 156
Emphasis, 222
Encirclement Attack, 58
Equal Opportunity, 153
Equivalent Advertising Value,
    61
Establishing Shot, 187
Euphony, 201
Event Marketing, 63
Events, 46, 47, 63, 86, 92, 106,
    135, 143, 158, 163, 189, 190,
    191, 207, 215
Exaggeration, 125, 141
Excess Capacity Pricing, 45
Excess Demand Pricing, 45
Exclusive Distribution
    Agreement, 48
Executive Summary, 88
Exhibitions, 63, 105, 106
Exporting and Importing, 52
Exposure, 36, 57, 98, 184, 185
Externally Stated Intention, 235
Extranet, 110

Extreme Close-Up, 187
E-Zine, 107, 115, 161
Facebook, 99, 112
Facial Expressions, 253, 254
Fade to Black, 191
Fake Interview Advertising,
  156
Fake Remote Advertising, 156
Family Life Cycle Stages, 20
FATQINS, 198, 204
Feature/Benefit Analysis, 150
Features and Benefits, 29, 75,
  76, 82, 156, 157, 165, 166,
  170
Feelings, 8, 10, 11, 12, 13, 14,
  34, 69, 119, 126, 156, 162,
  169, 232, 237, 238, 241, 242,
  249, 252, 254
Field of View, 188
Fill Light, 186
Filters, 191
Five P's of Personal Selling, 66
Fixed Position, 97
Flanging, 199, 200
Flanker Brands, 42
Flanking Attack, 58
Flanking Defense, 58
Flash Animation, 160
Flight, Advertising, 9
Flighting, 60
Flyer, 103
Focus, 8, 14, 15, 18, 23, 27, 83,
  86, 164, 165, 166, 184, 185,
  207, 235, 237, 238
Forgetting, 36
Fragmentation, 100
Frames per Second (FPS), 184
Framing, 188

Free Information Advertising,
  156
Frequency, 57, 60, 61, 67, 91,
  93, 96, 99, 103, 114, 152,
  194, 195, 197, 198, 199, 200,
  203, 205, 208
Frequency Response, 205
Freud, Dr. Sigmund, 120, 123,
  124, 125, 126, 127, 128, 130,
  133, 136, 139, 141, 143, 144,
  173, 261
Frontal Attack, 58
Full-Duplex Recording, 197
Gap Analysis, 42
General Appeal Advertising,
  155
Generation, 181
Generational Clustering, 19
Generations, U. S., 19
Geographic Areas, 86
Geographic Zone, 45
Geography, 17, 18, 20, 57, 92,
  93, 99
Gilad, Benjamin, 58
Global Marketing, 52
Google AdSense, 113
Google AdWords, 113, 160
Google Display Network, 113
Google Reader, 114
Grammar and Vocabulary
  Errors, 215
Gross Impressions, 96
Gross Rating Points, 98
Growth Strategy, 85
Growth/Share Matrix, 39, 58
GRP, 98
Guerilla Strategy, 58
Habitual Pitch, 216
Handheld Mics, 207

Handout, 103
Hanging Microphones, 207
Hard Limiting, 202
Harmless or Abstract Wit, 126
Harmonics, 198, 200, 201, 221
Harmony, 32, 201, 211
Head Voice, 221
Headline, 160
Headphones, 183
Hierarchy of Needs, Maslow, 23
Hook, 27, 35, 160, 164, 165, 213
Horizontal Diversification, 43
Horizontal Expansion, 86
Hosting, 111, 146
Households Using Television, 103
HP, 216, 230
HTML, 108
HTTP, 106
Human Behavior, 23
Human Reception Channels, 241
Human Vocal Ranges, 198
Humor, 119, 123, 124, 125, 126, 128, 129, 130, 131, 132, 134, 135, 136, 137, 138, 139, 140, 141, 142, 143, 144, 145, 168, 169, 170, 171
HUT, 103
Hyperlink, 51, 108, 114
Hypertext Markup Language, 108
Hypertext Transfer Protocol, 106
Image Advertising, 152
Image-Building, 57
Imagination, 248

Imaging, 29, 42, 53, 158, 164
IMC, 57, 96
Impact, 92
Impact Advertising, 152
Impedence, 205
Implication, 142, 143, 173
Inbound Telemarking, 61
Incentivized Traffic, 108
Indirect Channels, 48
Inflection, 218
Infomercial, 100
Infomercials, 59, 100
Infrasound, 198
In-Home Advertising, 60
Inner Child, 243
Inoculation Advertising, 154
Insert Edit, 193
Insertion Order, 97
Inserts, 59
Institutional Advertising, 152
Insult, 144, 145
Intangible Assets, 41
Integrated Marketing Campaign, 57, 96
Intellectual Motivating Factors, 24, 170
Intensity, 198, 201, 202, 203, 211, 216, 220, 222, 226, 227, 228, 230, 240, 245, 254
Intensity Dynamics, 221
Intentions, 235, 236
Intentions of the Moment, 235
Interactive Era, 8
Interactive Marketing, 16, 100, 107
Interest, 27
Interference, 36, 195
Interlaced Scanning, 184
Internal Marketing, 16

Internally Stated Intention, 235
International Phonetic
    Alphabet, 212
Internet, 9, 20, 50, 60, 65, 86,
    106, 131, 173, 179, 197
Interpersonal Communication,
    211
Interruption Advertising, 60
Intervals, 217
Intonation, 216, 219, 226, 227,
    230
Intranet, 110
Intrusiveness, 60
Inventory, 41
Inventory Control, 50
Invitational Advertising, 156
Island Position, 97
ISP, 161
Jib, 186
Jib Shots
    Boom Down, 186
    Boom Up, 186
Joke Structures, 126, 129, 136
Jump Cuts, 193
Key Light, 186, 187
Keywords, 112, 113, 114
K-Words, 134
Landing Page, 51, 99, 109, 114,
    160, 162
Language Merchant, 122
Lavalier Mics, 207
Law of Primacy, 34
Law of Readiness, 34
Law of Recency, 34
Layout
    Body Copy, 104, 160, 165,
        235
    Headline, 27, 35, 104, 160,
        164

Image, 104
Subhead, 104, 160
White Space, 104
Lead, 81
Lead POV, 188
Leader Pricing, 47
Leading Lines, 188
Leapfrog Attack, 58
Learning Domains
    Affective, 32
    Cognitive, 32
    Psychomotor, 33
Learning Levels
    Application, 32
    Correlation, 32
    Rote, 32
    Understanding, 32
Learning Personalities, 33
    Anxious, 34
    Attention Seeker, 34
    Dependent, 33
    Despondent, 34
    Impulsive, 34
    Independent, 33
    Silent, 34
    Tentative, 34
    Vulnerable, 34
Learning Process
    Aural, 32
    Emotional, 32
    Kinesthetic, 32
    Logical, 32
    Visual, 32
Least Effort Principle, 30
Life Cycle, Product Category,
    39
Lifestyle, 17
Lifestyle Marketing, 19

Lifestyle Segmentation, Family, 20
Lifetime Customer Value, 87
Lighting, 180, 183, 185, 186
  Hard, 186
  Soft, 186
  Soft Box, 186
LinkedIn, 112
Listening Skills, 14
Logical Motivating Factors, 24, 170
Logo, 41
Long-Term Impressions, 227
Long-Term Memory, 35
Lottery, 54
Lower Thirds, 192
Lowest Unit Charge, 153
Loyalty Program, 87
Macroeconomics, 28
Mailing List, 104
Management Methods
  Management by Objective, 83
  Top-Down, 83
Manufacturer's Suggested Retail Price, 47
Market Coverage Strategies
  Concentrated, 85
  Differentiated, 85
  Undifferentiated, 85
Market Research, 93
Market Share, 39, 53
Marketing Concept, 82
Marketing Mix, 39
Marketing Myopia, 7, 27
Marketing Objectives, 93
Marketing Plans, 81
  Formal Written Plan, 88

Informal Annual Marketing Meeting, 84
Marketing Stimuli, 34
Marketing Strategy
  Downmarket, 19
  Midmarket, 19
  Upmarket, 19
Marketing, Defensive Strategies
  Contraction, 58
  Counter-Offensive, 58
  Flanking, 58
  Mobile, 58
  Position, 58
  Preemptive, 58
Marketing, Offensive Strategies
  Bypass, 58
  Encirclement, 58
  Flanking, 58
  Frontal, 58
  Guerilla, 58
  Leapfrog, 58
Masking, 195
Maslow, Dr. Abraham, 23
Maslow's Hierarchy of Needs, 23, 56
Mass Market, 17
Mass Marketing, 16, 100, 151
Maximi$er, 101, 102
Maximization, 141
Media Audience Estimates
  Average Audience, 102
  Individuals Reached, 102
  Persons, 102
  Rating, 102
  Share, 102
Medium Shot, 187
Mehrabian, Dr. Albert, 8
Melody, 217
Memory, 35

Memory, Disuse, 36
Memory, Interference, 36
Memory, Long-Term, 35
Memory, Repression, 36
Memory, Sensory Register, 35
Memory, Short-Term, 35
Memory, Working, 35
Mental Flight, 25, 120
Mental Image, 82, 242
Mental Imagery, 119
Merchandising, 60
Merchandising Displays, 50
Message Development, 87
Message Retention, 35
Metadata, 111
Metaphor, 155
Meter, 236
Me-Too Advertising, 154
Metro, 18, 101
Metropolitan Statistical Area, 18, 101
Micro, 18
Microeconomics, 28
Micromarketing, 20
Microphone Construction, 207
Microphone Pickup Patterns, 205
Microphones, 183, 203, 204, 205, 206, 207
Micropolitan Statistical Area, 18
Middlemen, 48
Milking, 45
Mind/Body System, 255
Mind's Eye, 119, 120
Mind-Body System, 242
Minimization, 126, 141, 143
Minimum Advertised Pricing, 44

Mission Statement, 83
Misunderstanding, 138
MLM, 51
Mobile Defense, 58
Mobile Devices, 10, 60, 91, 100, 106, 107, 113
Mobile Marketing, 107
Mobile Media, 91
Modulation, 218
Monologue, 134, 143, 146
Mood, 186, 195, 233
MOSAIC, 20
Motion Graphics, 191
Motivating Factors, Emotional, 24
Motivating Factors, Logical, 24
Motivation, 31
Motivation, Extrinsic, 31
Motivation, Intrinsic, 31
MS, 187
MSA, 18
MSRP, 47
Multi-Level Marketing, 51
Multimedia, 115
Naiveté, 71, 247
Narrative, 167, 235
Narrowcasting, 100
Nat Sound, 187
Negative Advertising, 153
Negative Appeal Advertising, 154
Negative Motivations, 24
Network Marketing, 51
New Media, 2, 9, 91, 92, 99, 108, 113
Nielsen, 20, 93, 94, 101, 138
Nielsen Company, A. C., 20
Noise, 198, 203
Noise Filters, 203

Noise Floor, 205
Non-Destructive Editing, 197
Non-Price Competition
    Advertising, 154
Non-Production Overhead, 42
No-Reserve Auction, 115
Normalize, 202
Note Selection, 218
Nuke, 192
Objection, 76
Objectives, 82, 89
Obscene, 141
Observation, 171, 172, 246
Octave, 198
Odd/Even Pricing, 47
Off-Axis Coloration, 206
Offer, 21, 29, 42, 44, 66, 68, 73,
    74, 76, 97, 109, 114, 151,
    159, 166, 167, 169
Offshoring, 41
On-Axis Sound, 205, 206
Online Auctions, 115
Open Distribution
    Arrangement, 48
Opportunity Cost, 28, 86
Opt-In and Opt-Out, 161
Organization for Economic
    Cooperation and
    Development, 3
Organized Self, 34
Outbound Telemarking, 60
Outdoor Advertising, 91, 105
Out-of-Home Advertising, 60,
    105
Outsourcing, 41
Overstatement, 120, 125, 141,
    143
Over-the-Shoulder Shot, 187
Owned Media, 1, 7

PAC, 153
Pacing, 224
Packaging and Shipping, 52
Pantomime, 125
Paradigm Shift, 27
Parody, 125, 146, 147, 158
Particularize, 233
Patterns, 218
Payment Methods, 48
Pay-per-Click, 107, 112
Penetration Pricing, 47
Perceived Risks, 87
Perceived Value, 30
Perceptual Superimposition,
    231
Perfect Unitary Elasticity, 46
Performance, 69
Performance Triads, 249
Personal Selling, 2, 8, 10, 17,
    25, 48, 50, 51, 53, 56, 61, 65,
    66, 69, 70, 75, 86, 150
Personality Marketing,
    Definition, 11
Personalize, 233, 234
Persons Viewing Television,
    103
Perspective, 188
Phase Shifting, 199, 200
Phonation/Air Ratio, 221
Phonetic, 212
Piggyback Ads, 100
PIPPs, 216, 225
Pitch, 194, 198, 199, 211, 216,
    218, 219, 225, 226, 227, 228,
    240
Place, 16, 48, 86
Podcast, 107, 115, 229
Point of View, 119, 121, 153,
    167, 170, 241

Point of View (POV), 188
Point-of-Purchase, 50, 60, 106,
    160
Polar Pattern, 205
Polishing, 133
Political Action Committee,
    153
Political Advertising, 54
Population Estimates, 102
Pop-Up Ads, 108
Pop-Up Blockers, 108
Portraying Characters, 247
Position Defense, 58
Positioning, 12, 25, 27, 29, 42,
    53, 57, 74, 85, 87, 89, 156,
    158, 159, 173, 182
Positive Motivations, 24
Postproduction, 181, 187, 189,
    195
PR, 61
Predatory Pricing, 44
Pre-Emptible Rates, 97
Preemptive Defense, 58
Premise, 130
Premiums, 62, 87, 105
Premiums, Self-Liquidators, 62
Premiums, Semi-Liquidators,
    62
Preproduction, 181
Present Situation, 89
Presentation, Personal Selling,
    71
    Action, 76
    Appointments, 71
    Attention, 73
    Canned Pitch, 72
    Cold Calling, 71
    Consultancy Selling, 72
    Desire, 74

    Farming, 71
    Hunting, 71
    Interest, 74
    Relationship Selling, 72
    Step Plan, 72
    Wrap-Up, 77
Press Conference, 61
Press Pack, 61
Press Releases, 61
Pressures and Motivations, 67
Prestige Pricing, 47
Preview Window, 190
Price, 16, 43
Price and Quality Perceptions,
    46
Price Elasticity, 46
Price Lining, 47
Price/Quality Equation, 28, 46
Price-Item Advertising, 157
Pricing, 42, 43, 44, 45, 46, 47,
    49, 57, 58, 82, 89, 150, 157,
    164
Pricing Strategy, 30
Primary Research, 18, 93
Prime Time, 97
Print Advertising, 103
Print Insertion, 103
PRIZM, 20
Product, 15, 30, 39, 40, 41, 42,
    43, 59, 65, 66, 71, 84, 150,
    151, 162, 163, 165, 166
Product Awareness, 27, 42, 57,
    85, 151, 158, 159, 164, 182
Product Category, 39
Product Category Life Cycle,
    39
Product Knowledge, 66
Product Line, 40
Product Line Depth, 40

Product Line Expansion, 43
Product Line Extension, 42
Product Line Mix, 40
Product Line Retrenchment, 43
Product Line Stretching, 43
Product Line Width, 40
Product Placement, 101
Production Capacity, 41
Production Era, 8
Production Music, 196
Professional Advertising, 155
Program-Length Commercial,
    100
Progressive Scanning, 184
Projection, 221
Promoter, 81
Promotion, 16, 53
Promotional Budgets, 56
Promotional Pricing, 47
Propaganda, 153
Proposal, 75, 76, 152, 166
Proposition, 166
Prospect, 81
Prospecting, 67
Proximity Effect, 206, 207
PSA, 154
Psychic Income, 28, 47
Psychographics, 17, 52, 92, 93,
    113, 151
Psychomotor Domain, 33
Psychophysical
    Communication, 242, 252,
    255
Public Relations, 56, 61, 86, 90,
    109, 149, 150
Public Service Advertising, 154
Public Solitude, 248
Publicity, 16, 53, 56, 61, 90, 150
Pull Marketing, 49

Pull Production, 49
Pulses, 232, 235
Punchline, 129, 131, 132, 133,
    134, 135, 140, 142, 146, 172
Puns, 140
Push Production, 49
Push-Pull Marketing, 48
PVT, 103
Qualified Prospect, 67
Qualitative Data, 17
Qualitative Research, 18, 94
Quality of Sound, 200
Quantitative Research, 18, 94
Question Types - Open and
    Closed, 73
Question-Based Advertising,
    157
Questioning Strategies
    Confirming, 73
    Leading, 73
    Probing, 73
    Rhetorical, 73
Radio Advertising Bureau, 155,
    238
Radio Spots, 161
Range, 217
Rate Card, 96, 97
Rate of Speech, 226
Rating, 98, 102
Ratings Book, 101
Reach, 60, 95
Reach and Frequency Plans
    Diagonal, 103
    Horizontal, 103
    Vertical, 103
Reaction Shots, 193
Readership, 60
Reasonable Access, 153
Reason-Why Advertising, 157

Rebate, 47, 62
Rebate Advertising, 157
Recall, 36
Reeves, Rosser, 29, 166, 259
Referrals, 57, 72
Reflection, 194
Refraction, 194
Register, 216
Relationship Marketing, 57
Relative Positioning, 158
Relaxation/Tension, 220
Reminder Advertising, 152, 163
Repeat Customer, 81
Repeat Sales, 57
Repositioning, 27
Reputation Management, 30
Resale Price Maintenance
    Agreements, 44
Research, 18
Research Terms
    Qualitative, 94
    Quantitative, 94
    Universe, 94
    Validity, 94
    Variable, 94
Retail Selling, 49
Retention of Ad Message, 35
Retention of Learning
    Association, 36
    Attitude, 36
    Human Senses, 36
    Praise, 36
    Repetition, 36
Reverse, 43, 137
Rhythm of Speech, 227
Rhythm of the Setting, 237
Ries, Al, 29, 58
Ripple Edit, 190
Risqué, 137, 141, 142, 143, 144

Robinson-Patman Act, 49
ROP, 97
ROS, 97
Rough, 133, 136
Rule of 300, 104
Rule of Thirds, 188
Rule of Threes, 134
Run of Publication, 97, 104
Run of Site, 97
Run of Station, 97
Sales Era, 8
Sales Forecasting, 68
Sales Promotion, 62, 150
Sales Promotions, 53, 62
Sales Quotas, 68
Sample Rate, 197
Sample, Non-Probability, 95
Sample, Probability, 94
Sample, Random, 95
Sample, Strategic, 95
Sample, Weighting, 95
Satire, 127, 147
Saturation Campaign, 97
Saver, 146
Scene, 14, 129, 183, 185, 187,
    189, 193, 195, 216, 234, 235,
    248
Search Engine, 50, 108, 111,
    113, 114
Search Engine Optimization,
    112, 162
Search Engine Ranking
    Criteria, 112
Secondary Research, 18, 93
Segmentation, Demographic,
    19
Segmentation, Geographic, 18
Segmentation, Lifestyle, 19
Segmentation, Psychograpic, 19

Segmented Market, 17
Selling frequency, 96
Selling-In, 49
Sense Memory, 248, 249
Sensory Register, 35
SEO, 162
Setup, 129, 131, 132, 133, 134, 135, 140, 142, 145, 146, 172, 186
Sex/Age Groups, 102
Shadows, 186
Shape, 220
Share, 16, 33, 39, 40, 47, 85, 89, 102, 103, 107, 163
Share-of-Voice, 96
Shift, 219
Shock, 137
Short-Rate, 97
Short-Term Impressions, 227
Short-Term Memory, 35
Shot, 34, 67, 72, 135, 141, 180, 182, 183, 185, 187, 188, 189, 193, 213
Shrinkage, 50
Simile, 155
Skim Pricing, 45
Slant, 120, 121, 122
Slice of Life Advertising, 157
Slippage, Coupons, 63
Slogan, 41
Slow Motion, 187
Smartphones, 107, 183
Smutty, 141
Social Media, 50, 61, 91, 97, 107, 108, 111, 112
Sound Effects, 161, 196, 197
Sound Pressure Level, 205
Sound Wave, 193, 194, 195, 198, 199, 200, 205

Soundfile, 197
Spam Filters, 161
Speakers, 204
Specialty Advertising, 105
Specialty Goods, 47
Speed of Sound, 200
Spiders, 113
Spine of a Character, 232
SPL, 205
Splash Page, 109
Split Edit, 190
Spokesperson, 211
Spot, 100
Stakeholders, 3
Stanislavski, Constantin, 70
Stanislavski's Triad
    Concentration, 71
    Relaxation, 71
    Truth, 71
Stereo, 198, 203, 204
Stereo Placement Regions, 204
Stickiness, 109
Story, 61, 122, 125, 144, 161, 177, 183, 188, 252
Straight Character, 135
Strasberg, Lee, 70
Strata, 101
Strategic Elements, 89
Strategic Subtext, 232
Strategy, 57, 82
Streaming Media, 115
Stress
    Moderate, 222
    Primary, 222
    Unstress, 222
Subconscious, 119, 130
Subhead, 160
Subtext, 231, 238, 240
Suggestive Selling, 63

Superconscious, 130
Superiority, 127, 146
Superobjective, 232, 236
Surface Mount Mics, 207
Surprise, 119, 127, 133, 134,
    135, 136, 137, 254, 255
Switching, 131, 132, 133
SWOT, 82, 84
Tablet Computers, 39, 60, 91,
    107, 183
Tactic, 83
Tactical Communication, 232
Tactical Subtext, 232
Take, 183
Talent, 12, 31, 32, 120, 187,
    188, 192, 207
Tapscan, 101
Target, 81
Target Market, 17
Target Market Segments, 86
Target Pricing, 45
Targeted Marketing, 85
Targeting, 9, 17, 18, 23, 82, 93,
    113, 114, 151, 163
Teaser Advertising, 157
Technology, 41
Tempo of a Character, 237
Tendency, 26, 27, 75, 83, 92,
    126, 127, 151, 229
Tension and Muscle Memory,
    247
Test Mailings, 104
Testimonial Advertising, 157
Texting, 107
Through-Action, 232, 236
Tie-In Promotion, 155
Timbre, 200
Time Element of Sound, 200
Time Lapse, 187

Time Signature, 224
Timeline, 82, 189, 190, 191,
    194, 197
Titles, 192
TLD, 108
TOMA, 29
Top Level Domain, 108
Topical, 135
Topical Advertising, 158
Top-of-Mind Awareness, 29,
    53
Toppers, 135
Tracking Shots, 59
Trade Marketing, 49
Trade Show, 51
Trade Shows, 63, 105, 106
Traditional Media, 9, 10, 91, 93,
    95, 97, 99, 108, 112, 113
Trait Analysis, 242
Trait Categories, 244
    Emotional, 245
    Mental, 245
    Physical, 244
    Social, 245
    Speech, 245
Trait List, 242
Transducers, 204
Transfer of Learning, 36
Transit Advertising, 61, 105
Transitions, 189, 190, 191
Trial Close, 76
Trial Offer, 62
Trick Banner, 108
Tripod, 183, 185
Trout, Jack, 29, 58
TRRS, 183
Truth in Performance, 247
Truth-in-Lending Act, 44
Tune-Out, 92

TV Spots, 161
Twitter, 112
Two-Step Marketing Process, 160
Tying Agreements, 49
Ultrasound, 198
Understatement, 125, 141
Unfair Advertising, 163
Unique Positioning, 158
Unique Selling Proposition, 82, 89, 158, 166
Unique User, 60, 109
Unique Visitor, 109
Unit Objectives, 235
Unity Gain Amplifiers, 198, 199
Universal Resource Locator, 108
Universe, 102
URL, 50, 108
USP, 29, 158, 166
Variable Gain Amplifier, 202
Vehicle, 10, 50, 63, 107, 115, 159, 169
Verbal Invective, 127, 144
Vertical Expansion, 86
Vertical Integration, 41
Vertical Price Restraints, 44
Vertical Scheduling, 96
Video Clip, 190
Video Hosting
    Vimeo, 180
    Wistia, 180
    YouTube, 179
Video Shoot, 183
Vimeo, 161
Viral Marketing, 115
Visual Aids, 75

Visualization, 82, 119, 120, 121, 132, 133, 136, 171, 247
Vocal Performance, 211, 230
Vocal Skills Exercises, 229
Vocal Support, 220
Voice Acting, 211
Voice-Over, 192
Vowel Sounds, 212, 213
Wait Order, 60
Waltz Time, 225
Wanamaker, John, 2
Want, 24
Warranties, 41
Wavelength, 194, 200
Web Advertising, 60, 108
Web Browsers, 107, 108
Web Page, 108, 114
Website, 8, 16, 30, 50, 51, 59, 92, 108, 109, 110, 111, 114, 152, 160, 162, 166, 170, 182, 187, 189
Website Stickiness, 109
Whimsy, 126, 141
White Balance, 184, 185
Why People Laugh
    Defense or Escape Mechanism, 126
    Superiority, 126
    Surprise, 126
    Victory, 126
Wide Shot, 187
Wireless Microphones, 207
Wit, 119, 120, 123, 124, 126, 127, 128, 129, 130, 133, 136, 138, 139, 141, 143, 173
Word Association List, 168
Word Play, 124, 137, 138
Word-of-Mouth, 57, 72
WordPress, 110

Wordsmith, 122
Working the Mic, 207
Worldwide Web, 107, 108
WS, 187
XCU, 187

YouTube, 112, 129, 161, 182,
    187, 189
Zebra Stripes, 185
Zipping, 92
Zone Pricing, 45

www.ingramcontent.com/pod-product-compliance
Lightning Source LLC
Chambersburg PA
CBHW051943090426
42741CB00008B/1251